THE
TRANSFORMATION

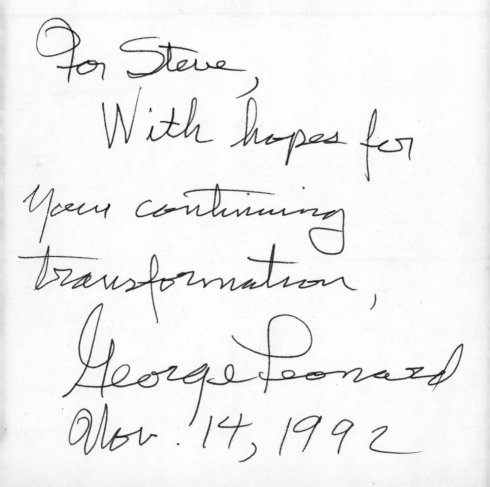

For Steve,
With hopes for
your continuing
transformation,
George Leonard
Nov. 14, 1992

THE TRANSFORMATION

A GUIDE TO THE INEVITABLE CHANGES IN HUMANKIND

GEORGE B. LEONARD

J. P. TARCHER, INC.
Los Angeles
Distributed by Houghton Mifflin Company
Boston

Library of Congress Cataloging in Publication Data

Leonard, George Burr, 1923–
    The transformation.

    Includes bibliographical references and index.
    1. Twentieth century—Forecasts. 2. Civilization,
Modern—1950– 3. Self-actualization (Psychology)
I. Title. CB161.L48 1981   303.4   80-53151

ISBN 0-87477-169-2

Library of Congress Catalog Card No.: 80-53151

Manufactured in the United States of America

Published by J. P. Tarcher, Inc.
9110 Sunset Blvd., Los Angeles, Calif. 90069

10 9 8 7 6 5 4 3 2 1
First Edition

for Lillie Pitts Leonard

*. . . no transformation is either permanent or desirable which
does not forward the spontaneous life of the world, advancing
those issues toward which it is already inwardly directed.*
—GEORGE SANTAYANA, REASON IN RELIGION

*Earth, isn't this what you want: an invisible
re-arising in us? Is it not your dream
to be one day invisible? Earth! Invisible!
What is your urgent command, if not transformation?*
—RAINER MARIA RILKE, DUINO ELEGIES

Contents

Publisher's Note

IT IS A rare privilege to reissue George Leonard's *The Transformation* nearly a decade after its first appearance. For those who read the first edition, the book served as an entry point, a sneak preview, an affirmation of personal experience, a campfire lit in a darkening world. The intervening years have made it increasingly clear that this is one of those prescient works that both inspire and suggest directions crucial to our very survival.

The author's challenging of mainstream thought and his unconventional views have been adopted and elaborated on by other writers in such diverse fields as science, public policy, health, education, psychology, sports, and theology. In fact, the title itself has passed into the language and is often used to name the period of transition in which we are now involved as well as the epoch that awaits us, we may hope, beyond the current crisis.

The book's history in the literary marketplace is worthy of mention as it illustrates significant changes of the past decade. *The Transformation* was originally published in 1972 just as Richard Nixon was amassing an unprecedented reelection victory. American auto manufacturers were at work devising ingenious ways to enlarge most models, while utility companies were sponsoring media campaigns urging increased consumption; all for the ultimate promise of an endless supply of cheap energy.

These events and the notions on which most public policy was predicated suggested business as usual. Conventional beliefs concerning prosperity, material growth, our global omnipotence and our hopes for solving social problems, even definitions of what it meant to be a man or a woman, were based on the assumption of an unchanging world. As if to reaffirm this view, there was a new silence following the noisy demands of the sixties and early seventies for social and institutional change.

Therefore, it is not surprising that given the timing of Mr. Leonard's messages—that energy shortages were inevitable, a turn in the growth curve was inevitable, and a significant change in our way of life was inevitable—they were largely ignored or greeted with skepticism and denial.

There were notable exceptions, but it was not until the times caught up with the book that his vision was widely acknowledged. Watergate . . . gas lines . . . the invention of the misery index . . . stagflation . . . the Chrysler crisis . . . problems in the Persian Gulf . . . all are familiar and painful symptoms of a deepening malaise Mr. Leonard had described. With each day's headlines, his ideas for positive change, which previously might have seemed fanciful, gain new relevance.

The author's personal background and seventeen-year career as a Senior Editor for *Look* magazine provided a rich and unique perspective for examining the undercurrents of the early seventies.

At the end of the Korean War he went to work for *Look*, initially covering Cold War stories because of his intelligence background. But soon there were assignments on labor strife, urban affairs, music, religion, education. In 1956, at the height of the westward population shift, Mr. Leonard was transferred to San Francisco to continue covering national and international affairs from the vantage point of the western edge of the American continent.

Less than a year later the desegregation riots broke out in Little Rock, and he began commuting to his native South to cover the Civil Rights movement.

Moving away from the traditional journalist's detached stance, he became a participant-observer, a style that was later to evolve into what was called "the new journalism." Instead of basing articles on sociological studies, other media reports, and opinion polls, Mr. Leonard went out into the cities and suburbs and hamlets and isolated farmhouses of the nation and talked for hours, for days, with the people. Instead of watching the Selma demonstration on television, he joined the march. Instead of learning about a school system by interviewing its administrators, he went into a classroom and sat in a child's seat and became a child for weeks on end. He was drawn to stories not only for their newsworthiness, but by the dictates of his heart.

During this period he wrote extensively about education, and won numerous awards. However, his habit of questioning conventional wisdom led him to believe that, because his articles were so highly regarded by the National Education Association and the Education Writers Association, he might be missing something. The result was *Education and Ecstasy*, published in 1968, a work about schools not as they were, but as they might become. Over 300,000 copies of the book were sold.

From his California viewing post at *Look*, Mr. Leonard began to see the United States as a huge social laboratory. This led to his design, supervision, and editing of a number of special issues, identifying trends before they became popular media topics. In 1960, when most were speaking of the silent generation, his special issue was entitled "Youth of the Sixties: The Explosive Generation." Two years later his special edition, "California: A Window Into the Future," predicted that many of the changes occurring in his new home state would spread to the rest of the United States and on to other advanced industrial nations.

During these years Mr. Leonard began a systematic study of individual human capabilities. *Look*'s editorial board allowed him nine months to research an article that was to be called "The Human Potential." He met at length with neary forty leading philosophers, psychologists, and brain researchers. Even in this case, he avoided the role of unmoved observer. He took a position on the board of trustees to Esalen Institute, where he co-led the first of the marathon interracial confrontation groups.

Cultural change became his main beat and questions about the survival of the individual and society the center of his thinking. His associations, experiences, and concern for the future eventually prompted his decision to devote full energy to the writing of *The Transformation*. It was this voyage that led to his radical thesis that we were coming to the end of one line of human development and approaching the beginning of a new one, one almost beyond our imagining.

So, it is our particular honor to provide an opportunity for the reader to experience this remarkable man's vision, to provide the outlines of a positive scenario of human transformation, and to keep alive this bright flame whose warmth has given so much courage and whose light has allowed us to see a bit further into the darkness.

A Note
from the Author

I HAVE BEEN urged by friends whose counsel I most respect to write an introduction listing the numerous events that have occurred since 1972 that tend to confirm the thesis put forward in this book. I resist their advice not only because any such list would necessarily be incomplete and debatable, but because *The Transformation* was intended primarily as a general theory of social and personal transformation rather than a detailed blueprint for reform or a specific outline of the future.

In any case, as T. S. Kuhn points out in *The Structure of Scientific Revolutions*, the cry for immediate practical applications of a new theory is a mistake, as applications do not develop directly from a theorist's words but from a complex process involving trial and error, feedback and "reality fit." Such a process, stemming not from any one person's theory but from a deep historical necessity, is now underway throughout the world and, most visibly, in advanced industrial nations. The outcome is far from clear, but there is little doubt that we are involved in a thoroughgoing transformation concerning the ways in which we deal with matter and energy, organize society, and shape consciousness. My purpose in *The Transformation*, as I state early in the book, is simply "to help the reader recognize the changes that already have occurred and are occurring, to help bring about the kind of understanding that may render the changes less painful and abrasive, to warn of hazards along the way, and to attempt a few glimpses at transformed behavior and being."

It should also be noted that *The Transformation* is not a "theory" in the classical sense, one with formal definition, proposition, and agument. Although this book is heavily undergirded by canonical material from such fields as anthropology, psychology, and the history of science, it is a work of the heart as well as the head, and is perhaps at its best in questioning the conventional wisdom of

Western culture. I might justify my inclusion of affective material by pointing out that cognition spans only a few octaves in the vast range of possible human knowing. I might even propose, with Gregory Bateson, that "mere purposive rationalty unaided by such phenomena as art, religion, dream and the like is necessarily pathogenic and destructive of life; and that its virulence springs specifically from the circumstance that life depends upon interlocking *circuits* of contingencies, while consciousness can only see the short arcs of such circuits as human purpose may direct."

But justification is beside the point. This book was conceived and written in passion and must eventually stand or fall on more than formal argument. The impassioned thesis of *The Transformation* is that beyond the dying of our present culture lies the possibility of a new and better culture, that the energy crisis and the end of material growth may be blessings in disguise, leading to greater development of human resources, and that fascinating adventures await us in a transformed world—adventures that do not burn excessive quantities of fuel, do not exploit other people, do not rape the planet or poison the biosphere.

The years that have passed following the original publication of this book have brought us closer to the end of one way of life and closer to the birth of new ways of life. And though the hour is late and catastrophic possibilities confront us wherever we turn, I still believe that we as individuals and as groups of individuals can help shape a humane future. If we use our heads and hearts wisely and somehow learn to bear the pain and terror of change, each of us can become consciously involved in one of the great adventures thus far in the human journey on planet Earth.

Jeremy Tarcher's decision to publish this beautiful new edition of *The Transformation* at a moment of *kairos*, of time alive and crackling with tension and possibilities, stands as the greatest thrill of my writing career. I offer it to you, the reader, in that spirit.

Acknowledgments

A SPECIAL acknowledgment goes to Richard Cowan, who acted as research associate for this book. Cowan is not only a gifted anthropologist and filmmaker, but a human being of wide, compassionate and informed interests. For his constant support and encouragement, his ideas, his editorial suggestions, and for his companionship during hikes on Mt. Tam, family picnics and aikido practice, I thank him.

Three other people are also due very special thanks. Michael Murphy, Leo Litwak and my oldest daughter, Ellen Leonard, were deeply involved in the making of this book. They offered ideas, criticism and encouragement at what always seemed the right moment. A part of them is in these pages.

For exemplary support and guidance, my gratitude to Ross Claiborne, Richard Huett and Sterling Lord.

For critical readings, my appreciation to Robinette Bell, Price Cobbs, Alan Dundes, Paul Ehrlich, T George Harris, Edward Leonard, Jerry Mander, Lisby Mayer, John and Julia Poppy, Jean Stein, and Brendan O'Regan.

And for the full and useful index, my thanks to Ellen Leonard.

The Beast
at the Gates

To discover the truth in anything that is alien, first dispense with the indispensable in your own vision.

—LEONARD COHEN

AN UNCOMMON and persistent malaise afflicts the advanced industrial nations. Along with this malaise, which dates at least from the first World War, there has recently arisen a widespread feeling that a change of large dimensions is in the air. The anticipatory sense of the coming of a new age is shared by soothsayers, astrologers, and others of a visionary turn of mind. At the same time, social observers of various persuasions have examined the possibility of a forthcoming overturn in the way society in the industrial nations is organized. These observers—Daniel Bell, Kenneth Boulding, Herman Kahn, Alvin Toffler, Marshall McLuhan, Jean-François Revel, William Irwin Thompson, and Buckminster Fuller among others—have engaged in the difficult task of describing the world of tomorrow in the language of today. The difficulty shows up in those very terms they have chosen to characterize the future —"post-civilization," "post-industrial society," "Global Village," "super-industrial society."

We should not be surprised at the resurgence of prophecy, or even eschatology; perhaps the approach of the year 2000 alone is enough to trigger millennial thoughts. There is, in fact, an old tradition of millenarianism accompanying the collapse of established social values or the fear of natural catastrophes. Apocalyptic visions arose among the Jews during the two centuries preceding the birth of Christ. And there were numerous millenarian movements such as the Joachimites and Free Spirits in medieval Europe. This Western fantasy of destruction and transfiguration has more recently appeared in the culture of the oppressed, setting off, for instance, the Ghost Dance of the American Indians, the messianic native migrations in Brazil, the Cargo Cults of the South Seas. Many non-Western cultures—notably the Aztecs, the Hindus and the Jains—organized their existence around the concept of great cycles that end with the cataclysmic destruction of the entire culture followed by the birth of a new age. The Aztecs created smaller cycles within the epochs of destruction and rebirth. Every fifty-two years, they destroyed all their furniture, extinguished all their fires, and on the final night of the cycle waited fearfully to see if the sun would come up.

So it may be that the current anticipation of the end and beginning of a way of life is a delusion, or simply the manifestation of an expectable cyclical notion. It is possible that the dislocations and disquietudes of the times will be remedied by ameliorative measures that will leave the basic structures of our culture unchanged.

It is my thesis, however, that the current period is indeed unique in history and that it represents the beginning of the most thoroughgoing change in the quality of human existence since the creation of an agricultural surplus brought about the birth of civilized states some five thousand years ago. I am using the term "Civilization" (with a capital "C") to designate that mode of social organization marked in general by political states, markets, legal sanctions and social hierarchies, wherever in the world it occurs. (The dynamics of Civilization will be discussed in detail in Chapter 4.) I take the term "Transformation" to stand for both the process that spells the end of Civilization and the period during which the process takes place.

At this point I must stress that the Transformation as I see it does not entail any sort of return to a primitive state, though a man or woman of the Transformation may someday seem as far removed from Civilization as a civilized man or woman now seems from primitive society. Nor does the Transformation entail overthrowing all of our civilized values and practices, though it does mean subsuming most of them under a higher order.

I shall attempt to demonstrate that the Transformation, despite surface similarities, is neither utopian nor millenarian, that it is not only possible but inevitable, that it is, most significantly, already well under way, that it proceeds out of historical necessity, amenable to validation both by intuition and by reason. This theme will be approached from several different angles, some quite traditional, others less familiar. I shall begin and end with personal experience, out of my strong feeling that even the most theoretical apprehension of the galaxies cannot stand entirely apart from the consciousness of the observer.

I shall also argue that most of our current troubles, from free-floating anxiety to the breakdown of craftsmanship, can be traced ultimately to the lack of a vivid unifying principle or belief system; the biblical dictum that where there is no vision the people perish is by no means merely metaphorical. I believe that the time is overdue for the emergence of a new vision of human and social destiny and being.

My purpose here, however, is not to specify the Transformation's outcome or to fabricate a new organizing myth. No person or organized group can do that. My purpose is simply to help the reader recognize the changes that already have occurred and are occurring, to help bring about the kind of understanding that may render the changes less painful and abrasive, to warn of hazards along the way, and to attempt a few glimpses at transformed behavior and being.

❧

This is no moment in history for simple reassurances. The Transformation will be a difficult time. No one can promise easy transcendence. Repression growing from fear of change may well get worse in the years to come. And even if the old fears and dangers pass, there is nothing familiar or comfortable in store for us. The guardians of Civilization warn of what may be waiting just outside the gates. And there is something in us all that resonates to Yeats' vision of the rough beast slouching towards

Bethlehem to be born. The beast that waits beyond Civilization, however, may turn out to be neither rough nor dark but far more awesome. Someday, just possibly in our own lifetimes, we may gain eyes to see it full face: the radiant and terrible beauty of humankind transformed.

PART ONE
Given

one

A Morning on Mt. Tam

Man has no Body distinct from his Soul: for that call'd Body is a portion of Soul discern'd by the five senses, the chief inlets of Soul in this age.

❧

Energy is the only life, and is from the Body; and Reason is the bound or outward circumference of Energy.

❧

Energy is Eternal Delight.

—WILLIAM BLAKE, THE MARRIAGE OF HEAVEN AND HELL

DURING MY childhood in Georgia, going up a mountain on a summer day was a reliable experience. The air always became cooler, lighter and sweeter as I rose to soft greenery and birdsong. Ascending Tamalpais, an unusual mountain only thirteen miles northwest of the center of San Francisco, is entirely different. The lower slopes are often covered with fog sweeping in from the Pacific, calling for heavy sweaters. Breaking out above the fog, the hiker soon removes his sweater. The air is hot, dry and utterly still. The grasses on meadow and knoll have turned to bronze, setting off the hard, dark, metallic green of trees and shrubs. Few birds sing, though now and then you may hear the echoing cry of the scrub jay, the yellow-shafted flicker, the red-tailed hawk. A faint smell of bay and sage hangs in the motionless air, and beneath the steady vertical rays of the sun all life seems held in the pressure of an immense silence.

7

On Mt. Tam all expectations are overthrown, even those seasonal certainties from which we draw the rhythm of our deeper longings and the references in our literature. Somehow this mountain, a sacred and forbidden place for countless generations of Indians, survives as both desert and rain forest. For about half the year, April to October, the rainfall is negligible. Then for six months the mountain is swept by gusty rainstorms with winds that sometimes exceed one hundred miles an hour. Even then, the newcomer is not reassured by the familiar. When the autumn rains bring the summer desert to an end, the grassy knolls and meadows start their yearly shift in hue, turning from bronze to a vague greenish-gray, then deepening to the unequivocal green of winter. There comes a brief November spring: While the scattered deciduous trees are slowly shedding (maple leaves lie like damp golden stars on the lower trails), all else rushes towards greening and blossoming. By mid-January the major streams have become cataracts. Water gushes in every small gully. The meadows have turned to marshes. Before that winter month has passed, more than a hundred species of native plants may bloom on and around Mt. Tam. To fly home from New York City on a January night then walk up a redwood canyon by a loud stream the next morning is to experience a happy disorientation for which no drug has yet been conceived.

By late March most of the blossoming is over, while some of the leafy trees are only just finishing their fall. The rains lessen. In May the summer pattern of cool fog below and hot desert above is well established. Gradually the green hills lose their brilliance. Tall grasses turn to straw, curing through the summer to an ultimate bronze. And the moment comes at last, in mid-October, when all living things are stretched to their limits—dry, thirsty, waiting.

❧

I sit on a bare knoll westward of Tam's west peak watching the stars fade. Now and then I glance at the faint emanation of pale gold along the eastern horizon. The ground is hard and dry, for the rains are overdue. Though it is cool now, the clarity

8

of the sky promises another hot day. Just to the west of me there is a clump of California oaks, and a forest of firs seventy-five yards downhill to the south. If I am still enough I can sense the soft respiration of the trees. I toy with the idea of sharing a tree's existence—foliage spread out to receive the sun, trunk thrusting downward in sexual union with the earth, roots feeling their way towards moisture. I focus my attention on one of the gnarled oaks to the west, a silhouette against the grasses beyond. I try to enter its double life of light and darkness, air and earth.

For a brief moment I experience the tree's being, then I am thrust back firmly to my separate existence, capable of seeing the tree at a distance, touching it, cutting it down, analyzing it. I have been given names for each of its constituent parts, terms for its processes, and ways for relating it with the other elements of the biosphere. But I have been made incapable of entering its being and sharing its life. The dryads have long since been banished from the forests, and metaphor itself is suspect; the pathetic fallacy is, after all, a fallacy. I am left with logic and separateness, and can bring to mind no myth-heroes of the woods except Paul Bunyan and Smoky the Bear.

But something is wrong with this mode of perceiving and being, even in strictly scientific terms. The physicists have taught me that the tree, so substantial and impenetrable, actually is mostly "empty space," if we conceive the subatomic elements of which it is made as particles. It is certainly quite transparent to radiation of wavelengths longer than one meter (including all radio waves) and shorter than one angstrom (including X rays and gamma rays). Only a conspiracy of my genes makes the tree opaque to me. In the experience of the living beings from which I am descended, electromagnetic radiation within the narrow band we call visible has proved to be useful for guidance and survival in a particular terrestrial mode of existence. Through long evolution we have developed eyes sensitive only to the radiation vibrating between 10^{14} and 10^{15} times a second. Therefore the tree appears impenetrable to my sight just as it would be impenetrable to my physical body, a handy correspondence. Its opacity, however, is operational, not ultimate. Physics and mathematics have provided us a respectable way of acknowledging what primitive peoples have always known: The tree is not really solid. There is room in it for spirits.

But this too—the idea of the tree as composed of empty space between tiny particles—is obviously an oversimplification. Bertrand Russell once defined matter as whatever satisfies the equations of physics. Ever since the early 1920s, it has become increasingly clear that the elementary particles can be treated mathematically and experimentally as energy waves. Even earlier, light waves and other forms of radiation were shown quite clearly to consist of particles. All discussion on whether photons and the basic stuff of matter are "waves" or "particles," however, simply demonstrates the limitation of human language and the bankruptcy of the conceptual framework upon which language is based. Both "object" and "space" are constructs. The constituent stuff of what we call matter exists entirely apart from "visible" and "invisible," far beyond conventional concepts of "real."

The dark dome of sky above me on this mountain morning is transparent. Beyond the darkness, layer upon layer of luminosity. Of what is the world made? Surely we need no concrete building blocks, however infinitesimal, to explain substance. We know that matter is pent-up energy. Surely we need no concept of tiny bodies to bind this immense energy. What may seem to be small moving bodies constituting matter—the "particles" of physics—can be conceived, in Einstein's words, as "pulselike concentrations of field, which would stick together stably." Indeed, we may go on to imagine the elementary particles as resonant centers of vibrancy which can combine with others to create new centers of vibrancy which may combine again in varying pitch and pattern. The interplay of all this vibrancy manifests itself in the spangled diversity of common experience.

Of what is the world made? Underlying everything, forming itself into what we now call electrons, protons, neutrons, and all the rest, obliterating basic distinctions between matter and energy, substance and spirit, joining all manifestation in common origin and cause, there is the elemental vibrancy. Let us say that substance is vibrancy tending towards transformation. All existence—whether mountain, sky, star, shaft of sunlight, thought, song, or self—is vibrancy. And the oak tree (if only I had eyes to see) is a particular arrangement of vibrant energy. The oak tree (if only I had ears to hear) is a consummation of its constituent vibrations, thus a perfectly harmonious strain of music. The oak tree (if only I had ways to learn) is available for me to enter and experience fully.

But I have been taught that it is a "thing," solid and separate from me. The perceptual mode bequeathed me by my particular culture denies me identity with the tree and insists that it and I remain forever walled off from one another. In the same way, I and all of us who live and breathe and take our psychic sustenance from this culture are convinced that we are solid and separate, forever walled off from our wives and lovers, brothers, fathers, friends and children, sisters, mothers; forever alone and alienated; locked for life in the prisons of our skins. And this is it, we are assured by pessimists who delight in the glitter and safety of the negative vision: The Human Condition!

Actually, there is nothing essentially human or natural in our present situation. The illusions of separateness and alienation have been created only by enormous, exhausting efforts. The walls between us and our fellow beings are merely one aspect of the ruins of a dying culture.

❧

A band of sky along the rim of the east is turning a rich deep gold. Only a few stars remain. Beneath me to the southeast, the north leg of San Francisco Bay picks up a faint reflection of the predawn colors. Farther south, the distant lighted buildings of the city appear translucent against the gentle glow of morning. Lines of miniature red lights move southward on the freeway by the bay. The more distant Bay Bridge stretches, an amber-studded spider's strand, from Berkeley and Oakland to the city.

I consider the quality of the human energy and spirit moving along with the tiny red lights on the freeway below. I consider the significance of those lives or mine here on the mountain, so infinitesimal beneath the stars. It is easy to bring to mind the familiar formulation, passed along uncritically from writer to writer, about how the human individual has been successively reduced and dethroned by the discoveries of Western science—removed from his honored place in the center of the heavenly bodies by Copernicus and others, removed from his special position as king and curator of the animal kingdom by Darwin, removed even from command of his own acts by Freud and the behaviorists, thus rendered puny, insignificant and impotent, vulnerable to further reduction with each further discovery. But this formulation has always seemed wrong to me. Perhaps the whole idea of dethronement is a function, not of the discoveries, but of the rather bizarre consciousness of a culture that has held distance, size, rank and manipulation to be the essential marks of honor, a consciousness doomed to dethronement because it conceived itself as enthroned.

A culture that compares itself favorably to a mountain only when it climbs it or moves it is certain of eventual deflation. We'll not likely move a galaxy physically, and journeying to the distant stars, if possible, will require not just a new technology but a radically altered consciousness and mode of being. In any case, we have moved enough mountains, rechanneled enough rivers, leveled enough forests, gathered up enough gross physical energy. There must be some larger destiny for humanity.

On this luminous morning, I want to shake off the prevailing sensibility of the age, at once ironic, smug and cautious. I want to dream of some great adventure in consciousness. I want to dream of the kind of personal and communal transformation that may lead to the unification of the world, not by conquest or politics, but by the emergence of a new human nature. The old culture has no respectable tradition that allows such dreams. The respectable tradition, demeaning our essential nature while encouraging us to go out and move the world, isolating us within our own skins then glorifying this tragic condition in literature and art, obviously did not anticipate the peril posed by such a monster armed with twentieth-century technology. *Not* to dream more boldly may turn out to be, in view of present realities, simply irresponsible. By conceiving of the human individual as an aggressive mover of things and other people, yet severely limited and flawed, we take a crucial step in assuring that he remain so. And the concept is clearly incomplete, if not totally false.

Most of us, I believe, must admit a timid sense of recognition when we come across the trail maps left for us by such voyagers as the Indian seer, Sri Aurobindo, who writes about the emergence of "an inherent, intrinsic, self-existent consciousness which knows itself by the mere fact of being, knows all that is in itself in the same way, by identity with it, begins even to see all that to our mind seems external in the same manner, by a movement of identity or by an intrinsic direct consciousness which envelops, penetrates, enters into its object, discovers itself in the object, is aware in it of something that is not mind or life or body." Aurobindo, like other master voyagers in these realms, writes with the assurance of one who has been there. He is not simply a dreamer when he tells us of higher states of consciousness, in which "a universal beauty and glory of being begins to manifest; all objects reveal hidden lines, vibrations, powers, harmonic significances concealed from the normal mind and the physical sense. In the universal phenomenon is revealed the eternal Ananda." [1]

Yes, I'm small, a speck on an ordinary planet in the vastness of space. But physical size is in many ways an irrelevant dimension. My consciousness, and yours, can move with the dance of energy in the atom's heart, the first invisible stirrings of life, the march of epochs. "A small galaxy only a few light-years across" is an idea that I can envelop. I have, if only on rare moments, entered other lives, merged completely. I am not inevitably separate and alone. In a real sense, I *am* all that I know. The galaxies exist in me, not printed as mere images inside my skull, but vibrating in the larger self that defines me and all beings. This self is by no means confined to the limits of the skin, which is only one of the lesser boundaries of the individual being we call human.

❧

The gold has just drained from the eastern horizon. Now the sky is pale yellow rising to pale blue then a deeper blue above. The last star has disappeared. To the southwest and west, the calm slate-gray Pacific merges with a slate-gray sky. A veil of light fog stretches out beneath a crescent point of land south of San Francisco, creating the illusion that the land is floating in air.

Dramatic changes now. Just a few moments ago the city was a maze of twinkling lights. Now it is a silhouette. Suddenly the air seems cooler. The call of a crow affirms the change. I feel a slight movement from the west, then the south—a wandering morning breeze feeling its way along the mountain's undulating ridges and hollows. My attention is drawn to a dark red glow just south of Mt. Diablo, some thirty-five miles to the east. Seven tiny birds pass over me in pulsing flight, propelling themselves in short bursts of energy. And without warning the dark red glow on the horizon becomes a blazing spot of sunlight. After all the waiting, it happens in a rush, and all the world is transformed. Diablo is rendered invisible. The sky is transfixed with light. The trees around me are rudely awakened. Only a moment later the sun, though only half-revealed, has become too bright to look at. A bee hovers before me, throbbing with energy.

In this light I know that we are not reduced by the insights of Copernicus, Darwin, Freud, and the others, only freed from the trivial anthropocentric arrogance. Each insight offers us further proof of our kinship with all existence, and a more immediate possibility of merging and ecstasy. We are neither petty geocentric tyrants nor existential ciphers. We are strange and radiant creatures, flesh of the sun's flesh, most favored visible heirs of the primal consciousness.

Nothing about our existence is really ordinary. The sort of matter we deal with must rank with the rarest and most exotic manifestations in the known universe. The substances we consider most commonplace actually are the most extraordinary.

Water is exceptional. Air is a gift of grace. A piece of wood is an exotic rarity. Stone is locked energy or the frozen music of the Pythagorean brotherhood. No wonder the cathedral builders were drunk with the grandeur of dominating so much heavy matter and enclosing so much resonant space.

And yet, on this exceptional planet, in the midst of all this beauty, situated at the leading edge of a particular fashioning of life, mind and higher consciousness from the inconscient stuff of existence, I am forced to admit that I am restless. The ground seems hard and uncomfortable. I think of things I should be doing. The sun's up. Why not go down the mountain and get on with the day's trivia? My culture has done a good job on me. I'm torn from the present moment. My consciousness is positioned somewhat to one side of my own being. I have been made, in Heidegger's phrase, forgetful of existence. Could it be true that we spring into full authenticity only when confronted with death? I know that moments of vibrant awareness are rare in our culture and that it is difficult to find them in our literature except where associated with long deprivation, tragedy, or the approach of death. Yet who among us hasn't experienced at least a few of those rare interludes when we quite escape the puppet strings of social conditioning, when our being seems perfectly synchronized with the rhythm of a larger existence, when all things flow and there is neither waiting nor satiation?

Maybe such moments seem rarer than they really are due to the fact that we have no words for adequately expressing them. One of the more powerful taboo mechanisms is simply not providing a vocabulary for the experience to be tabooed. In this case, you are forced into surrogate vocabularies that can be categorized as mystical or nutty, and easily dismissed, leaving you shamed and doubtful that you really had the experience after all. How many contemporary films, plays, or novels can you bring to mind that deal with unadulterated ecstasy? Positive, unconditional joy may, as a matter of fact, turn out to be the real pornography of these transition years—strange, embarrassing, titillating.

I consider how often the moments of bliss in my life have

been associated with rhythmic activities—dancing, running down a long mountain trail, playing drums, paddling a canoe for hours —an affirmation, perhaps, of the essentially rhythmic nature of the universe. There is a scene in *Anna Karenina*, based on one of Tolstoy's personal experiences, in which Levin mows hay with his serfs. At first he mows with conscious effort. He forces the scythe to do his bidding. The rows come out badly. Gradually, the work becomes easier:

> He thought of nothing and wished for nothing, except not to fall behind the peasants and to do his work as well as possible. Behind him he heard only the swishing of the scythes and ahead of him he saw only the receding figure of Titus, the convex half-circle of the mown piece in front of him, the flower heads and grass slowly and rhythmically falling around the blade of his scythe, and ahead of him the end of the swath that would bring him rest.
>
> Suddenly, as he worked, he had a pleasant sensation of cold on his hot, sweating shoulders, without understanding what it was or where it came from. He looked up at the sky while whetting his scythe. A low, heavy cloud had come up, and fat raindrops were falling. Some of the peasants went over to their coats and put them on; others, and Levin too, merely wriggled their shoulders joyfully up and down beneath the delightful freshness.
>
> They did another, and still another row. They went on mowing—long rows and short rows, with good grass and bad. Levin lost all awareness of time; he had absolutely no idea whether it was late now or early. A change had begun to take place in his work now that gave him an enormous amount of pleasure. In the midst of his work moments would come over him when he would forget what he was doing; it became easy for him, and during these same moments his row would come out almost as even and as good as Titus's. But the instant he would

recall what he was doing he would feel the full
burdensomeness of toil, and the swath would come out
badly.[2]

Lunchtime comes, to Levin's surprise. He had not been aware
that four hours had passed. After lunch, he takes his place among
the mowers again:

> In the heat of the day the mowing did not seem so difficult
> to him. The sweat he was soaked in cooled him off, and
> the sun that burned his back, head, and arms, bare to the
> elbow, lent him firmness and tenacity; more and more
> frequently those moments of unconsciousness would
> come on him when you didn't have to think about what
> you were doing. The scythe sliced away on its own
> accord. These were happy moments. Even more joyful
> were moments when on reaching the river where the
> swaths ended up the old man would wipe his scythe with
> some wet grass, rinse the blade in the fresh river water,
> ladle out a little in his whetstone box and offer it to Levin.
> "How about some home-brew? Good, eh?" he said
> with a wink.
> And as a matter of fact Levin had never had a better
> drink than this warm water with green stuff floating in
> it and the rusty taste of the tin box. Then came the slow
> blissful walk back, with his hand on the scythe, during
> which you could wipe off the streams of sweat, take a
> deep, deep breath, and watch the long line of mowers
> and everything happening round about, in the woods and
> fields.
> The longer Levin kept mowing the more often he
> would feel the moments of oblivion when it would no
> longer be his arms that were swinging the scythe, but the
> scythe itself, like a body full of life and
> self-consciousness, would move forward of its own
> accord, and the work would perform itself, accurately
> and carefully, as though by magic, without a thought

being given to it. These were the most blissful moments.[3]

All natural manifestations share this quality of periodicity—cycle, wave, pulsation, vibration. There is rhythm in the incredibly high-pitched singing at the atom's heart, the shimmer of sound, the ten-cycles-a-second alpha wave in the brain of ant and man (echo of a faint pulse in the sun), the beat of the heart and the sea, the wax and wane of tides, the predator-prey cycles of forest, field, stream and sea, the turn of the earth, the return of the rains, the elliptical swing of planets and stars, the rhythmic travels of galaxies, and, beyond conceivable time and space, the expansion and contraction of the universe itself. Only humanity under the conditions of Civilization has dared try to step outside the pulsing flow of nature. Only one species has marched across the earth in contrary rhythms, superimposing rigid rectangles over the curves of life, pressing forward deaf and blind to nature's clear and urgent pleas. Only the human individual has been thrown out of phase with the rhythms of life, so that he can serve as a sort of component for collective man, while the self is left, betrayed and nearly forgotten, in a state of constant discontent and dis-ease, longing for something never fully experienced, lacking words to ask for a nameless grace.

But no organism can entirely escape the rhythms of existence. The familiar episodes of earthy intensity—laughter, physical exertion, crying, orgasm—call forth pulsations from sanctuaries deeper than thought, reminding us of the throb of existence. Indeed, when any action achieves a certain focused intensity, the formation of waves or pulsations seems inevitable. Traffic engineers were hard put to explain the stop-and-go pattern of cars on absolutely unimpeded expressways, until their studies showed that all such traffic, upon reaching a certain intensity, forms into longitudinal waves somewhat more than forty-four cars in length; in each wave, the cars speed up in the center and slow down at the ends.

For every such overt, quantifiable rhythm in our lives, there are many vibrations and sinuosities hidden from our senses and our instruments. From the vantage point of any individual at any moment in time, all the rhythms join in a single sinuous flow. This flow may best be defined by the converse, as being precisely that which is most forbidden us by our social conditioning. Our attention and energy are repeatedly directed away from the flow of the present and towards what has not yet happened or what is finished. By age four we have been plucked out of the natural stream of existence by a series of unacknowledged manipulations so traumatic that we generally suffer total amnesia of the early childhood past, rarely if ever again to experience the immediacy of unpostponed life.

By the late middle years, the typical American has become completely allergic to the present. The long-awaited European trip constitutes a busy, distracting period of planning and describing the plan to friends, followed by a period of recounting the event to the same friends and showing them pictures. The trip itself is a wearying and uncomfortable, if necessary, inconvenience. For most tourists everywhere, the camera serves as a surrogate experiencer. Busying himself with exposure settings and focus, the traveler avoids having to make the pretense of enjoying present perceptions. He aims his camera into the abyss of the Grand Canyon, unaware of the futility of the act or of the pathetic figure he makes. At Disneyland he follows directions on markers that show him exactly where to point his camera to get the "best" angle, so that his pictures will be almost identical to those of his neighbors. Thus, he will gain comfort that existence does have an approved and recognizable pattern, and may even be real. If he is a good citizen, he travels always through time in the same manner, planning ahead, doing his job, gaining perspective in the approved way, by distancing himself from events and beings, including himself. Only at the approach of death does he realize, perhaps for the first time, that he can no longer plan ahead. If not dulled by drugs and the false reassurances of professional routine, he may be forced at last into remembrance of existence. He may spend a few urgent moments of authenticity, flowing with the natural waves of life and being.

No wonder so many people flirt with death in the Hemingway

manner, and that so many people in recent years have risked the discomfort and possible nightmares of psychedelic drugs. "I want the world to change, so that it will be what it is," the seeker's reckless action cries. "Take the chance. Let my mind be blown. Let me suffer the winds of madness or feel the chill of death, if only for a few precious moments I can see colors in their original splendor, if only for a moment I can just *be*, neither anticipating nor recapitulating, perfectly at home with myself." How sad that people must resort to reckless or illegal acts simply to feel natural. How ironic that joy should seem so far away, requiring such strenuous pursuit, when the crux of the difficulty lies in the fact that it is so close at hand. Ecstasy is here, now. It is we who have been removed.

Having no tradition of ecstasy, we hardly know where to begin in reclaiming it. Our culture does allow one exception, however. We are granted the possibility of transcendence in the area of erotic love. If we can get over the fantastical childhood and adolescent obstacle course that places difficulties in the way of almost every natural sexual urge, we may hope for tenuous erotic connection with a larger vibrancy. In this area we have at least a tradition and a vocabulary, however truncated and debased. Indeed, some people can conceive of such a word as "ecstasy" *only* in the sexual sense. One editor never reconciled himself to the title of my book, *Education and Ecstasy*, since for him it invariably evoked images of Hedy Lamarr running nude across a field of flowers—in an educational context apparently. That our culture, through neglect, allows a word with the power and utility of "ecstasy" to be captured by a movie star is commentary enough.

Still, sex remains one of the most readily available ways of sampling the primal consciousness. The knowledge contained in the full orgasm is considerable. And we may read in the yearning of lovers a parable of all creatures' yearning to join—not to return to a lower, more primitive state, thus reducing tension, as Freud would have it, but to attain a condition of grace in which all beings great and small, "higher" and "lower," feast upon the elemental vibrancy.

Moments of transcendence have come to me in various forms.

I bring to mind a night of walking the streets of Berlin with a friend shortly after the Wall was erected, not just understanding the separation of families, but experiencing it with every cell of our bodies. And there was a hazy May afternoon in Selma, Alabama, after a sleepless all-night journey across the country. The scene in Brown's Methodist Church Chapel, where Martin Luther King, Jr., and other civil rights leaders were preparing a great throng for a historic march, burst upon me with such overwhelming brilliance that I felt I must hold firmly to the back of the last pew or else actually float away. And there was a dazzling July noon in Big Sur when thirty-five people of different races, after twenty-four hours of struggling with the bitterness, resentment and rage that generally isn't even acknowledged, suddenly dropped every barrier and came together in tears of understanding, love and joy. Joining after separation.

I have been fortunate. I have experienced more than my share of the events that the culture has chosen to chronicle, and have been involved in movements and causes that call forth strong passions. But I am a child of my culture. The most transcendent events in my life have been associated with the erotic.

There was once a moment in the deepest hours before dawn, after a night of love, when consciousness itself began to change. Awareness of the different parts of our bodies which earlier in the evening had brought such delight had faded away, leaving only a generalized awareness of luminescent smoothness and sinuosity. Separate acts had blended into a prolonged single movement. Even the divisions between waking and sleeping had become unclear. Please do not misunderstand me. I offer no expertise in these matters; such nights may be rarer for me than for you. But I must tell you that the moment did come when our own once separate and private emotions began to appear on each other's faces. Just that. Every flicker of feeling I might expect to originate inside me appeared instead on her face. I was left no sensation, no emotion, no existence apart from her. There was nothing metaphorical about this merging. In the faint light from another room, each of us could see our actual selves embodied in another—and we were terrified.

That was some years ago. Since then I've learned more about

such changes and have been introduced to disciplines through which the blending of selves may sometimes be achieved without such intense and intimate stimulus. But we were ignorant then, and we grasped for the old objective consciousness as drowning swimmers might reach for any solid object. We returned, rather shaken, and the remaining hours before dawn could be described in more familiar language.

But that wasn't the end of it. We had been there, if only for a moment, in another sphere of being, and thus to some extent were to be forever changed. The following afternoon a delightful little miracle occurred. We were having late lunch in a modest restaurant by the Pacific, seated at a table by a window overlooking a narrow strip of beach. It was a soft blue day with thin sheets of high white clouds. We merely toyed with our food. Gradually we became aware that the experience of the previous evening was coming back, only now it was happening gently and unthreateningly. We held hands across the table and surrendered. Little by little our separateness faded and with it all possible restlessness and unease. As my body stopped being "mine," every part became a deliciously tingling cloud of energy. I knew hers did, too, since we were one being. The waitress, the proprietor, the other patrons and the objects on the table also became part of us. Finally, everything was joined, perfectly related in time and space. The waitress couldn't possibly think our behavior strange, for "she" was "us." Nothing could be "wrong." And, as a matter of fact, the waitress did smile when we smiled. We smiled each other's smiles.

On the beach just outside our window, about seven or eight sandpipers were running back and forth looking for food. Sometimes they would run out on their incredibly fast tiny legs after the receding water, then rush back just a fraction of an inch ahead of the incoming wave. But we didn't perceive them as separate from the wave. They and we and wave and sky and beach and sea and all in it and all existence was part of a single flow. One of the sandpipers didn't run with the rest. This particular bird would make great sweeps around the others, covering twice as much territory, or suddenly dash off to make a joyful figure eight, then shoot back to startle the others with his sudden reappearance. An ethologist might argue that the bird was merely establishing his dominant position in the pecking order. We might respond by characterizing his actions as "play." Both ideas would miss the point because they entail separation into categories. As we entered the sandpiper's very existence, as we literally became one and the same, all such considerations became irrelevant. He *was*. We *were*. Everything flowed together. We couldn't be surprised by any of the bird's wild sweeps because we were of his consciousness, just as he was of ours. And yet it was an unfamiliar delight to be one with such sporty vibrancy, and we often laughed aloud. We had no doubts that the bird knew somehow he was one with us. I'm certain even now that, to whatever extent the sandpiper "knew" anything and to whatever extent "knowing" is really important, the bird did know.

We stayed there all afternoon, flowing perfectly with the rhythm of existence, not wishing to be anywhere else or to do anything else, seeing straight through the cardboard illusion of separateness and thus perceiving all colors and sounds in their infinite perfection and clarity. A rare afternoon. When the sun touched the Pacific the birds flew away. The tables were set for dinner. The cocktail crowd came in. And we were awakened from reality to the demi-existence of wanting and waiting that we all know so well.

❧

Sitting now in some discomfort and impatience on Mt. Tam, I wonder why we can't spend more of our lives in such harmony with time and being. I know the objections: We can't have people sitting around contemplating their navels or grooving with birds; there's work to be done. But those who object do so without knowledge. The states of heightened awareness can also be states of heightened performance. There is the well-known tale of a Zen master sitting motionless in what seems to be a trancelike state of *satori*. A Western visitor wonders whether the master is aware of the outside world. At this point the master's hand darts out and he catches a fly with a pair of chopsticks. It may seem a profane comparison, but the greatest of athletes the world over are no strangers to unusual states of consciousness. Lacking the vocabulary and the sanction to talk about it, American athletes sometimes refer to a sort of self-hypnosis that accompanies their most remarkable feats. They speak of projecting themselves with the ball, of just blending with a play rather than reasoning about it, of letting the bat do the work.

Indeed, the human organism in a condition of heightened awareness, experiencing the connectedness of all things, flowing with universal rhythms, can perform wonders. But such an organism is next to worthless as a standardized component in a social machine. Then, too, heightened states of awareness produce fascination and contentment, thus reducing the insatiable urge to consume. It has been consumers and components, unaware and out of tune with nature, that our culture has for the most part needed and produced.

And then there is India, a blot on every argument for adventuring in the realm of human consciousness. But is it, really? India has created what might be called an effective technology of inner consciousness change along with the rich and varied vocabulary that goes with it—and has ended up with impotent starving masses. But India has been as unbalanced and one-sided as the West, in the opposite direction. India, by and large, has neglected Brahman as manifested in what we call matter and energy and has failed to realize the marriage between contemplation and action. These failures are acknowledged by some spiritual leaders in that country. It becomes increasingly clear that an individual or a culture must be balanced before beginning the difficult evolution into new forms.

No, I can't envisage a transformed humanity that is passive, nonphysical, nonerotic. The laws of equivalency between physical and psychic states are not yet widely understood, but surely will be. The sense of oneness with all existence (a first step in the Transformation) entails not just blending with animate things and seas and stones, but also with buildings and ships and

24

airplanes and electronic networks. All these must eventually balance and flow together. All are part of evolution. All are manifestations of the elemental vibrancy and the primal consciousness. In the hands and under the will of the old culture, machines have proven how fast they can rape and poison the earth (while helping prepare it, we must also acknowledge, for the Transformation). But there is another way of thinking about machines, expressed by Richard Brautigan in his poem "All Watched Over by Machines of Loving Grace." Brautigan imagines a cybernetic forest that can accommodate both pines and electronics, "where deer stroll peacefully/past computers/as if they were flowers/with spinning blossoms."

During his lectures, Alan Watts sometimes chides his audience: "What is all this talk about *going* to heaven? We live on a beautiful blue and white ball floating in the heavens. *We are in heaven now.*" Sometimes I fear that Watts, in spite of his enthusiasm and charm, may be tarred and feathered for saying that. In a world of poverty and racism and war and suffering children, such a statement might rouse frustration and anger. If taken seriously, it might soothe the outrage that is considered prerequisite to social action. It might invalidate personal experience. After all, a constant, nagging unhappiness is somehow reassuring. We learn to equate it with normality.

Yet Watts is quite right. Heaven is available, not somewhere else, but exactly where we are. I would add, however, that we are also in hell, the hell of pain and injustice, the hell of potential wasted and bliss unnecessarily renounced. Neither heaven nor hell exist somewhere else, in separate spheres. Both are right here. The angels and demons are superimposed on every cubic centimeter of *this* world. We can never deal with either by placing them at a distance. The journey towards further human evolution is first of all a journey towards a place and time that has become for us somehow remote and clothed in mystery. That elusive destination is the eternal present, where, transcending demons and angels, we may exist in the pervasive fullness of the elemental vibrancy. We cannot travel there fragmented, but only with body, senses, intellect and spirit together, all one.

The West, however, has never before attempted that journey. Its history has been the history of an escape attempt. Somehow, through abstraction, fragmentation, renunciation of bodily and sensory knowledge, and through the technological realization of the old dream of magical manipulation, this culture has attempted to thrust its way up and out of the stream of life. In this respect, as in most others, the United States achieves an extreme. As Alan Watts has pointed out, Americans are not really materialists but abstractionists, showing their contempt for the realm of ordinary matter by promiscuous and careless use of all materials, including their own bodies.

It's hard to say just when or where the Western flight from the flesh began, but it shows up clearly in Platonism, then even more vividly in neo-Platonism, in which a human being's greatest hope is to free himself from his body. Plotinus, the leading neo-Platonist, whose vision illumined centuries of Western mysticism, constructed a Ladder of Being with pure matter at the bottom and pure spirit at the top; a good man's task was to climb. We glimpse other beginnings of the flight in the passionate asceticism and oriental mysticism of early Christianity and, perhaps most significantly, in the earlier dualism that came to us from Persia. Zoroastrianism was, in fact, the first thoroughly dualistic religion in the history of the world, with one great deity, Ahura-Mazda representing all that is good and light, and another, Ahriman, representing all that is evil and dark. This religion strongly influenced Pythagoras, who was in turn a significant philosophical influence on Plato. These two philosophers gave us a majestic vision of underlying unity and form. But, unfortunately, the dichotomies in Plato that served the dialectic tension became rigid and irreconcilable in the neo-Platonic tradition.

Meanwhile in Persia other dualistic religions succeeded Zoroastrianism. The most extreme among them was founded around A.D. 250 by a Mithraistic priest named Mani, who (as this philosophical version of *La Ronde* continued) had undoubtedly been influenced by Platonism. Manicheism conceived the entire universe as divided into two kingdoms, each the utter antithesis of the other. The kingdom of spirit was ruled by a totally good God, while Satan held sway over the kingdom of matter. God created only spiritual things such as light, fire and human souls, while Satan created all matter, including the human body and its desires. Inevitably, human nature was seen as totally evil, since the first parents of the race had received their physical bodies from Satan.

The man who was to become St. Augustine spent nine years of his life as a Manichean, was then attracted to neo-Platonism and finally, at age thirty-three, was baptized a Christian. Bringing together three strains of thought that vied with one another in demeaning the flesh, Augustine raised up a powerful dualistic structure of philosophy and religion in which man's fate is predestined, his nature totally depraved. On the Day of Judgment, the fortunate few predestined to dwell in the City of God will be transported to their heavenly immortality. All the rest, the inhabitants of what he called the Earthly City, will burn in hell. We can hardly expect these doomed inhabitants of the Earthly City (which would include most of us) to hew to the highest ethical and spiritual standards. Most people can, as a matter of fact, get on with the business of the world. Thus the spiritual and temporal leaders who followed Augustine justified the prodigious manipulations of the physical that have characterized the Western flight from matter.

Drawing upon Augustine, John Calvin refined and improved the justification by contriving an ingenious reconciliation between the worldly and other-worldly. Calvinism manages to despise the flesh and the world while simultaneously measuring each individual's heavenly standing in terms of his worldly success, surely one of history's neatest doctrinal tricks. The significance of this justification can hardly be overstated. Indeed, Max Weber has speculated that capitalism developed in the West rather than elsewhere primarily because the West possessed the Calvinistic justification for it.

There is a long-standing argument about the efficacy of ideas. Can a new philosophy really influence the course of history or is it only a reflection of events, cultural confluences, and technological developments that already are unfolding? The argument takes force and relevance only for the kind of dichotomizing intellect that insists upon viewing ideas as *separate* from life and matter. We can look at it differently. Ideas are neither unreal nor the only true reality. They are simply another manifestation of the elemental vibrancy. Neither more nor less real than a tree or a bird or a mountain, ideas join inevitably with the total flow of existence. An idea is something like a virus. A virus consists of strands of RNA within a cover of protein. It contains none of the material stuff necessary for assimilating matter, fixing energy or reproducing itself. For all intents and purposes, it is simply an idea. The strands of RNA possess coded information that can direct a cell or group of cells to do their bidding, including reproducing more viruses. Similarly, the DNA that directs the fabrication of each living organism is pure information, pure idea, but it is passed down directly from generation to generation. A virus must come in contact with an appropriate host under appropriate circumstances. Some viruses may lie dormant for many years before favorable ecological conditions arise. We do not deny the virus reality because at a given moment it is not influencing matter and energy. We do not categorize it as separate and apart from the web of life. The same thing is true of an idea. The words on the pages of a book, even if unread, are still a manifestation of the elemental vibrancy. An idea arises from life. It can influence life. It is life.

Calvinist capitalism, idea and actuality, found a perfect host in the West. And then, in science and technology, the West found its most promising and desperate means for escaping itself, and maybe even its planet. The way towards escape has been up and out, the mode has been separation, abstraction and manipulation. And when Freud, bearing the imprimatur of science, turned at last to the inner being, what he purported to discover was really the same old dualism: the id forever at war with the higher needs of the social order, a "scientific" justification of civilized repression.

Symbols may reveal historical directions. The West has long been fascinated by the rising vertical. We see this in the extreme skyward thrust of the Gothic steeple, and then the Gothic skyscraper, pointing always towards a destination up there, out there, somewhere *away* from the roots of life. And at last it stands on its launching pad, ultimate symbol of frustrated escape: an immense Gothic spire denuded of its bristling ornamentation and gargoyles, made aerodynamically clean, ready to launch dehumanized young men *out there*, from which they will try to comfort us with spiritless readings from the Bible or mechanical mouthings of party slogans.

The escape attempt ends here, in the pollution of this planet and the futility of flight from it. The space program is a triumph of Newtonian physics, but its leaders have failed to understand the psychological laws of motion. Any decisive outward movement of human consciousness requires an equal and opposite movement to greater depths. In the long run, there can be no successful outer trip without an inner trip. A space capsule is not a very good escape vehicle. We cannot escape ourselves. The space program falters to the extent that the culture fails to explore its own roots—the endless spaces of individual and communal consciousness, the deep rhythms of existence embodied in the natural world.

❧

The sun is higher now. I can sense its power. Another hot dry day is in store, a hard one for the plants and animals of Mt. Tam. There is a strangeness about this mountain on the edge of a continent that has shaken my assumptions about flora and fauna and climate and "the way things are." But its rhythms are becoming familiar to me; I know that eventually the rains will come. I stand and stretch, still rather restless. I'll not flow with the mountain's rhythms on this morning, nor merge with the life of a tree. But I know such things are possible, and they will doubtless happen on another day.

I walk eastward down the slope of the knoll, aware of the sun's energy. I am a particular manifestation of that energy—all of me, not just flesh, but consciousness and all. And the sun, insofar as our present science can tell us, is a particular manifestation of the energy that once was gathered up in the primordial fireball. On one incredible, infinite instant some ten billion or more years ago, all the vibrancy that was to become matter and energy sang together in a single high trilling of ecstasy and potential, being somehow the elemental stuff that was to transform itself into stars and stones and trees and flesh and the consciousness of Bach and other things beyond our conceiving. Once this elemental vibrancy began to expand and cool, all the rest was inevitable. Huge eddies formed in the surging vibrancy. The smallest of these that could be held together by their own gravity were approximately the size of a galaxy. Vibrancy coalesced in glowing clouds of gas in the shape of these eddies. Stars condensed out of the clouds, and then planets —form unfurling in the cooling.

As heat is lost, organization increases. As the universe as a whole moves outward, its particular elements move towards new centers, drawing closer in ever more complex and elegantly interrelated forms. Outward and inward movement. Entropy and disentropy, perfectly balanced.

I can't possibly be separate and apart from all of this. My consciousness, mind, spirit can't possibly be separate and apart from me and all of this. Like all else, consciousness, mind, spirit existed, *in potentia*, in the primordial fireball (or in whatever process of being and evolution the universe presents us) and thus must respond to the general laws of existence. The first of these on this planet in this solar system in this universe is transformation to more highly ordered states. Existence is transformation. The consciousness, mind, spirit of humankind will be transformed or humankind will pass out of existence.

There is nothing startling about this. The wonder is that humanity has managed, under cultural constraints, to resist significant evolution for so long, and that we have been conditioned to view our present aberrant and extreme condition as normal. It is true that most cultures that we know of have seen it as a primary task to keep individual consciousness stuck at a certain point. But the history of this type of culture has come to an end. Perhaps we can sense new beginnings that involve regaining our balance, mending the artificial splits between mind and body, spirit and matter, man and nature, the individual and the social. Perhaps, as our vision clears, we shall see just how far we have already traveled on the journey of the Transformation. But first let us look at our origins, at the very roots of the fading Civilization in which we now live.

two

Some Notes on Being Alive

Sometimes the women would sit together beside their shelters in the long level light of the evening sun, their beads and necklaces like gold upon them. Each would hold a handful of long, straight, dry grass and sing all together, beating time with the grass and stroking the stems with the tips of their fingers like the strings of a guitar. The melody was charged with all the inexpressible feelings that come to one at the going down of the sun over the great earth of Africa. They called the song "The Grass Song" and with the difficulty of interpretation neither Dabe nor the singers could readily explain it. I can only recall the feeling and render the words inadequately:

> This grass in my hand before it was cut
> Cried in the wind for the rain to come:
> All day my heart cries in the sun
> For my hunter to come.

They would sing this over and over again, the song becoming more charged and meaningful by repetition, as if the heart, too, was enjoined to a constant act of importunity, as in the New Testament injunction to prayer, in order to make life and its powers accessible to its deepest entreaties. The song put us all under a spell, so that I was not surprised that often the young men hearing its crescendo of longing could contain themselves no longer. They would drop what they were doing and come out of the bush, their feet pounding the desert sand like a drum, their hands stretched wide and their chests heaving with emotion, crying as if the sound had been torn alive and bleeding from the centre of their being, "Oh, look, like the eagle, I come!"

—LAURENS VAN DER POST, THE LOST WORLD OF THE KALIHARI

IT IS THE beginning of the second act of *Don Giovanni*, possibly the most sublime sustained piece of music our culture has ever created. All around the semicircle of boxes at the opera house the patrons of the arts are beginning to fall asleep. It is mostly the men's heads that slump forward as if stunned by a heavy blow. A majority of the women remain rigidly upright, encased in their makeup, their jewelry, their expensive gowns. A long passage on strings reveals Mozart's measured passion and presages the tragic events to come. The somnolent breathing in the boxes increases in tempo and effort. The breathers sleep without dreams, waves of music lapping at the edges of their unconsciousness. Their bellies and blood are heavy with the food and alcohol of the pre-opera dinner, along with two more drinks during intermission. Their livers have grown large and flabby from the continuing assault of liquor and excess fats. Their metabolic systems reel under the repeated shocks administered to their systems by the rewards of our rich way of life. Sometimes these sleepers rise to a familiar way station of semiconsciousness in which is contained the faint click of metallic wheels of time on an endless track, flickering images of the abstractions they call "business," and a pervasive but unfocused tumescence. Their hearts pound heavily, not with the urgings of lust or the passions of music, but simply to maintain a vital oxygen level in the body and brain. Millions of capillary blood vessels have collapsed in the girdles of fat that have gathered around the waist, the neck and shoulders, the joints. Hundreds of thousands of brain cells strain for survival on a minimal supply of oxygen. Half clogged with fat, the heart labors to send blood through heavily lined arteries and veins to keep alive the slumping, slack-jawed patron of the arts. Unheard, the music soars.

("Oh, look, like the eagle, I come!")

The men who sleep in the opera house represent an extreme. But millions more sit before their television sets in varying states of lowered consciousness, literally forgetting themselves. Many are surrounded by material plenty, evidence of the highest standard of living in world history—wood, glass, metal, fabric, plastic, paper, chemicals, pipes, valves, wires, intricate circuitry, cleverly concealed electric motors. And there are the cars and the power saws and the power mowers and the snowmobiles and the dune buggies and the motorboats and the private planes—all idle and temporarily forgotten as the evening's programming presses on through time, cutting it into segments of synthesized laughter and plasticized adventure for those who would embark upon an adventure only if they could take out an insurance policy guaranteeing its success. Here are the favored people of the rich civilization, people who pay professionals to live their lives for them, people who are pumped full of vitamins and antibiotics so that they will survive and grow to consume more and ever more.

Others among the television viewers are not so fortunate. They lack the spacious houses, the power mowers, the boats, the vitamins. They live in ugly, cramped quarters, are unsure of medical care or police protection, and are by no means certain of the food they need to live. But they, too, watch the same programs and the same commercials. And they burn with resentment. They are being cheated and they know it. They want their share of the goods and action of the rich civilization. They want the green lawns and the clean white houses and the shiny plastic credit cards. And surely they should have their share. For every American knows (he is repeatedly reminded, in countless subtle ways) of his inalienable right, not to be happy, but to be unhappy in style.

Much is made of how effectively American merchandisers and advertisers have programmed gullible people to become insatiable consumers. But high effectiveness in this regard is not required. The key factor here is that, until recently, no alternative aspiration has been available. The alternatives that have popped up in recent years have been tolerated by the established order precisely to the point at which they begin to affect the demand for goods and services; then they have been firmly resisted. Without words or other conscious formulation, the established order knows that most people will go on consuming at an increasing rate (with or without the help of advertising) so long as no other mode of satisfaction is readily available. It is best, in fact, for the people to be totally unaware that other modes exist. To this end, the culture devotes itself to the creation and maintenance of a strange and unprecedented "self" almost entirely cut off from being and thus condemned to ceaseless doing and getting. For such a self, the quality of being alive is simply irrelevant. Progress or success thus becomes associated entirely with changes in matter and energy external to the self. And "standard of living" comes to mean the use and accumulation of goods and services, nothing more. All of this is so bizarre that it is difficult to write about. The main trouble is that we find it hard not to consider our present mode of life and consciousness as "practical," "reasonable," "commonsensical," and "solid," when actually it stands as a historical aberration.

It is natural that people throughout the world would envy the material plenty of America—this raw and extreme end of Civilization—and it is easy to understand that most people would choose, other things being equal, to be physically secure. But it is doubtful that anyone, including ourselves, can long tolerate the peculiarly deprived consciousness that prevails over most of this nation. Suffice it to say that the life of the Bushmen described by Laurens van der Post, people living under material conditions we would consider shockingly low, clearly contains more power and intensity, more laughter, more music, more challenge, more joy than does that of a typical American.

Few of us would change places with a Bushman, which is just as well, since we lack not only the necessary physical and mental skills, but also the capacity for emotion and joy which is as much a part of the Bushman's existence as is his bow and arrow. Americans once faced a more realistic choice. During the long period when whites and Indians lived side by side on this continent, thousands of individual whites chose to go to the Indians and adopt their way of life. It is significant that voluntary transculturation was more likely to take place in this direction than the other.

We may as well face it: In terms of how it feels to be alive, we have a very low standard of living indeed. Surrounded by our shares of the spoils from the plundered planet, we must be judged among history's deprived people. There is something especially poignant about our condition. We have achieved a certain material plenty. We have eliminated many of the more obvious forms of physical suffering. We have realized many of the ancient sorcerers' dreams of power over matter, energy and distance. We are, in fact, heirs to all those benefits of Civilization that are so often proclaimed they need no elucidation here —the refinement of certain sensibilities, the creation of diversity, the multiplication of options, the evolution of humor and irony, taste and style. And yet we are likely to live strangely numbed and isolated in the midst of these riches, bereft of feeling, ignorant of the joys of the senses, dispossessed of vision and barely able to breathe.

This last point discloses much about our particular society, for relatively few people in it have taken a truly full breath since early childhood. Our way of living elicits a high shallow breathing which, in turn, serves to reduce the flow of feeling and thus perpetuate this way of living. Even in periods of high exertion or in mortal combat, breathing usually is concentrated high in the chest, which "steels" the individual to "meet his challenge." This matter rarely comes to conscious awareness, much less to discussion or study. And yet other cultures, especially those of the East, have long been aware of the relationship of breathing to psychic and physical states. And there are those teachers of yoga and other disciplines here in the West who realize that practices involving the breath can help students achieve an unfamiliar variety and richness of emotional and mental states. But the very notion of systematic study and practice in something as "natural" as breathing too often elicits a quick and scornful dismissal. Significantly, those who dismiss the notion generally have not tried the practice, nor would they consider trying it.

There is a seventeenth-century parallel. The picture of the solar system revealed to Galileo through his telescope was new and startling. It threatened established doctrine. It was dismissed and scorned by the most respected academicians of the period. During the debates on the subject, Galileo asked his opponents only to look through his telescope and judge for themselves.

Many of them, as has been recounted many times, steadfastly refused. Others looked and claimed to see nothing. One critic maintained that the ancients, who excelled at everything, must have developed the telescope and then discarded it as worthless.

Eventually, of course, the scientific view prevailed, dispelling scholastic dogma and medieval superstition. But even science can lead to blindness. Today we are in the midst of what Willis Harman of Stanford Research Institute terms a New Copernican Revolution. Understanding it involves looking through unfamiliar windows of feeling and being. Many of the most respected members of the established order simply refuse to look. (To return to the matter of breath: I have spent some time in the practice of breathing under the tutelage of Magdalene Proskauer, one of the pioneers in the field. This practice has opened up new vistas for me, as vivid as a first look at the moons of Jupiter or the mountains on the moon. I have witnessed new worlds opening, with impressive reliability, for Miss Proskauer's other students. But the stuff of these worlds is subjective. It cannot yet be recorded on a photographic plate or measured by an instrument. Efforts to do so are now under way, but their outcome will not alter the value of the experience.)

The new view of the universe by no means excludes objective observation and replicable verification, only their tyranny. The new view is not invariably clarified by the routine backward step for perspective or by the interposition of an instrument between perceiver and perceived. It is now becoming clear, as Michael Polanyi, Lewis Mumford and others have argued, that the whole concept of the detached and unmoved observer is simply a fallacy. We begin to realize that nothing is entirely impersonal.

To view the universe anew is to change in feeling and being. Just as there is no mind without body, no spirit without matter, there is no cognition without affect, no observation without personal change, no unmoved mover. And there are neither medical nor economic indicators that can measure the quality of being alive. Before we can begin to comprehend our present condition, we must be willing to look through windows that have been clouded over for several centuries.

three

An Introduction to Mass Murder

The human heart gets into a frenzy at last, in its desire to dehumanize itself.
—D. H. LAWRENCE, STUDIES IN CLASSIC AMERICAN LITERATURE

WE ARE WELL aware of what generalization and abstraction, classification and categorization have gained us—how these modes of thought have helped us control matter and energy and create man-made environments and organize ever-larger social entities. And we need only be introduced to one of the familiar biological taxonomies (Gray's *Anatomy of the Human Body*, Peterson's *A Field Guide to the Birds*) or begin to understand one of the great mathematical constructs (Euclid's *Elements*, Newton's *Principia*) to realize that the abstract, ordering intellect has added a certain majesty to our perceptions of the manifest vibrancy. What it has cost us is perhaps less clear.

Once the perception is firmly locked to the generalization "green," a particular bush can never again be quite so vivid and unique. Once a hunter accepts the generalization "brown," he may find it more difficult to distinguish the stag from the dry foliage in which he hides. Primitive hunters and gatherers indeed do not generalize colors. According to ethnologists Brent Berlin and Paul Kay, all languages, even the most primitive, have words for black and white. If a language has three color terms, they will be black, white, and red, the colors rarest in nature. Primitives avoid generalization, not because their color sense is less sophisticated, but because their ecological sense is far more sophisticated than ours. Berlin points out that abstract color terms are relatively useless concepts in societies living close to nature. Indeed, our present-day color concepts may serve primarily to separate us from our environment. Children of four to five can generally distinguish more subtle gradations of color than can adults. The children have not yet begun the process of formal education that embalms experience and prepares all the stuff of perception for interment.

Whether hunters and gatherers or simple farmers, the peoples we call primitive are highly sensitive to the attributes of being. Anthropologist Dorothy Lee writes of the tribal farmers of the Trobriand Islands which lie to the east of New Guinea:

> If I were to go with a Trobriander to a garden where
> the taytu, a species of yam, had just been harvested, I
> would come back and tell you: "There are good taytu
> there; just the right degree of ripeness, large and perfectly
> shaped; not a blight to be seen, not one rotten spot;
> nicely rounded at the tips, with no spiky points; all
> first-run harvesting, no second gleanings." The
> Trobriander would come back and say "Taytu"; and he
> would have said all that I did and more.
>
> Even the phrase "There are taytu" would represent
> a tautology, since existence is implied in being. . . . And
> all the attributes, even if [the Trobriander] could find
> words for them at hand in his own language, would have
> been tautological, since the concept of taytu contains
> them all. In fact, if one of these were absent, the object
> would not have been a taytu. Such a tuber, if it is not at
> the proper harvesting ripeness, is a bwanawa; if overripe,
> spent, it is not a spent taytu but something else, a yowana.
> If it is blighted it is a nuunokuna. If it has a rotten patch,
> it is a taboula; if misshapen, it is an usasu; if perfect in
> shape but small, it is a yogogu. If the tuber, whatever its
> shape or condition, is a post-harvest gleaning, it is
> an ulumadala. When the spent tuber, the yowana, sends

its shoots underground, as we would put it, it is not a yowana with shoots, but a silisata. When new tubers have formed on these shoots, it is not a silisata but a gadena. An object cannot change an attribute and retain its identity.[1]

Only an advanced technology permits us the sloppiness of our present-day perception and terminology where being is concerned. Now that technology is itself creating a dangerous jungle, we may find ourselves in urgent need of a more precise terminology. For example, we could well use a word for the tough-skinned, rubbery plants sold in supermarkets as "tomatoes." These plants were developed by agronomists for the express purpose of withstanding the trauma of mechanical harvesting devices. They bear only small resemblance in taste, feel or essence to the original plant. We also might invent separate words for tomatoes force-grown with harsh chemical fertilizer and over-irrigation, for those ripened after picking, for those permeated with pesticide.

And surely "smog" is a sloppy generalization for the many kinds of poisoned air, each of which affects us differently and *is* different. The term "polluted water" only begins to inform us of the particular disease or damage we may suffer from the various biological and chemical solutions that we insist on classifying under the noun "water pollution." But for us neither plants nor air nor water possess life. As our language clearly tells us, they are simply *things* to be *used*.

In his novel *Little Big Man*, Thomas Berger accurately summarizes an essential difference between primitive and civilized sensibility. His hero asks the Cheyenne chief, Old Lodge Skins, if he hates the Americans:

> "No," he says . . . "But now I understand them. I no
> longer believe they are fools or crazy. I know now that
> they do not drive away the buffalo by mistake or
> accidentally set fire to the prairie with their fire-wagon
> or rub out Human Beings because of a misunderstanding.
> No, they *want* to do these things, and they succeed in
> doing them. They are a powerful people." He took

something from his beaded belt at that point and, stroking it, said: "The Human Beings believe that everything is alive: not only men and animals but also water and earth and stones and also the dead things from them like this hair. The person from whom this hair came is bald on the Other Side because I now own this scalp. This is the *way things are*.

"But white men believe that everything is dead: stones, earth, animals, and people, even their own people. And if, in spite of that, things persist in trying to live, white men will rub them out.

"That," he concludes, "is the difference between white men and Human Beings." [2]

When everything is alive and unique and particular, perceptions are finer and more intense. All of existence is more immediate and poignant. Questions of "meaning" never come up, since being and meaning are one.

We have a word, "animism," for the primitive belief that all objects possess life or are endowed with indwelling souls. Having defined the belief, we can dismiss it without further understanding or feeling. Jean Piaget devotes a major portion of his seminal book, *The Child's Conception of the World*, to animism in the children of his culture (Swiss, mostly middle class). In questioning the children, Piaget writes, "It is naturally necessary *and this is the most important part of the experiment*, to ask 'Why' or 'Why not?' after each answer." [3] I have supplied the italics in this sentence to point up what Piaget may never have considered. The repeated use of "why?" with young children constitutes one of our most effective ways of insuring that they *not* endow objects with vital force. Piaget was testing the children for animism and simultaneously influencing them against it. For there are no real "whys" in nature, and all the "hows" are strictly provisional. The barrage of "whys" directed at our children helps shape our particular brand of objective consciousness—this mode of thought built of boxes, armored with schedules and rulers and clocks and counters, capable of dissecting and distancing, skilled in a simple geometry of judgment and love.

41

The years have passed and we have had a chance to observe Piaget's excellent scientific work put into practice. The filmed laboratory demonstrations have become classic: the obviously scientific-authoritative surroundings, the white lab coats, the yardsticks and beakers and scales. And the bewildered little child, his eyes darting around as he tries desperately to come up with an answer, *any* answer, that will please the man in the lab coat and the horn-rimmed glasses. Children are paraded in and out of the test chamber, hopelessly naive, undeniably darling. (My youngest daughter, at age four, was asked a series of the Piaget questions and answered, among other things, that the sun is alive and could feel the prick of a pin "if God had a pin," that a candle is alive but can't think, since "it doesn't have a thinking place," and that thought itself is "pretty strong. My thought can grow flowers. Daddy couldn't break it. With an ax he could, but he wouldn't.")

At the end of the documentary, we must nod in agreement with the man in the white coat as he explains that the child confuses thought with body, fails to see himself as objective and separate from nature, imbues things with life and is pretty poor at abstraction, conceptualization, and the like. Some sort of equation is often drawn between the child's animism and that of the primitive—generally quite misleading, since the adult primitive's concept of aliveness is precise, coherent and wise. About our own children: no worry. If we are patient, they will come around to our mature way of thinking and everything will be all right. But there's one thing the commentators never mention: The development of abstract, generalizing, "objective" thought does prepare people in this culture for what the culture terms success. It also prepares the way—whether through the maturation of children or the evolution of cultures—for mass murder.

It prepares the way for mass murder, first of all, in the literal sense. Abstraction and generalization tend to precede territorial warfare and genocide in social evolution. American Indians learned mass war from white men. They learned it late and were never very good at it. Even the practice of scalp-taking probably was started and certainly was spread by whites. Scalping was known in Europe from the time of the ancient Greeks, and quite possibly did not exist in the New World before the arrival of the white man. In any case, the early settlers of eastern North America cleared whole statewide areas of Indians by a system of bounty payments. Governor Kieft of New Netherland is generally credited with the idea of using scalps as proof of dead Indians, thus avoiding the bulk and inconvenience of whole heads.

But that masterpiece of generalization "The only good Indian is a dead Indian" has turned out to be only a prelude to some of the generalizations of recent years. One of the broadest is summed up in the terms "combatant" and "noncombatant." If a village in Indochina is officially declared to be occupied by "combatants," some junior officers, according to their own testimony, seem unable to distinguish women, children, and even infants from fighting men. They are all combatants and they are treated as such.

Throughout the course of Civilization, those capable of the highest abstraction have often been the most humane. But abstraction can also exist entirely apart from high intellect or humane purpose. Let us view the highly trained young abstractionists sitting at the controls of giant bombers, many miles removed in height and psychic distance from the consequences of their acts. They address themselves to grid coordinates which first were expressed abstractly on pieces of paper, then encoded in electronic-inertial devices. At a certain point in the sky, the abstractionists actuate the devices, which then release hundreds of tons of high explosives. Neither the abstractionists sitting in their orderly, antiseptic surroundings in the sky nor those on the ground who conceived the operation are motivated by personal malice. They are concerned only with clearing out specified rectangular areas of jungles. The planes wheel in the sky and fly away, and that's all there is to it.

But the great bombs continue downward and murder is done, not only to every man, woman and child who happens to be in the rectangle marked out so neatly in grid coordinates, but also to all manner of living things that fly and walk and crawl and swim and burrow, and to strong trees and tender shoots and fruit and flowers and fungi and the rich humus of many seasons. And later there may be a small newspaper headline: BOMBS BUST JUNGLE.

Are there greater horrors in store for us? Possibly. For we have had a Secretary of Defense who has written that "mere biological survival" isn't really as important as whether our good Godly side wins out over the evil Godless side.[4] Let us acknowledge our situation: Abstractionists, men for whom most things already are dead, control the actuating code that could wipe out life on this planet. Let us not ignore the blank dead despair behind their eyes. Late one night, after dinner and many heavy drinks with one of these men, I looked into this deadness, and it chilled my heart.

"Just tell me one thing," I said, after a long debate, "you wouldn't really, under any circumstances, risk a nuclear war that would kill everybody—I mean, including you and me and our families, our children?"

"Why not risk it?" He looked straight into my eyes and paused. When he resumed talking, I heard his voice as a sort of echo, utterly flat, distant and metallic. "Why not? Sometimes I just want to get it all over with, one way or the other."

Don't underestimate—as did the American Indians—this despair, this alliance with deadness.

During the siege of Marseilles, the ancient poet Lucanus tells us, Caesar ordered his men to cut down a grove of sacred trees so that they might build a machine of war. When they refused, Caesar himself took an ax and struck the first blow. The men followed his example. Though Caesar failed to overwhelm the defenders in the subsequent battle, he went on with "reckless rage and stern heart" to bring Civilization to the benighted peoples of Europe.[5] Caesar's example continues to inspire us, except that now the bulldozer, the power saw, and the bomb have replaced the ax. The benighted people of primitive times generally had no single word for "tree." Each type, sometimes each individual tree, was separately named. The primitives felt compelled to offer an apology to any part of nature that they used in any way. Generalization has increased our efficiency. We can replace a forest with a shopping center without so much as a thought, much less a word of acknowledgment. A tree,

44

after all, is just a tree. A dust bowl is just a dust bowl. Asphalt, cement, concrete are graded according to technical specifications. Never mind what is pushed aside or buried underneath or denied the life of sun and air.

Once categorized, all things, whether literally buried or not, are set in a sort of perceptual concrete. Even events are sorted and graded. Our newsmagazines are structured around departmentalization. Any event or trend which doesn't fit into one or another of the departments is assumed not really to exist. I know of stories that actually were denied publication because the editors could not find an appropriate department for them. A similar difficulty plagues the fixed departments and disciplines of academia. Interdiscipline, cross-discipline, and nondiscipline studies proliferate as the old culture breaks down.

Actually, nothing that lives can be assigned a permanent generalized category. The old culture murders things and events so that they will be still. To the extent that we continue to perceive them as dead, we are involved in the murder. Perceiver and perceived are one. The ultimate victim of the murder committed by unthinking abstraction and generalization is our own perception, ourselves.

I am by no means suggesting that the Transformation involves renunciation of generalization and abstraction, classification and categorization. These modes of thought are extremely useful. I am using them in this book. The new culture will continue to use them. But I suspect they will be recognized for what they are: dangerous instruments that should be used with caution. Please do not mistake anything on these pages for a dichotomy setting "animism" and abstract generalization in opposition and mutual exclusion. The Transformation involves both, and much more. As the lifeless world comes back to life, the abstract and the general don't desert us, but they lose their hypnotic power over our perceptions. The first step in our liberation is simply to become aware of possibilities that have long been hidden from us. This alone triggers new perceptions, unfamiliar intensities of feeling and being, and a heightened sensitivity as to what is live, particular, and unique.

45

four
Hunters and Farmers

"You insist on explaining everything as if the whole world were composed of things that can be explained. Now you are confronted with the guardian and with the problem of using your will. Has it ever occurred to you that only a few things in this world can be explained your way?"

—WORDS OF DON JUAN, A YAQUI SORCERER, QUOTED
BY CARLOS CASTANEDA IN A SEPARATE REALITY

FOLLOWING the trail that leads back to humankind's emergence on this planet, we are soon confronted with difficulties. Even the relatively recent beginnings of Civilization are tangled over with uncertainties and ambiguities. Continuing backwards through prehistory to the origins of farming and thence to the birth of the earliest social forms, we are compelled to proceed by conjecture and extrapolation. Thus, every description of social and cultural evolution partakes of the mythic. We ourselves are revealed in our attempts to reveal our distant past.

Still, it will be my purpose here to establish what may be called an anthropological scale of social and cultural change, starting with the views of representative Western anthropologists. I am not treating the possibility that some lost Atlantis existed in prehistory and that most social evolution consists of relearning forgotten lore. Even if this tantalizing suggestion were true, it would not change my main point, that wherever certain social and environmental conditions are present, large-scale human transformations inevitably do occur.

46

CONCORDANCE OF SOCIAL CLASSIFICATIONS

Classification							Author
Savagery	Barbarism		Civilization				**Lewis Henry Morgan**
Primitive Culture	Simple Farmer	← Agriculture → Great Cultures of Antiquity (S.E. Eurasia)	Varied Ways of Life Based on Farming	Fuel Age			**Leslie White**
Band	Tribe	Chiefdomship	State				**Elman Service**
Egalitarian		Rank	Stratified State				**Morton Fried**
Hunter & Gatherer	Simple Agriculture	Theocratic States	Industrialism				**Julian Steward**
Hunter & Gatherer	Horticulture / Pastoralism	Agriculture		Modern Technology			**Yehudi Cohen**
Hunter & Gatherer	Simple Farmer	Early Urban Civilization	Capitalism	Industrial Revolution	Cybernetics		**Richard Cowan**
Primitive Communism	Pagan Society	Ancient Classical Civilization	Feudalism	Merchant Capitalism	Finance Capitalism	Communism	**Marx & Engels**
Free Wanderer / Restricted Wanderer / Central Based Wanderer	Incipient Pastoral Nomad / Diverse Pastoral Nomad / Semi-Permanent Sedentary	Simple Nuclear-Centered	Advanced Nuclear-Centered	Supra-Nuclear-Integrated			**Beardsley & others**
Nomadic Gatherer / Semi Nomadic Predator / Semi-Sedentary Collector / Semi-Sedentary Collector	Pastoralism — Shifting Cultivation / Rotating Cultivation / Permanent Cultivation	Peasantry	Commerce				**Philip Wagner**

The chart on the previous page, prepared for me by Richard Cowan, shows how several well-known anthropologists have classified societies. On the chart, complexity of social organization increases from left to right. Some anthropologists argue that societies do not evolve. The most compelling evidence, however, is on the side of social evolution. I see the chart as revealing a dynamic and ultimately inevitable movement from past to present, from less complex to more complex. The divisions are obviously not drawn to time scale. Hunters and gatherers have existed in bands for well over a million years, while farming is thought to have had its crude beginnings around 9000 B.C. in the eastern Mediterranean region and the Zagros highlands of Iran, or perhaps even earlier in Southeast Asia. Urban civilization or states probably began around 3000 B.C. in the Middle East and by 1200 B.C. in the New World in the lowlands of the present-day Mexican states of Veracruz and Tabasco.

Though the time scale is not indicated graphically on the chart, the vertical lines between the types of societies are significant. The chart is a concordance, showing how the different classifications relate to one another, and revealing that anthropologists of our culture, whatever their orientation, tend to perceive the same great cultural turning points. You can see that all these scholars except Fried (who is primarily concerned with freedom and equality irrespective of the other markers of social evolution) noted a significant change either between the band and the tribe or between the corresponding shift from hunting and gathering to simple farming.

Anthropology, however, being a study of things human, is beset with exceptions, contradictions, and fuzzy areas. Some researchers point out, for example, that the Northwest Coast Indians, like the Eskimos who lived not far north of them, were primarily hunters and fishermen. And yet, rather than remaining at the level of the band as did the Eskimos, they evolved complex chiefdoms with elaborate ceremonies and systems of rank and status. But this comparison is rather specious. The Northwest Coast Indians were blessed with an unusual abundance of fish and game; fishing for these Indians was as certain as harvesting a crop. The Northwest coast dwellers also had developed means of preserving and storing their surplus food. Unlike the Eskimos, they did not have to expend large amounts of energy just to survive a hostile environment. Their main problem lay in distributing surplus wealth to a relatively dense population rather than perpetually questing after food. Status became associated not with hoarding but with giving. During potlatch ceremonies, the greatest chiefs gave away most of what they owned. In the end, when whites pumped more wealth into the system than it could handle, the ceremonies became competitive orgies of destruction. Blankets, canoes, and jewelry were thrown into great bonfires before thrilled and horrified onlookers, all for the sake of status —and as an unacknowledged attempt to maintain economic stability.

The Northwest chiefdomship was an anomaly. (It has been pointed out that history will probably consider our present-day Western consumerism, with its continual potlatch of planned obsolescence, rockets shot off into space, and billions tossed into the "defense" wastebasket, just as anomalous.) The exception helps prove the general structure of the concordance: Over most of the planet most of the time, according to the research graphically summarized here, hunters and gatherers are organized in small bands. Simple rainfall farmers are joined in tribes. The beginnings of permanent cultivation and irrigation goes along with the beginnings of urban civilization, from which has emerged statism, commerce, capitalism, industrialism, modern technology, and the megastate of today.

Cowan's concordance starts out with Lewis Henry Morgan's breakdown of human societies into savagery, barbarism, and civilization. This first great classification is based on complicated correlations of technology, social organization, and other factors. Now out of date, it remains a bold and remarkably accurate attempt at synthesis as of the 1870s. Leslie White is interested in mankind's per-capita use of energy; his classifications lead up to the recent beginning of a Fuel Age, a significant turning point in humankind's capture of the earth's power. Elman Service, a leading student of White, bases his classifications on sociopolitical organization. Morton Fried focuses on the rise of social and political hierarchies, which he sees as overriding the division between hunter and simple farmer. Julian Steward, a major influence in the evolutionary school, is concerned with humanity's relationship to its environment; he emphasizes how the adaptive core of man's culture interacts with the natural ecology. Yehudi Cohen comes up with somewhat similar classifications, though he calls himself a social ecologist. Richard Cowan's own classification system follows Service, Steward and Cohen and will be used as a basic guide in this chapter.

Karl Marx's evolutionary social theory, first proposed in 1857, is presented here as a significant curiosity. Based on Morgan's out-of-date anthropology (Primitive Communism as Marx conceived it never really existed), it nonetheless reveals a clear if biased picture of the development of the West.

The final two classifications are more complex than the others in the concordance. Both volumes from which they are drawn attempt to classify every possible way societies can function rather than tracing the broader sweep of evolution. Richard K. Beardsley's scheme is based on community patterning (i.e., demography), while Philip Wagner's tries to combine economics, technology and demography. Both contain categories that are, for our purposes, far too neat and fine. Significantly, however, they show that even when microscopic analytic categories are utilized, the large-scale phases of evolution still can be recognized.

What do these anthropologists have to tell us about life in the major types of societies? The hunters and gatherers live in small bands generally composed of only a few families. Their material culture is extremely simple. Since they are often on the move to follow the seasonal flux of their plant and animal food supply, they accumulate only such property as they can carry. Their religious or spiritual culture, however, is extremely rich and sophisticated, though it is so closely interwoven with their daily life that an insensitive observer may miss it entirely. And they have ample time for play and contemplation. Peter Farb argues persuasively in his excellent book on the American Indians, *Man's Rise to Civilization*, that primitive hunters and gatherers are the world's most leisured people. Our schoolbooks tell us that only Civilization can give us the leisure needed for the production of art, literature, and the other "finer things." This is not necessarily the case. A ponderous and complex material culture is actually a millstone around the ordinary citizen's neck. By adopting the strategy towards scarcity now demonstrated in Zen practice, every member of the hunting band may gain substantial leisure time. Farb goes on to say that, "Where life is reduced to the bare essentials—it turns out that one of these essentials is art" [1]—not art for art's sake, but artistic creation as an inseparable part of living. And it is possible that the part-time shaman, practitioner of those subtle, powerful arts of the spirit now lost to most of us, may be considered the world's first specialist—though not in the modern, formalized sense of the term.

Hunting bands, in fact, have no government, courts or laws, no formal leadership, no social classes, no full-time economic specialists or trades. Labor is divided on the basis of age and sex. Rights to the band's territory are collective. Society is based on kinship ties and is egalitarian. Trade consists of reciprocity in goods, favors and labor. There is no warfare as we know it. Hunters tend to avoid abstractions and generalizations. Hunting and gathering societies rarely have words for numbers over five. Few have detailed time units like our minutes and seconds. Few have our linear sense of history. For members of the hunting band there is the Creation followed by a continual social equilibrium. Each individual life thus partakes of the mythic.

The next broad classification of human societies encompasses those generally known as tribes. The tribe classification may include some pastoral nomads and a few groups of unusually stable hunters, but is generally associated with early agricultural society. The primitive farmers live in permanent villages, joined together by complex ties of kinship. Indeed, kinship dominates all social and economic relationships. Some tribal societies are matrilineal; that is, lineage is calculated through the mother's side. Husbands in some cases move to the wife's family dwelling place. In many tribes, a system of totems and ritual avoidances based on extended kin groups assures that young people will "marry out," thus strengthening alliances between two totem groups.

Life in simple farming communities is still fairly egalitarian.

Leadership is usually based on charisma rather than inheritance or election. The independent economic, religious and political sectors that are so central to our lives simply do not exist in tribes. Tribal villages are held together, rather, by means of such pan-tribal sodalities as clans, secret societies and age-grade societies that combine all the functions of the many social sectors of Civilization in one institution. Tribal societies may war for booty and honor, but not for territory. There are no standing armies or extended military campaigns. Finally, religious practice is considerably more formalized and separate from daily life than in the hunting and gathering band, occupying great amounts of the tribesman's energy. A Pueblo Indian spends approximately half his waking hours in specifically religious activities.

The beginnings of early urban civilization often coincide with the building of large-scale irrigation works and the resulting creation of an agricultural surplus. The rise of male work forces with male bosses spells out the virtual end of anything approaching matriarchy; no longer can women hold sway over small, home-based plots for rainfall farming. Early urban civilization also spells out the end of egalitarianism. One of its earlier forms, the chiefdomship, has no class structure as such, but entails a a linear rank order in which each member of the group knows exactly where he stands, be it number 1 or 853. The chiefdom is limited in that it has no legal structure and no legal sanctions.

It may be said that with the coming of legalism the true state arises. At this point, for the first time, economics, politics, religion and so on are organized into separate institutions, and leaders rule by hereditary right rather than by charisma. Social hierarchies evolve. Status becomes a factor in human existence. Slavery takes its place among the other formal institutions. Priests begin to replace shamans. Art separates out from daily life. Full-time specialists emerge. Markets spring up and with them the beginnings of true money. Villages become cities, which serve not only as administrative centers but as redistribution points for the goods which pour in as tribute and taxes. Territory becomes power. Territorial war is born.

Lewis Mumford has argued that the large-scale machine was an invention of early urban civilization, more particularly of the ancient cities of Egypt and Mesopotamia—this "machine" being powered by masses of human components instead of engines and cogs. Mumford finds many apt parallels between the human machinery of the Pyramid Age and our own technological megamachine. But there are also differences. For example, individuals still controlled prestige and power in early urban civilization. The faceless bureaucracy that dominates our modern existence flowers fully, as Max Weber has pointed out, only with the rise of capitalism. *"The Malaise"*

The process of formalization, bureaucratization, alienation, fragmentation—call it what you will—has gone through many stages of wax and wane, development and intensification, over the past five thousand years. But the ultimate direction is now clear. We of Civilization are the direct heirs of the first man who was moved to think of another human being as a component. We are the heirs of that component himself.

❧

All of this is conventional, the kind of material found in the standard texts, drastically summarized, simplified in terminology, expressed, alas, in the inescapable dualism of our language. How can we cut through the dense layers of language, convention, conditioning and social hypnosis to breathe, if only for a few moments, the way a Bushman breathes, to sense, if only for a few fleeting pulsebeats, the rhythm of his living? Such an exercise may be difficult but it is by no means impossible. For there must exist in any consciousness echoes of every consciousness, the Bushman's song in our hidden memory. Physicists have detected a faint radio radiation that seems to fill the universe and bathe the earth from all directions—an echo, it is supposed, of the primal fireball, of a cosmic event that occurred ten billion years or perhaps much longer ago. If such energy is at large and detectable by the rudimentary electronic sensors of this age, how can we summon up the arrogance to rule out the perceivable existence of "alien" being and feeling? How can we deny to any human consciousness the ultimate capacity to feel as a Bushman feels, to experience the delicate sun-yearning of a flower, and even to summon up that echo of the elemental

vibrancy which is existence itself at the beginning of all beginnings? Claude Lévi-Strauss, burning with Continental intellec-
tualism, offers us clues in language and the structure of humankind's seemingly limited repertory of social behaviors which
may be said to link our mind with the savage mind. But we can
choose to go beyond the mere verbal and intellectual, and invoke
realms of knowledge that are at once broader and more precise.

It may begin with the fragment of a poem, a few notes on a
flute, the distant voice of drums, the silence that follows a koan,
the softness of a lover's mouth, an unforeseen glimpse of fig
leaves unfurling from the tip of a wintry twig like a flower from
a magician's wand, the fatal billow of thunderclouds, the smell of
summer rain or autumn smoke. These or less than these (a day
of joyful indulgence or denial) may trigger vibrations in some
lost and forgotten region of our being, vibrations which can
expand and set off sympathetic tremors throughout all of what
we term body, mind and senses. And for a time we are free of
the hypnosis. We are wide-awake and tingling, available to an
unfamiliar kind of knowing by direct experience.

Not long ago, I viewed a television documentary on the
Kalihari Bushmen. I began with hopes of gaining some new
knowledge, but soon succumbed to disappointment and then
annoyance. The two-dimensional image reduced the magnificent
desert to manageable dimensions. The commentary added only
authority and distance. The paid scientist on the sound track
spoke with a certain condescension and even distaste about what
hard work the hunting was, and how "none of us really likes
hard work, you know." He went on to offer the "enlightened"
viewpoint that "*we*" should "turn them into herdsmen."

In the midst of this disaster, however, there was one of the
unforeseen moments: a short sequence of a Bushman playing a
small hand lyre. The melody was simple—five notes repeated
again and again, unhurried, yet urgent and vibrant. Those notes
pierced straight to one of the buried centers of my being, telling
me what the commentary had missed entirely. All that I had
been reading and pondering about primitive humanity suddenly
made sense, literally "sense." I felt, tasted, smelled the hunter's
life with such unexpected immediacy that tears came to my eyes.

At the same time, a phrase I had read and "understood" before came to mind, but in a new way, so that verbal understanding became feeling and being: *Everything is alive.* While the Bushman music played, that world of *aliveness* unfolded for me, a planet other than my poor world, as strange as science fiction. The dead things of my daily life sprang to life around me—chairs and table, keys in my pocket, leaves at the window, the shimmering, living glass of the windowpane itself. A passage from Laurens van der Post's *The Lost World of the Kalihari* flashed into my consciousness:

> "But how d'ya know which zone is which?" I asked, thinking of the thousands of square miles of identical sand, dune and bush.
>
> They laughed at my innocence with that wonderful Bushman laugh which rises sheer from the stomach, a laugh you never hear among civilized people. Did I not know, they exclaimed when the explosion of merriment died down, that there was not a tree, expanse of sand or bush that was alike? They knew the frontier tree by tree and grass by grass.[2]

Everything is alive and, being alive, is unique and particular. For a few moments I experienced the living world which has existed for several million years of human consciousness, which indeed exists now for surviving primitive bands and, to some extent, for all young children, whatever their culture. Its incredible variety, immediacy and beauty were almost more than I could bear. I was overcome by a poignant sense of impending and inevitable loss. The music ended. The voice of authority, of generalization and abstraction, resumed. All around me things fell into that long sleep decreed by Civilization, each into its proper class and category. And I was surrounded once again by death.

Perhaps we need no charts to show us what we have lost. And yet we can use all our carefully gathered knowledge to help us regain and even surpass our ancient skill and sensibilities. For the very first time, most of the people in the world have become aware of each other's existence. The primitive societies wonder at our technology. We wonder at their richness of individual and group consciousness, realizing at last what we have paid in spontaneity and joy for the impressive technological structure that insulates us from spirits and natural chance.

Alvin W. Gouldner and Richard A. Petersen have applied a rather sophisticated mathematical technique called factor analysis to various traits of seventy-one primitive societies. They conclude that *"the higher the level of technology, the higher the degree of demanded impulse control."* Gouldner and Petersen use Nietzsche's well-known breakdown between the Apollonian (form, structure, cognition) and the Dionysian (rapture, intuition, instinct) as one way of analyzing the social effects of technological development. They find that as the level of technology rises, so does Apollonianism. Higher technology also seems to go along with social stratification—the proliferation of classes and castes and the decline of a sense of single community:

> Tensions and social conflicts between social strata grow,
> along with intensified sentiments of ambition as well
> as envy, greed, and other aggressive impulses. Since
> Apollonianism is associated with technology, and the
> latter with growing social tensions, it can scarcely be
> expected that Apollonianism will be associated with
> friction-free social relations. Indeed, to the extent that the
> impulse control required by Apollonianism induces
> cumulative frustrations, Apollonianism itself may be a
> source of aggression. Impulse control mechanisms may,
> therefore, create some work for themselves, heightening
> certain of the very impulses that it is their business to
> control.[3]

We should not be surprised that this mathematical analysis resonates with the general theme of Freud's *Beyond the Pleasure Principle* and *Civilization and Its Discontents*. In the latter, Freud comments upon the inescapable relationship between "progress" and ever-increasing guilt feelings. He writes eloquently about the repression of individual impulse which he feels is necessary for the maintenance of a civilized state. Philosopher Herbert Marcuse goes him one better with his concept of "surplus repression"—that is, the *additional* controls upon our existence over and above those really needed for civilized human association, "controls arising from the specific institution of domination." Gouldner and Petersen are by no means the only social scientists who have noted the relationship between technological progress and impulse control, nor Freud and Marcuse the only psychologist and philosopher.

The earliest origins of the impulse control that has led to today's surplus repression go far back into prehistory. But we can see one of the most striking landmarks on Cowan's concordance—that is, the shift from hunting and gathering to simple farming. Nine out of his ten classifiers of society make a significant distinction at this point. The beginning of farming almost always occasions a change in social organization (from band to tribe), a change in technology (pottery, farming implements and permanent dwellings), and an increase in religious activities separate from the ongoing activities of daily life. Farming also introduces a changed feeling and being, a different consciousness.

The leading behaviorist, B. F. Skinner, suggests that early agriculture had a traumatic effect on the human organism. He sees farming as the beginning of delayed reinforcement, with all that implies. While the consequences of the hunter's acts are reasonably clear and immediate, the farmer has to take strenuous action in the spring (plowing and planting), then wait several months for the rewarding consequences. More powerful means of control are thus necessary to bridge the gap. It is possible that the complex and pervasive religious rituals and sanctions of tribal life emerged to fill the emptiness between planting and harvest.

Skinner studiously avoids dealing with consciousness, feeling and the like. But if these aspects of life exist, we might suspect that they too are affected by modes of reinforcement. If farming separates a man from the immediate consequences of his actions, it also separates him to some extent from the natural world. It begins to change his perceptions. We may, indeed, look upon farming as the seed of alienation between humankind and nature from which has grown pollution, defoliation, "jungle busting" and potential nuclear holocaust. The primitive hunter's reluctance to take up farming was once looked upon as laziness. We could just as easily think of it as prescience. In any case, this aversion is widespread and deeply felt. The American Indian prophet Smohalla, who created the cult of the Dreamers in the mid-nineteenth century, preached that his people should go back to the old ways:

> It is a sin to wound or cut, to tear or scratch our common mother by working at agriculture. . . . You ask me to dig in the earth? Am I to take a knife and plunge it into the breast of my mother? But then, when I die, she will not gather me again to her bosom. You tell me to dig up and take away the stones. Must I mutilate her flesh so as to get at her bones? Then I can never again enter into her body and be born again. You ask me to cut the grass and the corn and sell them, to get rich like the white man. But how dare I crop the hair of my mother? [4]

The Dreamers failed. The dream is over. The earth has been cut and torn and mutilated and—even Smohalla might not have foreseen it—bombed and poisoned. And now satellites with infrared cameras ceaselessly circle the planet, sensing out likely areas that have not yet been plowed and sown or paved over. Thus "humanitarians" would provide more food to support the plague of humanity that wounds the earth.

But regret should detain us only for a moment. There is no going back to the huntsman's life. All of humankind's journey partakes of the inevitable. The farmer prevails. He plunges a knife into the earth and gains an edge of permanence and power over the roving hunter. Or he cultivates his herds, turning wild creatures into products to be harvested. His art turns abstract. The huntsman's vibrant animals and quivering spears in flight become patterns of repetition and variation, representations of the weathers of existence.

The early farmer's advantage is a slight one. He controls the earth but remains at the mercy of the sky. He turns his eyes to heaven and learns to wait. The sky can bring abundance or disaster; it is awesome. He laughs less often and deep, becomes serious, develops a sense of tragedy. Ceremony cures his longing and fear. Though he has removed himself one step from nature and the consequences of his acts, he remains connected through ritual. Planting is sacramental. There are songs and chants for the young maize or wheat. Pottery-making is sacramental. The pot externalizes a dream of enclosing. It is an egg that can contain the restless energy of seed or water. Its design and decoration offers us a glimpse, sometimes startlingly vivid, of innermost tribal consciousness.

The early farmer is thankful for the uncertain blessings of the sky. Ecstasy may not impregnate his every act but is available periodically during rites that pulse with seasonal rhythms. He is not set above or below his brothers. He is attracted to the particular. He is aware of the energy of the universe and shares the tingling connectedness of earth, sky and sun, night and day, animal and plant. He remains in mythic time and space.

Over the centuries, the farmer may increase his advantage. A considerable surplus may develop. Occasionally as with some of the inhabitants of the rain-washed South Seas, abundance is a gift of nature, in which case a softer, less "civilized" society may develop. Most likely, however, the surplus results from the farmer's ever-increasing control over nature, and over his brothers. He constructs irrigation systems. He becomes less susceptible to, more independent of, the vagaries of the skies. He organizes to build and maintain the mechanisms of irrigation. Bosses direct the teams. Specialists handle the surplus in various ways, from warfare to commerce to spectator sports to arts and crafts to pyramids and temples. Religion enters the realm of individual moral relationships.

The surplus of grain continues to increase, rich in vibrant energy, a silent bomb that will blow apart the matrices of human relationships. For the hunter and gatherer and for the simple farmer, kinship is the glue and balm of life; the word itself is akin to "kindness," not only in English but in many other languages as well. Kinship, however—even the clan-type, extended kin arrangements of tribes and chiefdoms—becomes too unwieldy and ineffectual to hold together the ever-larger social groupings organized around the agricultural surplus. Human beings are broken down into classes and castes. They learn to relate in terms of prestige markers—clothing, decoration, accent, neighborhood, wealth. Religion, ever more priestly and separate from daily living, validates caste and class, and sanctions formal, codified punishment as a means of social control.

As the web of kinship is torn asunder, money becomes a major means of human interchange. Some anthropologists have theorized that true money—the *dentalium* shell money of California tribes, for example—is used even by primitive societies. But *dentalium* is used in dealings between two *different* tribes, that is, in *non*-kin relationships. The usual primitive intratribal "money"—cows, pig tusks, and the like—is really neither abstract nor commercial. It has pedigree and personality, sacred uses, moral and emotional connotations. True money comes only with early urban civilization and the growth of markets. In the beginning it takes the form of any number of things considered valuable and nonperishable: the cocoa beans of the Aztecs, the sacred feathers of the Mayans, the clay tablets of the Assyrians. The first actual coins (pieces of stamped metal with token value used as a medium of exchange) do not appear until the time of the Lydians in Asia Minor around 700 B.C. The money of Civilization is impersonal. It replaces kinship ties in certain aspects of human interaction. It marks another step in the separation of humanity from nature. It is not so much cause as symptom and, as we shall see in a later chapter, preparation for a transcendent rejoining. The symptom spreads with the epidemic proliferation of markets, the growth of markets into cities, their growth into nations and empires. The conquest of nature. The conquest of consciousness.

Here is the hidden price of the material surplus: We have been taught in school that increasing human control of the nonhuman world has brought us leisure and art and culture and freedom from want. We have not been taught that control over nature has also meant an equivalent control over individual human beings. We have not been taught that whatever we have gained in dominance has been paid for with the stultification of consciousness, the atrophy of the senses, the withering away of being. We have not been taught because the whole business of being taught is itself part of the price we have paid and still are paying. The farmer's success has in fact brought us to the most eventful and agonizing segment of humankind's long journey towards Transformation: that epoch of splendid darkness we call Civilization.

❧

Ultimately, nothing is lost. The hidden dreamer remains among us. The dream of transcendence and mystical union that has died a million times still flickers in every consciousness. Now it flares in grotesque shapes, in hasty public prophecies and un-balanced outlines of destruction and rebirth. But gargoyles in the marketplace cannot invalidate the dream or the hidden dreamer. The grotesqueries of the time only testify to how long the transformation of consciousness has been delayed.

The ultimate tendency of all manifestations of the vibrancy (to reiterate) is towards ever more complex, more elegantly ordered entities. The vibrancy, as I use the term, includes all that *is*, all of what we usually call matter, energy, space, life, social organisms, culture, ideas. These manifestations take on what our consciousness perceives as their various natures because of rate and interaction and pattern of pulsation. In this mode of perceptual definition, time must be set off as a separate category from the vibrancy. For us, time is a matrix against which pulsa-tion and pattern reveal themselves. To place time in the same category with the vibrancy is to take a further leap of con-ceptualization and being. It is perhaps to enter the highest mysti-cal state, the *nirvikalpa samadhi* of the Hindus, in which case all things are experienced as identical, eternal and ecstatic.

But so long as we exist and perceive in time, at this moment, at this point in an expanding, cooling universe, we must expect the stuff of existence to keep joining together in ever more complex groupings. And this is exactly what has happened to the human race, in terms of culture and social organization, since the success of farming. In a period of a few thousand years, this planet has seen fantastic advances in technology and equally fantastic advances in the size of governed units. In these matters, Civilization constitutes a great transformation, incredibly fast in terms of anthropological time.

But the transformation of the various aspects of the vibrancy does not necessarily take place at the same time or the same rate. The farmer's success set off a huge, accelerating wave of growth and development in what we may call the externals of the social organism. No such development has been seen in human consciousness. Indeed, individual consciousness may have suffered a retrograde movement during Civilization. For the sake of the efficiency of the ever-expanding social machine, the human individual has in many respects been reduced to a mere component—standardized, specialized, reliable, predictable. Some of the most exquisite capabilities of the hunter's consciousness—ecstasy, communion, even those commonplace skills we now classify as extrasensory—have been censored, punished, or simply left fallow.

And still, none of these is entirely lost. A single human brain, according to the most conservative scientific measure, is incredibly more complex than is the external organization of any conceivable social system. And the brain itself accounts for only a part of human consciousness, which includes body and being, social and perceptual field, and more. Consciousness is not exempt from transformation; its best capabilities cannot be permanently denied. Simply to *regain* what has been temporarily lost—*and to regain it in a new context of modern technology, computers, worldwide communications*—is likely to set off the most startling changes ever seen on this planet. Regaining what is lost, of course, is only the beginning. I foresee no "retribalization." The Transformation, being a part of history, does not constitute a return to the past but moves with historical necessity towards a shape and condition of human life never before known on this planet.

❧

We are all farmers. We are also hunters. Civilization may be viewed as successive applications of the principles of successful farming. Those principles may be summed up in terms of delayed reinforcement, regularization, the manipulation of things and people, and the desire for a large surplus product. Thus, the pyramid builder is a farmer, and so is today's salaried bread-winner with his regular hours, his periodic salary and incremental raises, his profit sharing and health insurance and retirement benefits. Bureaucracy is farming. All mass production is farming. Indeed, the early factories so literally mimicked the agricultural model that we should not have been surprised when mechanized factory methods were successfully applied to agriculture. Mass armies, mass education, mass media—all things mass and collective, —share the farming mode, the farming consciousness, which has altered us all.

Jailing and rehabilitation is an agricultural application, though not a successful one. Seduction in the European sense is farming, the cultivation of the feminine field with flowers, bonbons and poetic entreaties against the possible rewards of a later reaping. All religions that promise specific, significant rewards in an afterlife are agricultural adaptations. The penitent fingering rosary beads, the hymn singer, the doer of good works are, with-out exception, farming. And even the most adventurous of us retains some secret hope for regularization and a surplus. Even the criminal may shift into agricultural consciousness. We see the agricultural spirit in the clan-like "families" of the Mafia—patient, thorough collectors of favors and fears, culti-vators of the random, neglected, sometimes illegal crops of our overorganized, technological society.

We are also hunters. Even the most prudent and regularized among us harbors the secret seed of a consciousness that, being its own reward, seeks no external reinforcement: the conscious-ness of the hunter who perceives existence as whole and mythic. There are also those rare individuals who have not concealed the hunter in them. Civilization has often called them rogues. I have written elsewhere of four main types of these indispens-able seed-bearers of an ancient learning—the picaresque rogue, the technologist rogue, the mystic rogue, and the artist rogue.[5] They are by no means ordinary criminals. They are far more dangerous to the civilized condition since they do not recognize rectangular boundaries of our categorizing perception, have

63

no limiting sense of historic time, and desire no large surplus—
thus are invulnerable to the hooks of social conditioning. Look
closely and you may discover them among your friends, by a
certain liquid gleam of the eyes, an elusive aura that is at once
soft and strong, and a way of seeming sometimes to be on another plane of existence. Wherever they move, these people seem
to create a warp in the gravity of Civilization; they are surrounded by unfamiliar lines of force that may attract or repel
according to the particular condition of whoever may come near.
It is exhausting to be with them for very long, since they tend
to draw us out of the hypnosis in which we commonly sleep.

Marooned between two states of consciousness is no comfortable place to be. To tingle with a sense of total awareness,
to experience the vibrant *spirit* in all things (after all the drowsy
years) is frightening. We tend to retreat, calling out for the
formulas of our bizarre "ordinary" consciousness, having been
taught in childhood the familiar hocus-pocus that gets us back
into the civilized hypnosis: "Take it easy now. Don't lose control. This is silly. It's *only illusion*. Be reasonable. There are
no such things. Be rational." The magical incantation generally
works. The flowing, glowing world of the hunter fades. The
frightening spirits vanish in thin air. And we are home safe,
rational and blind again, ready to continue our pursuit of the
dead surplus.

But—*again!*—there are the moments, and the hunters: The
scientist exploring the wilds of abstraction for a vibrant form
never before glimpsed by a human being. The entrepreneur seeking new ways of combining energy, just for the sake of doing
it. The psychic voyager descending through the labyrinthine
caverns of lost awareness, from which there may be no return.
The Congo drummer staying with a rhythm, pursuing it relentlessly, following its spoor for hours if necessary until at last he
becomes one with it and, through it, with all of existence; finding
then that "he" is no longer striking the drum but that his hands
are being thrust upwards by some force that seems to be concentrated in the drum's head, in the beat itself. And there is
romance, not seduction but that condition of sanctuary the West
provides for brief ecstasy and the hunter's consciousness: the

64

lover journeying with his love on the ancient arcane plane of
being where the two of them together can walk through fire,
through the most hostile and dangerous part of a city, through
custom and taboo, unscathed, untouched. And there is physical
nature itself—mountain, jungle, desert, swamp, wood and water.
How we need it to recall us to wholeness, to whisper the word-
less hunting lore, to cloak our consciousness in soft transparency
so that we are no longer hard and separate and unavailable to
those portions of ourselves that we—pathetically, tragically—keep
calling *the other!*

❦

The rains came at last to Mt. Tamalpais; it was the wettest
November in memory. At the end of the first week in December, there was a day of respite from the downpour, a day of
perfect stillness and heavy, clinging fog. On such days, Cataract
Creek makes its climactic run from Laurel Dell Camp to Alpine
Lake in splendid rush and roar, tumbling over huge boulders,
coursing through rocky sluices, gushing out in countless water-
falls. A group of us hiked around the silent meadows near the
mountaintop for a while, then started down the trail that follows the creek. The fog was particularly heavy in the depths of
Cataract Gulch. Only the lower trunks of the redwoods were
visible, massive columns supporting the gray ceiling above us.
Even the sound of the water was somewhat muted by the moist
air, the bough-carpeted earth.

When we reached the first steep, almost precipitous stretch of
the trail, my oldest daughter, who was leading the way, broke
into a run. I was not surprised. This young woman in her
early twenties, slim, smooth-muscled, glowing with a particularly lovely and delicate strength, can bound up the steepest
trails of Tam, seeming sometimes simply to fly from one boulder
to a higher one, leaving the rest of us far behind. Now several
members of our party followed her pace down Cataract Trail.
After only a few steps, it became apparent we were going too
fast to stop. The way down was crooked and often twisted back
on itself. There were roots, loose rocks, slippery spots. A few
fallen trees lay across the trail. I was aware of these hazards, but

almost immediately realized I could not afford to *think* about them. If I was to avoid a spectacular fall, all I could do was surrender myself to the total environment—to gravity, air, fog, trees, rocks, roots, earth, the sound of water, breath, movement, the multitudinous rhythms that linked me to *all of this*. Without becoming passive in the least but rather entering an unfamiliar mode of heightened awareness, I *let* my legs carry me down the trail at a dead run. I *let* my feet pick out the best spots. I *let* myself fly up over the fallen trees. My precipitous course down the steep trail became an integral part of the totality of Cataract Gulch. Without words to express it, I became aware that motion is not necessarily separate from stillness.

We came to a more level stretch of the trail and I had a chance to slow the pace. But my daughter only flew faster, and so did I, sailing down the next segment of steepness in perfect harmony with this winter rain forest, one with the white water, the liquid air, the fine jeweled droplets on the ferns and the laurels. Too soon, we came to the bottom. And there a cluster of laurels shimmered—across a deep round pool at the foot of a waterfall and also in me—cluster of silver-green leaves against black shadows, as bright as Christmas. We stood there without words, breathing deeply, and I wondered if for these last few moments I had shared, and would share again, the consciousness of the hunter.

❧

If in these pages I have seemed to praise the hunter at the expense of the farmer, it is only because I feel we have mislaid so much that is good about the former and have suffered quite enough from what is worst in the latter. As I have said, I foresee no simple "going back" to the hunter's life. The Transformation is something new. It frees us from a single vision, from the single mode of feeling and being ordinarily assigned us by Civilization. It offers us the farmer's consciousness and the hunter's consciousness, and more. It allows an intertwining of historic with mythic time. It joins immediacy with delayed reinforcement. It involves ecstasy and discipline (the former requiring the latter). It makes possible a rebirth of the particular and unique within the general and abstract. And when the dead world comes back to life, it will be more than trees and stones and stars and other "natural" things; machines will come to life, too—cars and washing machines and computerized communications networks. Exclusivity is a hallmark of a dying consciousness, a dead civilization. Existence is vibrant and it is filled to the brim. How can we live deprived and discontent in such a rich world?

five
The Gift

"*Beauty is a terrible and awful thing! It is terrible because it has not been fathomed and never can be fathomed, for God sets us nothing but riddles. . . . The devil only knows what to make of it! What to the mind is shameful is beauty and nothing else to the heart. Is there beauty in Sodom? Believe me, that for the immense mass of mankind beauty is found in Sodom. Did you know that secret? The awful thing is that beauty is mysterious as well as terrible. God and the devil are fighting there and the battlefield is the heart of man. But a man always talks of his own ache.*"
—FYODOR DOSTOYEVSKY, THE BROTHERS KARAMAZOV

❧

[*The liberty of the individual is no gift of civilization.*]
—SIGMUND FREUD, CIVILIZATION AND ITS DISCONTENTS

IT IS WELL known that some beggars in India and the Middle East mutilate their children so that they may lead more successful lives. The practice, however, is not limited to those regions. Begging itself has always accompanied a fairly advanced stage of urban civilization, wherever it has occurred, and is closely associated with the emergence of private property. During Civilization's earliest stages, the poverty-stricken managed to exist through such socially accepted institutions as prostitution, voluntary and enforced slavery, vassalage and clientage. The first beggars were mendicant holy men, members of respected religious orders. Purely economic begging became common only when social structures began breaking down. There was no economically oriented begging in Israel until commerce replaced pastoralism, and none in Rome until after the social upheaval of her foreign wars.

68

Large-scale begging in Europe followed on the heels of a series of cataclysmic events that ripped apart the fabric of feudal society and prepared the way for capitalism—the Crusades, the Black Death of the fourteenth century, the explorations of the fifteenth century, the enclosure of common land for the grazing of sheep. By the sixteenth century, begging in Europe was so widespread that beggars had organized into fraternities, each representing a different type of beggar. It was during this period that child-maiming appeared on the European continent. The anonymous author of the *Liber Vagatorum* (or *Book of Vagabonds and Beggars*), which was first published in Germany around 1509, commented that "there are some beggars who treat their children badly in order that they may become lame—and who would be sorry if they should grow straight-legged." The *Liber Vagatorum* typified the revulsion against begging that came with the Reformation and that entailed considerable persecution of all who begged. The book reappeared in 1528 with a laudatory preface by Martin Luther. Over the years, we of the West have indeed managed, by various methods, to reduce begging to a manageable minimum. And overt physical child-maiming for profit is practically unknown in our part of the world.

We might, however, pause for a moment before congratulating ourselves on our purity in this matter or censuring those in less affluent lands who still maim their children. Each mutilation is, after all, a gift from parents to child, perhaps the most valuable gift the parents have it within their power to bestow. In the beggar's foreordained specialty, that grotesquely twisted arm represents real economic value. We may imagine comparative lifetime earnings figures for maimed versus unmaimed beggars, similar to those familiar, unintentionally cynical comparisons having to do with educational levels and financial success in our own society.

No, we of the dying culture do not offer our children such a highly visible endowment as an obviously twisted arm or leg. But we do wish for their success. And we know that, in order to achieve success, every child of Civilization must have at least one physical or mental deformity, one Gift from the culture.

So we find ways—and the best ways are those that are somehow veiled from them and us—to provide our children with what they so urgently need. We find ways to fix them so that the peculiar, generally joyless, dronelike work of Civilization will be not only bearable but actually *sought after, so that they will turn even from their own bodies and beings in order to pursue this work.* We find ways at the same time to dull their feelings and senses so that they will not know what they are doing to the world outside their skins—to other people, birds, animals, trees, rivers, snakes and stones—so that they will be unaware of the cries of dismay their actions are causing. The conditions of Civilization being what they are, in fact, we might demonstrate concern for our children most convincingly by completely excising their sensitivity in this regard.

We have no commonly recognized name for the Gift. We may think it strange that this, perhaps the central fact of civilized existence, continues to elude accurate identification. But that is its very nature. Sigmund Freud came closest to giving it a name when he turned his attention to the seemingly irreconcilable conflict between happiness and civilization. He first entitled the book he wrote on this subject in 1929 *Das Unglück in der Kultur* (*Unhappiness in Civilization*), but later changed the title to *Das Unbehagen in der Kultur. Unbehagen* is not readily translated into English. The French word *malaise* comes to mind. Freud himself suggested *Man's Discomfort in Civilization* as a title for the English translation. His translator, a Mrs. Riviere, finally solved the problem with the powerful and evocative title *Civilization and Its Discontents.* We see here a groping for terminology that encompasses "unhappiness," "malaise," "discomfort," and "discontent." We may also note with special interest that the literal rendering of *Unbehagen* is "dis-ease," a word listed as obsolete in our present dictionaries.

"Scientific objectivity," categorization, and the germ theory have made us forget the common origin of disease and dis-ease. Though respected men of medicine now assure us that up to 90 percent of all "physical" complaints are psychosomatic in origin (just as "mental" complaints have their somatic components), we have still failed to grasp clearly just how valuable these complaints are. We have still not acknowledged that most of the so-called physical diseases are actually *interchangeable* with what we call neurosis or simply human discontent—and that all of these, separately or in combination, most often contribute not to a person's failure, but to his success in the civilized state. That this is especially true for Western man will become clear shortly.

Terminology continues to be a problem. Since I can think of no one word that adequately expresses the common origin, nature and function of conditions often considered to be disparate, I must resort to the lamentable expediency of fabricating a single term, neurosis/disease/discontent, or NDD, to use in the following discussion. I begin with a few preliminary points:

❧ Civilization's most indispensable nonmaterial endowment to its children is some type of neurosis/disease/discontent.

❧ Each NDD, whatever its nature or origin, serves to keep the human individual in a state of dis-ease, to render each person's here-and-now being uncomfortable and distasteful. If properly programmed, the NDD also dulls the senses and cuts off the individual from nature and the cosmos. The best way of gaining temporary relief from dis-ease lies in forgetfulness of existence. This is generally achieved either by drugs or by the relentless getting and building that has characterized much of human life since the success of agriculture.

❧ The NDDs do not necessarily result (as Freud would have it) from a conflict between humankind's primal sexual and aggressive *instincts* and the realities of social life. They are created by Civilization. *Even if humans had no sexuality or aggressiveness whatever yet were sensitive beings capable of joy and harmony with nature, they would still have to be afflicted with dis-ease in order for Civilization's work to be done.*

❧ An NDD is more effective the more its origin is veiled. When one mode of programming dis-ease is widely revealed in a particular society, that mode loses much of its power. The society goes on to evolve a more subtle means of bestowing the Gift.

❧ Up to a certain remarkably high breaking point, the

71

NDDs are not maladaptive for the civilized individual but highly adaptive. A pre-ulcerous condition makes for success in this society; ulcers are a bit too much.

❧ Whether seemingly physical or psychological, every NDD is actually both. As we shall see later in this chapter, every NDD leaves some physical scar. To that extent we are all maimed and we are maiming our children.

❧ The NDDs are essentially incurable in any civilized society and perhaps in any society that has advanced as far as agriculture. Symptoms may shift and particular forms of dis-ease may be exchanged for others. The basic condition remains. Transformation of society is the only real cure.

❧

Frederick S. Perls, the founder of Gestalt therapy, was a master showman. He was also a master craftsman. Even his critics have had to grant that he could get to the heart of a neurosis with stunning speed and accuracy. We are not privileged to view Freud at work with his patients. Even if electronic recording devices had been widely available in his time, Freud's mode of treatment probably would have precluded their use. Perls, on the other hand, believed that the presence of a group or even a large audience is necessary, for one thing, to keep the therapist honest. Thousands of people watched him work, and his sessions were recorded on hundreds of hours of tape, video tape and film before his death in 1970.[1] His dreamwork demonstrations were particularly spectacular, since he would work with his "victim" before a sizable audience, making explanatory asides at key points in the procedure much in the manner of a surgeon describing a tricky operation to a group of medical men in a surgical theater. Those in the audience could see, in a few minutes, just how much a person loves his neurosis, how desperately he clings to it, how cunningly he manipulates the environment to keep it propped up, how he will resort to charm, humor, intelligence, deafness, blindness, dumbness, confusion, pity, outrage, amnesia, *anything* to avoid the loss of this, his most precious possession, his adored dis-ease.

A pleasant sense of anticipation pervaded the dining room at

Esalen Institute on the California Coast on those nights when
Perls was scheduled to give one of his demonstrations. Tables
were quickly cleared away. A partition was moved to expand
the gallery where he would perform. Chairs were set up and a
fire was built in the large brick fireplace at the end of the room.
As soon as the doors were opened the room would fill to over-
flowing. Perls, an Old Testament prophet in a white jump suit,
would take his place on a low platform near the fireplace. In
addition to his easy chair, the platform was provided with two
empty straight chairs—one the "hot seat" for the victim, the
other a place where the victim would sit while enacting one of
the phantom cast of characters with which he keeps his neurosis
alive and active.

After a brief talk, Perls would ask for volunteers. About a
third of the hundred or so people present generally would raise
their hands, eager to be diagnosed, dissected, stripped of their
most intimate pretenses before curious onlookers. A victim
would mount the platform, take the hot seat and start to describe a dream. Perls would miss nothing. He would find clues,
not just in the cognitive content of the words, but in the voice,
the gestures, the breathing, the posture. Sometimes he would
make the victim aware of what his hands were doing, then ask
for a dialogue between the right and the left. Sometimes, hearing different tones of voice in different situations, he would
create a dialogue between, for instance, the victim's whining
voice and his domineering voice. The victim would move from
one chair to the other as he played the two parts.

The dream itself would come alive in a reconstituted present
tense. Instead of talking *about* the people and things in the
dream, the victim would be asked to *become* each person and
thing; the dream, after all, is entirely his and every element in
it some aspect of his being. Perls often commented that a neurotic is someone who does not see the obvious. He would make
the obvious explicit, then cut off the escape routes the victim
may have painstakingly and cleverly maintained over the years.
Relentlessly, Perls would follow the trail that leads directly to
the neurosis. If the victim began trembling, Perls would have
him *go into* the trembling, exaggerate it, personify it. He would

never shy away from the victim's anxiety or terror; he took this to be a very good sign that he was nearing a neurotic center. Finally the moment would come when the victim's escape routes were entirely cut off, when all the props that had supported the neurosis had been knocked out. Perls called this moment "the impasse." Here the victim is offered the opportunity for an existential leap past the neurosis, a sort of death of the ego structure and a rebirth, however temporary, into a state of pure being in the here and now. The impasse is a moment of high drama. Getting past it demands a headlong dive into unfamiliar waters.

Once Perls brought a heavy stammerer to the impasse by having him increase his stammer. As he stammered, Perls asked him what he felt in his throat. "I feel like choking myself," he answered. Perls gave him his arm and said, "Now, choke me." "God damn," the man said, "I could kill you." As his anger became explicit, his stammer disappeared. He spoke loudly, without difficulty. Perls pointed out that he now had an existential choice, to be an angry man or a stammerer.

These short demonstrations were by no means cures. But they were often remarkably powerful. They cast doubt on the efficacy, and the real function, of the five-year-long, five-day-a-week therapies. I once saw Perls bring a handsome and ingratiating young man to his impasse in a period of about fifteen minutes. Within ten minutes it was perfectly obvious to everyone in the room except the victim that he was keeping himself in a constant condition of dis-ease with a fear—clearly a false fear—of homosexuality. He was unwilling to confront this simple fact. His chief escape modes, his ways of squirming around the truth, were charm and humor. Fritz cut these out from under him. There was a tiger in the young man's dream, snarling and clawing up at him from a deep ditch. But when he *became* the tiger, the snarls and threats were less than frightening. The tiger was paper. The fear was false. We may balk at accepting the fact that a person wouldn't be quite happy to realize that his worst fear is false. But that is almost always the case when it is part of a neurosis.

As the charming young man was brought closer and closer to the truth, he was overcome with dismay. His once mobile, ingratiating countenance became blank. His memory failed. He couldn't hear what Perls was saying to him. At this point Perls turned to the audience and, in a classic aside, murmured, "Ah, the impasse!" The victim broke through in a flood of tears. The next morning, I met him walking on the edge of the cliff by the sea. His face was transformed, no longer ingratiating or "charming." His smile was fresh and real. He had the soft, tremulous, vulnerable look of one reborn. And all this from one fifteen-minute demonstration.

How often I have seen that look on the faces of friends and family who have had the good fortune to experience the little transformations that are offered at Esalen. I have seen how beautiful people can be. And I have seen that beauty fade within a period of weeks after reentry into the world we so thoughtlessly call "real." One Friday evening in the autumn of 1967 I came home to find a stranger sitting in the middle of my living room rug. I recognized him soon enough as one of my closest friends, Leo Litwak, who had driven straight from Big Sur after a five-day encounter experience with William Schutz. Litwak's early years as child of a labor leader in Detroit had been far from tranquil. His World War II service as a medic with General George Patton's forces in Europe was by all odds the most harrowing I had ever heard. These formative experiences, along with his long study of Western philosophy, had contributed to a habitual expression that lay between sadness and skepticism. But now he simply shimmered. His eyes—there is no other way to say it—were like stars. When he rose to embrace me, I had an impression of a butterfly just emerging from a cocoon—moist, trembling, unquestionably newborn.

Later, Litwak described his experience for *The New York Times Magazine*. The article has since appeared in over a dozen anthologies and remains one of the very best written on a subject that generally defies graceful description. Its final paragraph speaks directly to the subject of this chapter:

> The condition of vulnerability is precious and very
> fragile. Events and people and old routines and old
> habits conspire to bring you down. But not all the way

> down. There is still the recollection of that tingling sense
> of being wide awake, located in the here and now,
> feeling freely and entirely, all constraints discarded. It
> remains a condition to be realized. It could change the
> way we live.[2]

I too have experienced that tingling sense of being wide awake. And I have felt it fade under the relentless, often unrealized pressures of daily existence. Much criticism of some of the early Esalen-type experiences (Gestalt, encounter, sensory awakening) has centered on the proposition that they "don't last." *Of course they don't last.* It becomes painfully obvious that no one can live safely and successfully in civilized society without some kind of NDD. It's also obvious that some sort of long-term psychotherapy is needed to effect what is generally termed a "cure" for a neurotic condition. (The Esalen experiences, despite some popular misunderstanding, were never meant to "cure" people who consider themselves "sick.") But let us ask what the usual long-term therapy really accomplishes. It certainly does not take very long to isolate a neurosis and cast it out. Perls, among others, has demonstrated this point again and again. Diagnosing and casting out neuroses, however, is by no means the basic function of most psychotherapy.

According to Perls, "anybody who goes to a therapist has something up his sleeve. I would say roughly ninety percent don't go to a therapist to be cured, but to be more adequate in their neurosis." Let us at least consider this possibility: that the main function of the conventional therapies is not curing the patient of neurosis, but helping him build, polish tune up, and test a new neurosis to replace the old. The new neurosis will continue to keep the patient discontented with his own being (so that he will be successful in Civilization), but it will do so in a manner that is more acceptable to himself and those around him. Building an adequate neurosis takes time and care. Under the present conditions of life it may be viewed as a humane endeavor. We can thank the conventional therapists for their painstaking and patient work, which may rank among the most important in our fading culture. But let us not for a moment pretend that its main purpose is cure.

To be cured—that is, to be entirely free of all NDDs even if for only a short period—is a powerful and sometimes radicalizing experience. It provides a tantalizing sample of what human life can be. It opens up new territory on the psychic map. The awareness that this territory exists may change a person's personal and social goals. It may sharpen his dissatisfaction with the status quo, and give that dissatisfaction the kind of focus needed for social transformation.

And there is another answer to those who criticize experiences on the grounds that they don't last. To become one with beauty is of value for its own sake. We travel to Athens to see the Acropolis even though we are not going to continue to see it every day for the rest of our lives. I first climbed that hill on a clear October day. The sky was pale but luminous blue. A flotilla of soft white clouds sailed from north to south for as far as the eye could see. The breeze was only cool enough to soothe my heated cheeks.

Nothing had prepared me for the impact of those ruins. No photograph or verbal description had even begun to suggest the *liveness* of those stones. The Parthenon, it seemed to me, could not have been as beautiful when intact as it was now—skeletal and airy and free. The columns moved with the moving clouds. I could feel them vibrating. Their vibrations pierced to my bones, offering me direct experience of the brave and tragic vision of those who had raised them up.

I am not there now. Out of my windows I can see only a line of redwood-covered ridges, enormous waves of a sea-deep green —and to the west the flanks of Mt. Tam. Yet the Acropolis still vibrates in my memory. And so do many moments of voyages that involve no physical travel.

❧

Sigmund Freud spent the final twenty years of his life in hardship, sorrow and suffering. The privations of post-World War I Austria were succeeded by the death of friends and family members, bitter dissension among his followers and the onset of the mouth cancer that was to lead through an epic of pain to his death in 1939. It was during this period that he moved far beyond theorizing based upon clinical observation to produce a number of speculative works that deal with crucial questions of human purpose and possibility. This Freudian metapsychology —expressed most notably in *Beyond the Pleasure Principle*, *The Ego and the Id*, *The Future of an Illusion*, and *Civilization and Its Discontents*—is breathtaking in its penetration, sweep and boldness. It is also utterly uncompromising in its view that human unhappiness is inevitable in the civilized state. This view is so damaging to the idea of successful therapy that many well-known post-Freudian analysts have attempted to revise, minimize, or just ignore it. But the message is clear: Beyond the human drive for pleasure there lies the reality of the restraint of pleasure. Superseding joy there is toil. And underlying all Civilization there is the ever-more-powerful, nearly unbearable sense of guilt.

To summarize, Freud conceives of Eros, a life instinct operating in all things animal and vegetable, as continually striving to join life into larger entities, so that life may be prolonged and brought into higher development. In this process Eros works to "combine single human individuals, and after that families, then races, peoples and nations, into one great unity, the unity of mankind." [3] To make this larger unity possible, individuals have to give up certain rights. Their normal sexuality must be severely inhibited. Much sexual energy (one of the expressions of Eros) must be sublimated, i.e., channeled into socially useful activities such as work or artistic creation. According to Freud, an individual's failure to deal with the sexual frustrations that are inevitable in Civilization leads to neurosis.

But Freud was not satisfied with his discovery of Eros, the life instinct. Like many global theorizers of the West, he craved a dualistic symmetry, which would call for an equal and opposite force, a death instinct which he identified as Thanatos. Freud found this negative and destructive force continually striving to reduce the tensions involved in maintaining higher forms of life by attempting to reduce them to simpler forms—

the simplest, of course, being inorganic, thus dead. Manifestations of Thanatos may be seen in what Freud calls "the original nature of man"—brutal, destructive violence; aggressiveness that "reigned almost without limit in primitive times." [4] Civilization's most difficult work, according to Freud, lies in quelling man's primal aggressiveness. Civilization does this work by turning the individual's aggressiveness inward, back towards himself. During childhood, every civilized individual is provided with a superego or conscience, which "is ready to put into action against the ego the same harsh aggressiveness that the ego would have liked to satisfy upon other, extraneous individuals. The tension between the harsh super-ego and the ego that is subjected to it, is called by us the sense of guilt; it expresses itself as a need for punishment." [5]

Here Freud comes up against a puzzle. The superego or conscience is created by the internalization of external authority. Yet it seems much more severe and unforgiving than any external authority it might have replaced. Indeed, as noted in the previous chapter, the internalized whip is far more cruel and repressive than is needed for the maintenance of Civilization. And surprisingly, the more it is obeyed, the harsher it becomes. "Ultimately," Freud writes, "it is precisely those people who have carried saintliness furthest who reproach themselves with the worst sinfulness." [6]

Freud offers complex and admittedly tentative explanations for this peculiar feature of civilized existence. In order to justify the harshness of the civilized solution, however, he goes back again and again to his concept of man's overwhelming aggressiveness in the primal state. "Civilization has to use its utmost efforts in order to set limits to man's aggressive instincts and to hold the manifestations of them in check by psychical reaction-formation." [7] According to Freud, the "primal horde" of prehistoric times was organized around an authoritarian father who ruled by brute force and "was undoubtedly terrible." [8] The sons, motivated not only by a quite understandable rebelliousness, but also by a desire to possess the mother sexually, plotted to kill the father and often did so. After the father's death the sons quarreled over the paternal inheritance, then formed a sort of band of brothers (the prototype of democratic government) which eventually reverted to another despotic patriarchy. In Freud's primal horde, authority was cruel, external, and based entirely on force. "The fate of the sons was a hard one; if they excited the father's jealousy they were killed or castrated or driven out." [9] The primal horde concept is central to Freud's metapsychology.

Modern anthropologists are a contentious lot and it is hard to discover wide agreement among them. On one point, however, they are almost sure to agree. The primal horde as Freud conceived it simply did not exist. The brilliant classics scholar, Norman O. Brown, who uses Freud as a takeoff point for soaring metapsychological speculations, argues that Freud's primal horde is "not a historical explanation of origins, but a supra-historical archetype," [10] and perhaps a projection into prehistoric times of the constitutional crisis of seventeenth-century England. Philosopher Herbert Marcuse also uses Freud's anthropological speculation for its symbolic rather than scientific value. Marcuse points out that Freud's hypothesis "telescopes, in a sequence of catastrophic events, the historical dialectic of domination and thereby elucidates aspects of civilization hitherto unexplained." [11] In this light we may say, as others have said, that Freud has more to tell us about the nature of Civilization than about the nature of mankind. Perhaps Wilhelm Reich was close to the truth when he outraged Freud by proposing that what Freud called the death instinct was actually a product of the capitalistic system. For the capitalistic system, however, I would read all Civilization.

Still, we would be mistaken in rejecting Freud's basic insights. His concepts of the internalization of external authority, of the inevitable conflict between Civilization and human happiness and of the ever-increasing amount of individual guilt that goes along with the creation and maintenance of civilized society—these concepts and many others ring true now even more than when he conceived them. But the failure of his primal horde formulation throws doubt on the intensity and the quality, if not the existence, of *innate* human aggressiveness, and allows us to examine an even more tragic hypothesis.

It is clear that civilized man is often aggressive and that the conflict between this aggressiveness and his conscience is one of the things that contributes to his perpetual dis-ease. As we have seen, Freud believes that the human individual is born a cruel aggressor, constantly tempted to wreak his aggressiveness upon his neighbor, "to exploit his capacity for work without compensation, to use him sexually without his consent, to seize his possessions, to humiliate him, to cause him pain, to torture and to kill him." [12] Civilization is forced to use extreme measures against a creature who is at heart a murderer. These measures create guilt, anxiety, and thus perpetual dis-ease—the unfortunate by-product of an inevitable conflict.

Here I do not wish to debate the existence of some inborn human tendency towards aggression, but simply to examine a different possibility: What if the human individual were not really the born monster that Freud paints him? Would Civilization without individual unhappiness and discontent then be possible? I think not. We may come to the realization, in fact, that dis-ease, far from being an unfortunate *by-product*, is the indispensable *end-product* of civilized conditioning. Civilization does exert harsh, internalized controls against human aggressiveness. But consider the possibility that most of this aggressiveness was *created* by the social organism that then attempts to quell and channel it, and that the most important function of this whole process is to help keep the human individual in a constant state of discontent, without which Civilization itself would not be possible.

The convoluted machinery just described provides only one of the mechanisms for producing the neuroses/diseases/discontents. The socialization process of Civilization operates effectively (with the preferred modes shifting from group to group and time to time) to throw the human individual out of joint with himself—through otherwise unnecessary restrictions on erotic impulse, creation of false fears, intensification of anxiety, absolute taboos against the elemental joy of being. There is simply not enough innate aggressiveness in the anthropological record to fuel all these machines of discontent.

❧

If anyone should tell you that he can define the original biological nature of the human species in a narrow and specific sense, you would do well not to believe him. The hard evidence is not available and perhaps never will be. Every argument on this subject proceeds from inference. Such ethology-oriented writers as Konrad Lorenz, Robert Ardrey and Desmond Morris have reached a wide audience in recent years by arguing from analogy with other species. Many readers have interpreted these books as proposing that man is essentially aggressive. It seems to me, however, that much of what these writers call aggression in the lower animals (territorial displays, for example) actually constitutes evidence for a finely balanced, generally peaceful ecological homeostasis. (The word "threat" is a human invention; we read nature as a Rorschach.) Animal "aggression" against members of their own species bears little resemblance indeed to human warfare or to civilized man's rape and poisoning of the natural world. Reading these man-the-animal books, I am haunted by one fact: Man is the only animal (with the exception of the rat) that purposefully kills members of its own species. I am left with the feeling that, where aggression and natural harmony count the most, civilized man is entirely different from the other animals.

Another writer, a noted medical specialist on psychosomatic disorders named A. T. W. Simeons, approaches the question from another angle. Making inferences from the development of the central nervous system, he argues that long and successful evolution is generally associated with timidity. Once a species becomes a bold carnivore, its evolutionary development slows or stops entirely. Pre-cultural man, according to Simeons, was the most timid of mammals. His outsized brain developed during a period when his response to threat was early flight. Being on the defensive enormously enhanced his inventiveness. Simeons theorizes that the human individual's basic instinct—along with sex, hunger and sleep—is fear. It was only after the development of tools and human culture that this creature, whose biological nature is entirely pusillanimous, was forced to become fierce and brave. The conflict between his innate impulse to flee and his culturally induced resolve to ignore danger is precisely what causes his multitude of psychosomatic diseases, which Simeons describes in sickening detail.[13]

This may sound like Freud turned inside out, but it gains force when you consider the enormous amounts of cultural energy devoted to the establishment of aggression. If men were innate killers, you would think it easier to turn them into warriors. The distinguished military historian, Brig. Gen. S. L. A. Marshall, has pointed out that only one out of four combat infantrymen can be counted on to fire at the enemy during battle. "The 25 percent estimate stands even for well-trained and campaign-seasoned troops. I mean that 75 percent will not fire or will not persist in firing against the enemy and his works. These men may face the danger but they will not fight." In postcombat interviews with some 400 World War II infantry companies, General Marshall discovered that on an average not more than 15 percent of the men had actually fired at enemy positions or personnel during the course of an entire engagement. Marshall does not take this as a reflection on the men's courage or experience or discipline. The cause seems to go deeper. Marshall cites studies by Medical Corps psychiatrists of the combat fatigue cases in the European Theater. The psychiatrists found that "fear of killing, rather than fear of being killed, was the most common cause of battle failure in the individual, and that fear of failure ran a close second." Marshall goes on to state his belief that "the average and normally healthy individual—the man who can endure the mental and physical stresses of combat—still has such an inner and usually unrealized resistance towards killing a fellow man that he will not of his own volition take life if it is possible to turn away from that responsibility." [14]

Throughout civilized history, societies have been able to create aggressive killers only by the use of extreme social pressure, medals, harsh discipline, depersonalization, "a cause greater than life itself," threats, punishment, and finally the execution of those who fail to kill. If the individual is a born robber, raper, torturer and murderer, why doesn't he jump, when given the chance, to fulfill his destiny? Why all the expensive and time-consuming conditioning? Those individuals who do turn into killers without being carefully conditioned to do so are hardly natural, healthy biological specimens. We look beneath their rage and find frustration. Beneath the aggression, the inevitable fear.

The biological nature of our species is not known. Archeology and anthropology offer us only ambiguity and paradox. Characteristic holes in the fossil skulls of early man suggest ritual killing and possibly cannibalism. So we cannot claim that our forebears, after they developed tools, were entirely gentle and nonviolent. It is clear, on the other hand, that some of the surviving Stone Age cultures—the Bushmen and Pygmies of Africa, the Aborigines of Australia—are considerably more balanced than are civilized cultures. They bear no resemblance whatever to Freud's primal horde. Child-rearing practices are noncoercive. The father is by no means a despot; we must resurrect the old-fashioned word "gentlemanly" to describe his relationship with women, children and other men. These primitives live in delicate, sensitive interaction with each other and the natural world. Their life, in fact, is far more exquisitely modulated than that of any civilized group. This modulation does not appear to depend upon guilt or repression of constitutional aggressiveness.

All of this, I know, is open to debate. But already we linger overlong on matters that are not only unverifiable but unnecessary to our understanding of the present human plight. We do not need constitutional aggressiveness to explain murder. We do not need constitutional pusillanimity to explain the anxieties of the age. Humankind does have a biological nature, but it is by no means narrow or one-sided. In addition to various survival characteristics held in common with the other mammals, the human individual has an innate tendency to create language. (And perhaps, as linguist Noam Chomsky suggests, all languages share the same deep roots.) The human individual has an innate tendency to create cultures. (And perhaps, as anthropologist Claude Lévi-Strauss suggests, all cultures are related at some underlying level.) Within these broad limits the human individual has an innate tendency to learn, to change, to adapt. Adaptability, in fact, constitutes the central biological characteristic of the species. The human individual adapts beyond all reasonable expectations, beyond even what is good for him. Compared with his adaptability, all his other putative constitutional characteristics shrink to a lesser significance. I have written elsewhere that a key message in the genetic code for the human species may be summed up as follows: "Construct now an organism that will do most of its learning during its individual lifetime." [15] From this the organism derives its very essence. All the particularities that have been cited to distinguish person from animal—upright stance, opposable thumb, massive brain—may be viewed as means to this end. The chief agency for carrying the stuff of individual learning is not the genetic pool but culture itself.

We clarify our understanding by studying, not what has been called the "constitutional nature" of the human individual, but his potential. We know that the individual has a potential for rage, fear, flight, aggression, cruelty, selfishness, self-destruction and the rape of the world. He also has a potential for joy, sensitivity, empathy with nature and other people, the creation of beauty, and a transcendent merging with all existence. The human individual is born a builder no more than he is born a dancer. He is destined to transform the external physical world no more than he is destined to transform himself and out of the Transformation help bring into being a culture that elicits aspects of his potential that may seem quite startling in the light of the past five thousand years of human history (which are, after all, a brief moment in evolutionary time).

It was about that many years ago that the domestication of grain crops, irrigation, and other cultural factors in the fertile flood plains of the Middle East began creating a considerable agricultural surplus, out of which developed the social order I have been calling Civilization. Ever since then, the main thrust of this social order has been clear. We may view it in the simplest behavioral terms. The surplus brought with it a new security, a certain freedom from the uncertainties of nature. At the same time it allowed the drawing together of larger and larger social units. This drawing together, whether we call it Eros or simply a tendency of the elemental vibrancy, does seem to fulfill a yearning of all existence. Even more than security, it is highly reinforcing—so much so that it set humankind off on a course of social expansion that has lasted ever since early Egypt. All else has been subordinated to the pursuit of the means and material for an ever-larger surplus and the swift expansion of the social unit. The earth was plundered. Additional territory for plunder was gained by armed conflict. Peoples were enslaved. Man-made environments were superimposed upon the earth with little or no regard for the messages from the natural environment.

To build and maintain the civilized order, a very special, unprecedented kind of human individual was needed. The adaptability inherent in the species made the creation of such an individual possible—difficult, yes, but possible. The civilized individual needed a cluster of characteristics. The inculcation of each of these characteristics worked separately and in combination to create the general condition most essential of all: perpetual personal dis-ease.

To create and maintain a civilized social order required human aggressiveness. Thus, child-rearing and cultural conditioning in Civilization devotes much energy towards programming young males to become aggressive. The most cursory study of male upbringing in any society in the Western lineage reveals the extreme means employed to create or intensify aggressiveness. Once created, it is frustrated. Pressures are applied to force it into socially sanctioned channels—engaging in violent sports, destroying an enemy or a forest, becoming a murderously effective intellectual swordsman. This builds up an even greater tendency to aggress. The entire process contributes to personal dis-ease.

Civilized societies, always expansionist, needed a high birthrate, achieved with a minimum of dalliance. So these societies set about blocking off as much as they could of the individual's access to every sensory and sensual pleasure except one: specialized genital activity. Pursuit of this limited and limiting pleasure was thus greatly intensified. Far from modulating lust, Civilization inflames it. Civilized societies generally are preoccupied with sex in a more obsessive and unhealthy manner than are primitive hunting and gathering societies. The process of specializing, inflaming and frustrating the erotic impulse contributes to personal dis-ease.

Civilized societies needed predictable, standardized human

components. The early states shaped them with the whip, but soon worked out techniques for internalizing the whip. As technology developed and specialization increased, a rigid system of formal education evolved, devoted to fixing individual behavior at a preordained point, thus effectively blocking the individual's tendency to learn (change, keep adapting) throughout all of life. This process contributes to personal dis-ease.

Civilized societies needed individuals insensitive to their environment and to their own feelings. Individuals who could sense and feel what they were doing in the name of Civilization to nature and other people simply could not keep on doing it. So the social order set about turning off the sensitive ecological sense developed over millions of years of mammalian and early human evolution. By a variety of conditioning techniques, human components were trained to ignore the messages of the senses and distrust their own feelings. The ideal civilized component is one who can keep on doing its task, at the same rate, regardless of its feelings, or of what is going on around it. Being in such a condition requires and contributes to dis-ease.

There are, of course, other modes of civilized conditioning and other concomitants of dis-ease. The significant point, however, is that the two exist in a classic closed-loop interaction. Being in a condition of dis-ease drives the individual to find relief by doing Civilization's work, while doing Civilization's work (with its impersonal aggression, high-intensity genital sex, standardized labor and general rape of the natural world) contributes to dis-ease. The cycle feeds and builds upon itself, reaching "heights that the individual finds hard to tolerate."

Is Civilization's work inevitable? Must we go on building, expanding, exploiting forever? Obviously not. The earth is a limited system. The pursuit of an increasing surplus now promises more punishment than reward for those of us in the advanced nations. The continuing expansion of social entities in their present crude form can no longer be viewed as the work of Eros.

Why, then, does the old, outmoded behavior go on? Here we turn once again to a simple and obvious behavioral explanation. Any mode of behavior that once was reinforced goes on for a considerable time even after the last bit of reinforcement has receded into the past. (Herbert Marcuse argues that the super-ego, representing civilized authority, "enforces not only the demands of reality but also those of a *past* reality.")[16] Cultural inertia has never been more of a threat.

Here is where we now stand. Living in a world that demands not Civilization but Transformation, we are left with the personal souvenirs of humankind's most bizarre journey. There are more than enough to go around, at least one for every civilized individual. They limit us, separate us from the simplest pleasures, make us miserable in our own skins. Yet we fear, we fear perhaps more than anything other than death, to be without them. We categorize them, list them on charts, treat them as if they have different causes and different cures. In a deeper sense, however, all of them are one and the same: the hateful, cherished Gift of Civilization.

❧

A pre-ulcerous condition makes for success in this society; ulcers are a bit too much. A postnasal drip provides a salutary goad for the civilized component; a serious sinus infection reduces the component's efficiency. A touch of paranoia sharpens the sense of conspiracy needed for organizational politics; paranoid schizophrenia may be an embarrassment. The unrelieved anxiety that constricts muscles and blood vessels helps armor us against the outcries and enticements of the outside world; arteriosclerosis and coronary thrombosis bring the game to an end.

A 1962 survey in New York City revealed a "serious" mental health impairment rate of 23.4 percent of the population, with a "well" rate of only 18.5 percent. This left a majority of the residents, 58.1 percent, in the category of mild or moderate mental disorder. Thus the survey showed at least some impairment in the mental health of 81.5 percent of the population.[17] Such findings are not necessarily limited to city dwellers. A 1961 study of a rural area in Canada came up with approximately the same figures.[18] These surveys were undoubtedly considered rigorous if not severe in their definition of mental health. I consider it more likely, however, that the investigators involved were entirely too lax, which is altogether understandable. A scientific study of "sickness" can hardly proceed in the absence of "wellness." Investigators of such matters must bend their will and perception to maintain a "well" category. A truly rigorous investigation would doubtless uncover the embarrassing fact that *100 percent* of the population suffers from one or more of the neuroses/diseases/discontents, or is victim of one of the psychoses. How, then, are we to measure our madness?

A number of psychologists point out that overt symptoms appear in the individual only after a prolonged history of submerged neurosis. Robert W. White, author of a classic abnormal psychology text in the United States, stresses the role of anxiety and defense against anxiety in the formation of neurotic personality. He is quite clear on the limited, climactic nature of what we tend to *recognize* as neurosis. White points out that the

acute neurosis with its symptoms is now seen as the end result of a long process of development. The trouble starts with what we have called the *neurotic-nucleus*, a process by which anxiety, typically in childhood, is subjected to such radical defense that a new evolution of the danger cannot be made. The trouble continues with the formation of overdriven strivings, tendencies that are exaggerated in the effort to maintain security. Overdriven strivings are likely to conflict with each other and with other tendencies in the personality, a situation that we have called the neurotic conflict. Integrative efforts continue, however, and the person steadily builds for himself a protective organization, becoming a full-fledged neurotic personality. At any point along the way the situation may get out of hand: anxiety may increase, and the defenses may become much more desperate. The person feels much worse, and it is usually at such a point that symptom formation occurs. We shall refer to this as *neurotic breakdown*. In the older terminology it is at this point that the person starts to be sick and to "have" a neurosis. In our present understanding, the neurotic breakdown is a sort of climax that occurs when the protective structure is severely threatened and can no longer be maintained intact.[19]

To put it another way, White notes that, according to Otto Fenichel in *Psychoanalytic Theory of Neurosis*, neurotic breakdown occurs when circumstances bring about "the failure of an established equilibrium." [20]

Dis-eased equilibrium is indeed the *normal* lot of the human individual in Civilization. The specific conditions that we recognize as neuroses are actually only indicators, red warning lights. They let us know that the normal situation of dis-ease is out of hand, that it has at last become unbearable for the individual or has triggered behaviors that are socially unacceptable. Some form of treatment or simply the passage of time (which in most cases seems to be equally effective) may cause the overt symptoms of the neurosis to disappear. But this means only that an equilibrium of dis-ease has been reestablished at a more satisfactory level. For the individual who is working hard up against the edge of civilized efficiency, the warning lights may flicker frequently without staying on long enough for any significant break in his routine. He is, in fact, likely to be one of the heroes of our culture. You may recognize the face of dis-ease on the cover of your weekly newsmagazine.

The individual we identify as psychotic is different. Through a variety of circumstances, he has been unable or unwilling to establish the requisite equilibrium of dis-ease. Such an individual thus stands outside the machinery of Civilization. This is especially true in the West, where internalization of conflicts through neurosis/disease/discontent has reached historic heights. In recent years, more and more poets, prophets, and even psychologists have been telling us about the value to be found in the psychotic experience. The madman, they feel, may lend us eyes for seeing the reality that lies outside our present social hypnosis. The West is, as a matter of fact, the only known culture that commonly assigns no value whatever to those conditions of "madness" and possession that may lead to shamanistic insights.

There is danger here of romanticizing a condition that can be most painful and frightening. We would do well, however, to take a fresh, sympathetic look at all truly nonneurotic be-havior. It is quite possible that when the transformed individual appears—tingling and wide-awake, unneurotic, entirely healthy —he may be mistaken by a dis-eased Civilization for a psychotic or a rogue. As a matter of fact, anyone who has escaped the circle of civilized conditioning may appear to our ordinary eyes as something alien. He who by nature and not by mere accident lives outside the *polis*, Aristotle tells us, is either a monster or a god. And yet, we are somehow drawn to this creature. He may exist, if only for a short while, on the living room rugs of the world we call real. He lives always in the secret chambers of our yearning. Could it be that this creature, imaginary or real, is in fact the radiant, always fearful, ever-yearned-for beast at the gates of our dead world? Is the measure of our madness akin to madness itself?

❈

Let us go a step farther. Western psychologists spend a great deal of time and energy in classifying the neuroses and psychoses. And yet many of them realize that

> it is arbitrary, artificial and inadequate to place the
> conventional amount of stress upon *separate categories*
> of mental illness. There are infinite degrees of disturbance
> of the mental apparatus. The various pathological states
> are not irrevocably fixed nor (often) sharply demarcated
> from one another or from what is considered normal.[21]

From this, it may be less of a leap than it at first appears to suggest that the lines which ordinarily separate *mental* from *physical* disorder are also arbitrary, artificial, and inadequate. It has become commonplace to argue that the vast majority of physical illness is psychogenic. But it is not enough to say merely that the brain affects the body or that the body affects the brain. I would like to propose, rather, that behavior affects the total organism; that every so-called mental state has its physical equiv-alent; that an individual's life experiences create specific, measur-able changes in the body which are temporary or permanent to the same extent as in what we call the mind, and that the converse is also true.

I am overwhelmed here with the feeling that I am belaboring something that is quite obvious. The idea that mental and bodily states are closely related goes back to the beginnings of recorded history—for example, in the theory of the four cardinal humors that were once thought to determine an individual's physical and mental qualities. This central theory of the ancient physiology persisted throughout the Middle Ages and well into the Renaissance. The scientific revolution demolished such falsehoods but also created its own false dichotomies. The most significant medical research in recent years has tended to heal the mind-body split and thus close off debate on the question. I persist in this exposition only because certain segments of our society continue to make the human body inconsequential if not practically invisible.

A widespread attitude on this matter was summed up for me recently by a female editor of a major publishing house. I found myself in conversation with this woman at a New York cocktail party given by the publisher. She seemed to be in her midthirties, had a rather attractive face, and was, I soon learned, recently divorced. It was impossible for me not to notice that she stood in an exaggerated slouch. She hunched her shoulders forward and inward. She crossed her arms protectively over a caved-in chest, somehow keeping one hand free to hold her martini. The flesh around her arms and throat was surprisingly flaccid for one of her age. Her stance was somewhat unbalanced. Her knees seemed to be locked. In spite of all this, she managed to strike a fashionable note of wistful irony as she told about her marital breakup and the four years of psychotherapy that pre- and postdated the divorce. Recently, she told me, she had started going to her therapist five days a week. I asked if it were helping her. She raised an eyebrow and shrugged ever so slightly as if to say, not only, "Who knows?" but also, "That's hardly the kind of question one asks." Then she answered, "I do think it's given me insights into my problems." I agreed on the importance of insight, then asked if she had ever considered trying a therapy or discipline that would bring aspects of the body into play.

She looked at me a moment, then said, in all seriousness, "I've learned to consider anything other than talking a gimmick."

This remark rendered me speechless. If I had told her I found what she said both wildly hilarious and exasperating, I feel sure she wouldn't have had the faintest idea what I was talking about. But she is not alone in her judgment. Many respected practitioners still assume that most problems of the human psyche can be solved by talk and talk alone. And if the problem to be solved is complicated, the talk has only to get complicated, and long. The body remains in an entirely separate arena. In sickness and in health, the life of the mind retains its imperial status.

I seriously doubt that such an attitude can survive this decade. A growing body of theory, experiment and practice argues forcibly against further neglect of the nonverbal aspects of our dis-ease and continuance of the mind-body split. Even a summary of this work in progress deserves a large volume. I limit myself here to a few brief mentions. For instance, A. T. W. Simeons, previously cited in this chapter, has formulated a bold and convincing theory about how the conditions of civilized living are related to our physical ills. In his book, *Man's Presumptuous Brain*, he provides specific and detailed brain-body mechanisms which create peptic ulcers, gallstones, colic, gastritis, duodenitis, habitual constipation, diarrhea, coated tongue and bad taste, esophageal spasms, heart palpitations or aerophagia, essential hypertension, arteriosclerosis, angina pectoris, coronary occlusion, obesity, diabetes, rheumatism, gout, lumbago, slipped or ruptured disk, and various sexual disorders.

The distinguished biologist, René Dubos, marshals a great amount of statistical information to show that the presence or absence of germs is only a minor variable in the incidence of physical illness. He points out that the microorganisms of our most common diseases are with us always, and that generally they cause obvious harm only when the conditions of living create some sort of stress. Each society, Dubos reminds us, has its own characteristic diseases. When primitive Indians become civilized, the pattern of their physical ailments changes completely; they, too, fall prey to the diseases of Civilization. Among the cases Dubos cites is that of primitive African tribesmen, the

Mebans, who live in the swamps of the White Nile, "seared for six months by the blistering sun, pelted by rainstorms the rest of the time."

> Tests recently carried out by a group of Western physicians revealed that the Mebans enjoy low blood pressure from childhood to old age; they are virtually free of obesity, coronary thrombosis, duodenal ulcer, ulcerative colitis, allergies, bronchial asthma, and dental caries. Many of them are said to live to be 90 years of age. The Mebans' relative freedom from degenerative diseases is not due to racial immunity, as shown by the fact that these afflictions are common among the members of the tribe who have settled in Khartoum and other African cities.[22]

Dubos is clear, not only on the striking relationship between physical disease and societal behavior, but also on the prevalence of "submerged potential illness" in the population of the technologically advanced nations. He suggests that the conditions of civilized living are not likely to kill us off quickly. Rather it seems our life degenerates into chronic suffering and eventual decay. Furthermore, "All too often, the biological and social changes that enable mankind to overcome the threats posed by the modern world must be eventually paid for at a cruel price in terms of human values." [23]

Psychologist David Krech has used a different mode of inquiry to establish the close relationship between behavior and the physical. A few years back, Krech and his associates at the University of California at Berkeley provoked a certain amount of skepticism when they reported on a series of experiments with young rats. The experiments showed that rats reared in enriched environments ended up with significantly altered brain chemistry and even a heavier brain cortex than their littermates reared in silence and darkness. His findings have since been verified repeatedly and the experiments expanded to include other physical factors.

Psychology is linked with physiology in a fast-growing field of investigation known as bio-feedback. Researchers in this field are demonstrating that such autonomic or "involuntary" bodily functions as blood pressure, pulse rate, temperature, the distribution of blood to various organs or endocrine systems, muscle tension, and even certain overall brainwave patterns can rather easily be brought under voluntary control by human subjects. The method used is extremely simple: The appropriate instrument is linked to the bodily system to be controlled. The instrument not only measures the function but provides feedback, generally in the form of a signal light or audible tone, to let the subject know when the desired state is being approached. Just by following the indications of the light or tone, the subject can, for example, reliably alter his blood pressure by as much as 20 percent, and sometimes even more. Frequently, he retains voluntary control of an "involuntary" function even after the instrument has been disconnected. These experiments offer further evidence that the body is not—as some medical scientists have seemed to assume—merely an automatic, unconscious machine that operates apart from the higher levels of consciousness. They suggest that all mental states, particularly those identified as neurotic or psychotic, are reflected in the deepest, most elemental workings of the body.

A whole spectrum of current therapies and disciplines are based on the notion that behavior, mental attitude and, indeed, total life experience are written clearly in a person's posture and musculature. The theoretical precedent for some of this work derives from Wilhelm Reich's concept of body armor (though much of it predates Reich). This Reichian connection probably accounts for some of the resistance to prima facie data. Reich was a stubborn and eccentric man. Some of the discoveries of his later years ("bions," the orgone box) stand well outside the boundaries of current scientific thought. But this does not change the fact that habitual attitudes and habitual muscle spasms are related. This concept has achieved a rather broad consensual agreement in its particulars, and the process of conventional scientific verification is now well under way.

The theory holds that as an individual's behavior is frustrated and twisted to produce neurosis or psychosis, there is a corresponding distortion in musculature. Certain muscles contract, usually without the individual's conscious knowledge, in an attempt to hold back forbidden behavior or emotional expression, or to protect the self from real or imagined dangers. After some years, the muscle spasms become habitual. When this happens, especially when it happens during childhood, bone and tissue development is inhibited or distorted, the flow of blood to certain parts of the body is restricted, bodily chemistry is altered, and the passage of nerve impulses is impeded. Certain areas of the body, often those in the deep musculature, become rigid. Under the constant pull of spasmed muscles, the posture is often distorted, sometimes in a highly visible manner. At the same time, certain emotional states are effectively blocked. A vicious collaboration of mind and body renders the individual literally incapable of certain feelings, crippled in his entire emotional life.

A common case of this crippling often occurs when individuals are given their NDD through restriction of all pleasure or satisfaction in the pelvic area. The programming procedure for this dis-ease may include forced control of elimination, taboos on touch, sight, or mention of the genitals, and indeed any of a varied and ingenious armamentarium of erotic repression. The continual holding back of pelvic satisfaction, and of the pelvis itself, creates chronic clenching of the muscles at the small of the back, resulting in an exaggerated lumbar curvature. Corollary contractions may occur in the muscles of the lower abdomen which support the genitals and in the muscles of the upper thighs. The knees, in conjunction with the back thrust of the pelvis, may be habitually locked, with the resulting strain on ankles and feet. The back thrust of the buttocks often creates a corresponding forward thrust of the chest. In extreme cases, people in this condition are deprived of nearly all feeling in the pelvic area— doomed to sexual immaturity, plagued with the problems of the colon and rectum, highly vulnerable to serious back ailments. And yet, this culture in its blindness hardly notices the condition until it has become quite extravagant. There is even a tendency to regard the outthrust buttocks and breasts of a young woman suffering from this particular malady as sexually provocative.

Another common postural distortion results from recurrent

fright and constant anxiety. The shoulders are raised as if to ward off a blow or to shrink back from danger; sometimes one shoulder is raised higher than the other. With the muscles that elevate the shoulders perennially contracted, the individual is always a little off balance, unable to settle down into a serene state of centeredness. A physical condition created by anxiety thus locks anxiety into the very muscles and bones.

Body is indeed a mirror of mind. The experienced practitioner, following indicators similar to the two I have mentioned, can read much of an individual's psychological history merely by looking at his body. "Body therapies" based on this fact are proliferating. There are two main types: One derives from Reich, goes under the general designation "bio-energetics," and is most notably represented by Alexander Lowen on the East Coast and Stanley Keleman on the West. The other is a form of deep facio-muscular massage known as Structural Integration by its founder, Ida Rolf, and as "Rolfing" by everyone else. When a person's muscular blocks are released, even temporarily, by the strenuous exercises of bio-energetics or by the powerful manipulations of Rolfing, there is often a dramatic outpouring of the blocked emotion. Feelings of sadness, joy, rage, sensuality are released. Sometimes specific memories of key people or events associated with the block rise vividly to conscious awareness.

No esoteric knowledge is needed, however, to see the obvious. Simply to look with unscaled eyes at our own bodies and the bodies of our family and friends is to realize that we are all maimed. During some of the workshops I have attended at Esalen, an afternoon has been devoted to body reading. Participants divide up into pairs and strip to bathing suits or underwear. The leader instructs the partners to look closely at one another's bodies as he describes some of the more common blocks and distortions, starting with the head and going all the way down to the feet.

The results of these sessions, even for those who might question the idea of mind-body equivalence, are nothing less than astounding. The people involved are for the most part intelligent and healthy; they take regular physical exams. And yet, to my knowledge, every first-time participant has discovered something quite significant and unexpected about his own body that he had never before noticed. The retired navy captain finds that his left shoulder is slightly higher than the right, and that this imbalance is reflected all the way down his body. The former beauty queen becomes aware that she is unable to stand firmly and evenly on two feet, and that there is a constant tension behind her knees. The insurance executive discovers that the muscles at the top of his chest are so tense that the area is sore to the touch. He realizes that, incredibly, neither he nor anyone else has touched him there with any real attention or feeling for as long as he can remember.

It is as if all the sadness of our lives is stored, available to our sight but unseen, within the boundaries of our skin. There are no exemplars among us, only the maimed. There is the soft-fleshed girl whose underlying muscles are so rigid that further development of the surface muscles is unlikely. There is the athlete, dancer, model, actor whose body has become an instrument to be pushed around, used, displayed—the person who studies flaws in the instrument as coldly and objectively as one would diagnose a flaw in an automobile engine. And we realize the cruel irony in the designation of some poor muscle-bound monstrosity as "Mr. America," the celebration of one who has spasmed every visible muscle, the better to damp the flow of every possible feeling. Here indeed is a stylized, dysfunctional battering ram, a specimen for display in the windows of our discontent.

There is a hum of voices as we discuss the subtle maiming that marks us as good citizens. We could no more do without physical blocks than we could do without neuroses. We search our memories in vain for the supple flowing body that can move and be at home in the world. Even the idealized antiquities fail us. The stones of Pericles' Athens offer us a body that is noble, graceful and balanced, but it is a body shaped for war; the Elgin Marbles reveal again and again the hard belly, the inguinal ligaments taut as bowstrings, the lower half of the body cut off from the top by a muscular block (seen as a sharp horizontal crease) at the diaphragm.

And yet we still can hope. As we discuss our deformities (standing there, pathetic in our underwear and the ill-used clothing of our flesh), an etheric figure begins to take shape and form, if only in our hopes. Within the rough cocoon Civilization has spun for each of us there lives a secret and durable image of beauty. We have glimpsed it. We see its persistent gleam in some of the eyes around us now. We are not entirely convinced that our ugliness is inevitable. *We are becoming aware.*

Freud's first great insight holds. Clear conscious awareness of how a particular dis-ease is inculcated is likely to make that particular dis-ease leave us. Since Freud, we have chased symptom after symptom. But as each is brought to awareness and thus vanquished or reduced, it is simply replaced by another, more subtly veiled. We have now arrived on the threshold of awareness that *all* the dis-eases, whether "mental" or "physical," have the same origin, the same function and, in a larger sense, the same effect on us all. Acceptance of this awareness will take courage. It requires a subsequent acceptance of despair, or of the inevitability of transformation.

The Emperor's New Clothes may yet turn out to be the central metaphor of our time. I have never been satisfied, however, with Andersen's halfhearted ending. When the scales fall from the people's eyes and they realize their Emperor is naked, surely all of them will join him in glorious nakedness, and they will dance and sing. And what will happen to the Empire then?

six

Graham Crackers for Our Children

The victims themselves considered it a glorious death to be seized by the priests and stretched on their backs over a stone on the temple summit, an incision made in the chest with a flint knife, the heart ripped out and placed in the cuauhxicalli, *or "Eagle vase," to be burned for the consumption of the gods. Quickly the head was cut from the corpse, and the body flayed. Priests and those doing penance garbed themselves in the victim's skin, which was worn for twenty days at the end of which the god-impersonator (for they then represented Xipe, the Flayed One) "stank like a dead dog," as one source tells us. . . .*

Most horrible of Aztec practices was the mass sacrifice of small children on mountain tops to bring rain at the end of the dry season, in propitiation of Tlaloc; it was said that the more they cried, the more the Rain God was pleased.

—MICHAEL D. COE, MEXICO

❦

As long as the world exists
The fame and glory of Mexico-Tenochtitlán
Will have no end.

—MEMORIALS OF CŪLHUACAN

(1974 !

IT IS EXTREMELY difficult to know just what aspects of conventional wisdom will eventually come to be perceived as outrage. But it is likely to be precisely those aspects that are most revered and acclaimed, for which pennants are flown and songs are sung, to which the most intense service and sacrifice are dedicated. The Aztecs were a dutiful and dedicated people. Present-day Americans who profess admiration for what they call the old virtues would find much about them to admire—their self-restraint and humility, the austerity and rigor of their upbringing, the depth of their religious belief. By contrast, the Spaniards who conquered them seemed hasty, greedy and arrogant. It was obvious to the Aztecs that the white-faces cared very little for their God; they offered him not a single human sacrifice.

The Aztecs were well aware of the responsibility they bore. Of all the peoples of the earth it was they who had been chosen to keep the sun moving across the sky. Without an adequate fare of human hearts, the sun would surely fail to rise. The dutiful Aztecs provided the hearts—thousands of them a year—by taking captives in battle after battle. On the occasion of the dedication of the Great Temple of Tenochtitlán, at least twenty thousand captives gained in the Flowery Wars were sacrificed. It was said that the ranks of those waiting to be sacrificed stretched several miles and that the arms of the priests became at last almost too weary to wield the sacrificial knives of flint and mosaic stone.

The victorious Spanish put an end to these practices. They demolished the temples and built cathedrals on their foundations. They sought out and destroyed the books and records of all the Indian cultures. They plundered the treasures of Mexico, divided the land among themselves, and took the people as servants. Meanwhile, in Spain itself, the Inquisition gained momentum. Thousands of people were tortured, broken on the rack, decapitated, burned at the stake—all in the name of the gentle Jesus.

Chronicles of this sort are commonplace. Volumes could be devoted to the outrages of every civilized period. But the familiar spectacles of blade and skewer, water and flame, stretching and suffocation may only dull our perception to the outrages with which we live. The sacrifice of human life can take various shapes. The Aztec warrior sacrificed at the height of his powers may truly be fortunate compared to the individual kept alive to endure, through countless days and nights, mutilations he cannot understand or even acknowledge.

The illogic and cruelty of the sexual repression among our own middle and upper classes during the nineteenth century now seems clear to us, as well it should, since we still are living out the post-Victorian reaction. But that the outrages of that time should have been considered so respectable, so anointed with sweet reason, may yet boggle the mind. Contrary to popular belief, sexual puritanism in the United States cannot really be traced back to the Puritans. The Pilgrim Fathers brought an Elizabethan spirit to Plymouth Plantation in 1620, and the hard-nosed Puritans themselves, who established the Massachusetts Bay Colony in 1630, never went so far as to classify sexuality as a sickness. Some early Americans may have inveighed against adultery and masturbation, but the seventeenth and eighteenth centuries were marked by a scarcity of published warnings against sexual misbehavior. Indeed, John Demos has suggested that the early national period, the late eighteenth century, was probably the most open period in American history where marital sex is concerned. The sex manuals of that time and even of the early nineteenth century treated married sex as a happy and salutary activity.

All of this underwent a sudden reversal around 1830. As Stephen Nissenbaum points out in his fascinating paper, "The New Chastity in America, 1830–1840," that was the time when a number of temperance lecturers turned their attention to the evils of sexuality and indeed of all sensory pleasure. Their message swept the nation, which was just embarking on a period of unprecedented agricultural, industrial and physical growth. These lecturers were, of course, symptom as much as cause, and the sexual hysteria of the period was European as well as American. But their words set a particular tone for the nineteenth-century attitudes that still resonate in the NDDs of our grandparents, our parents, and ourselves.

The most popular and influential of the lecturers, according to Nissenbaum, was the man who invented the Graham cracker, Dr. Sylvester Graham. Graham's theories start with the premise that every human faculty must be marshaled to stave off the threats of a hostile external environment. The individual must pay as little attention as possible to sensations that arise within his own body. "When . . . we are *conscious* that we have a stomach, or a liver from any *feeling* in those organs," Graham wrote, "we may be certain that something is wrong." [1] Graham saw the human body as a fortress under siege. The five senses serve as its sentinels, warning of the approach of particular dangers. The individual cannot survive by living in harmony with the world around him, but only in strenuous opposition to it. Graham viewed life as a temporary victory over the causes which induce death.

To achieve this victory, according to Graham, the individual must censor every conceivable inner sensation and cling desperately to external reality. Ordinary dreams and fantasies are simply mild forms of insanity. Feelings of religious exaltation derive from physiological irritation and are not to be trusted. Even the mental images that arise from memory or imagination can be dangerous; they are certainly not to be confused with the images that come from the actual sight of external objects. A healthy person senses nothing whatever from inside his own being. He focuses all his perception and intelligence on the treacherous outside forces that besiege him as long as he can manage to exist.

In this context, it is easy to see why Graham would consider sexual desire a sickness and the sex act itself a catastrophe. Graham warned that only when a man reaches thirty is his body mature enough to withstand the trauma of copulation. Even then, he should restrict this activity to a bare minimum—once a month for the healthy and robust and less or none at all for the sickly and the sedentary. Graham wrote that the nerves of the sexual organs "are, in their natural state, entirely destitute of animal sensibility," and that truly healthy people could easily subdue their sexual propensities so that they would be wholly free of sexual feeling for several months in succession. He argued that "health does not absolutely require that there should ever be an emission of semen from puberty to death." [2]

The consequences of excessive sexual activity are dire indeed. It is difficult in limited space to do justice to Graham's catalogue of horrors. The following list covers only the difficulties caused by libidinal excess between wife and husband:

> Languor, lassitude, muscular relaxation, general debility and heaviness, depression of spirits, loss of appetite, indigestion, faintness and sinking at the pit of the stomach, increased susceptibilities of the skin and lungs to all atmospheric changes, feebleness of circulation, chilliness, headache, melancholy, hypochondria, hysterics, feebleness of all the senses, impaired vision, loss of sight, weakness of the lungs, nervous cough, pulmonary consumption, disorders of the liver and kidneys, urinary difficulties, disorders of the genital organs, spinal diseases, weakness of the brain, loss of memory, epilepsy, insanity, apoplexy;—abortions, premature births, and extreme feebleness, morbid predispositions, and early death of offspring.[3]

Graham goes on to detail the effects of sexual activity on each of the bodily organs. The liver, for example, is made susceptible to jaundice "in its worst and most unmanageable form." The kidneys fall prey to diabetes. The bladder may suffer spasmodic affections and ulceration, along with "purulent discharges from the penis." The muscles become weak, the bones dry and brittle. The bodily fluids become "crude, acrid and irritating," the teeth loose and decayed. The skin "loses its healthy, clear and fresh appearance, and assumes a sickly, pale, shrivelled, turbid and cadaverous aspect" along with a thick cover of boils, blisters, and pimples of a livid hue.[4]

Graham's most frightening forewarnings concern the effects of lustful excitement upon a bodily system already weakened by sexual indulgence. For instance, when the "over-excited and convulsed heart" pumps blood into the sex-debilitated lungs faster than they can handle it, there may be a "rupture of the vessels, hemorrhage of the lungs, and gushing of blood from the mouth and nostrils." The heart itself may suffer a similar fate. When persons who have already weakened their circulatory systems by venery are rash enough to risk copulation, then

"the violent convulsive paroxysms attending the acme of vene-
real indulgence often cause spasms in the heart . . . sometimes
producing aneurisms, or bursting of its walls, and suffering the
blood to gush out into the pericardium; and causing sudden
death in the unclean act." [5]

It goes without saying that, for Graham, sex impairs or even
destroys the five external senses, tortures and debilitates the
nerves, unhinges the mind, and results eventually either in habitual depression or a state of total idiocy. The first physiological
process to be affected by lust, however, is the digestive system.
The stomach "more directly and powerfully sympathizes with
the genital organs, in all their excitements and affections, than
any other organ of the body." [6] Not only does sexual activity
strike at the digestive system with the usual gruesome results,
but the digestive process also strongly influences the sex organs.
"All kinds of stimulating and heating substances, high-seasoned
food, rich dishes, the free use of flesh, and even the excess of
aliment, all . . . increase the concupiscent excitability and sensibility of the genital organs." [7] Graham warns against the use of
such spices as mustard, pepper, and even salt, and such stimu-
lants as coffee and tea. Alcohol is, of course, entirely out of the
question. Graham eventually called for an exclusively vegetarian
diet. His invention of Graham flour, consisting of the entire ker-
nel of the cleaned grain, was part of his attempt to provide a
nourishing yet bland nonmeat diet.

Graham's views, incredible as they may now sound, received
wide acceptance in the 1830s. His lectures were well attended.
The published version of his *Lecture on Chastity* appeared in
at least ten editions over the fourteen years following its publication in 1833. Graham Associations were formed in several
cities. "Graham tables" were set up in the dining halls of a number of colleges. Graham Boarding Houses were founded in Boston and New York during the mid-1830s; here men could live
regimented lives under a program designed to reduce sex desire
to a minimum. Graham himself fell from prominence in the
decade preceding his death in 1851, but his influence continued,
especially in the many sanitariums that sprang up in the second
half of the century. The most famous of them, Dr. John Harvey

Kellogg's Battle Creek Sanitarium, used Grahamite methods in treating neurasthenia. Cold breakfast cereal, invented and marketed first to his patients by Dr. Kellogg, was a direct descendant of the Graham cracker. According to Stephen Nissenbaum, every American manual of sex hygiene published between the 1830s and roughly the end of the century "was soaked in the increasingly archaic Grahamite bath." [8]

Sylvester Graham himself might have been shocked by some of the methods that arose in the second half of the century. The fear of masturbation reached such hysterical heights that respected physicians in the United States and Europe regularly recommended clitoridectomy, circumcision, infibulation (putting a silver wire through the foreskin), wearing of locked chastity belts or spiked penile rings, blistering the penis with red mercury ointment, cauterization of the spine and genitals, surgical denervation of the penis and, in extreme cases, removal of both penis and testes. In 1876 a doctor could report on the infibulation of mental patients in the following manner:

> The sensation among the patients themselves was extraordinary. I was struck by the conscience-stricken way in which they submitted to the operation on their penises. I mean to try it on a large scale, and go on wiring all masturbators.[9]

This was indeed an age when normal adults were advised by William Acton, one of the more humane of the Victorian venerologists, to sleep with their hands tied, and when piano legs were commonly concealed beneath dust ruffles so that the sight of them should not excite the baser passions. Naturally enough, such theory and practice took its toll in human health and serenity. Historian Page Smith devotes a section of his book on American women, *Daughters of the Promised Land*, to the epidemic of nonspecific sickness that swept over middle and upper middle class women in the nineteenth century. He cites an informal survey published in 1855 by Catherine Beecher, sister of Harriet Beecher Stowe. Miss Beecher wrote to friends and acquaintances in every town she had visited and asked them to report on the ten women in their community they knew best. In the over two hundred towns thus surveyed, only two had a majority of healthy women among the ten sampled. The "habitual invalids" and "delicate or diseased" outnumbered the "strong and healthy" by anywhere from four to one to ten to one. Catherine Beecher herself was unable to recall in her "immense circle of friends and acquaintances' all over the Union, so many as ten married ladies born in this century and country, who are perfectly sound, healthy, and vigorous." [10]

We should not for a moment consider this epidemic, or indeed any of the massive sexual anxieties of the time, as harmful to the national purpose. On the contrary, the inculcation of severe sexual dis-ease and the cutting off of every possible inner feeling was necessary to accomplish the tasks set for the peoples of America and Europe during that period. "Sickness" for women was perhaps the only acceptable and efficient birth-control method of the time, as well as being a way of reducing inevitable man-woman pressures to an endurable level.

During this period, the Western nations were occupied in an orgy of growth and exploitation unprecedented in world history. While the European nations gobbled up the resources and "civilized" the peoples of their expanding colonial empires, the United States swallowed the American West whole in pursuit of what journalist John L. O'Sullivan in 1845 called "our manifest destiny to overspread the continent allotted by divine Providence for the development of our yearly multiplying millions." Between 1820 and the outbreak of the Civil War, American farm produce rose, in current value, from about $300 million to nearly $1.5 billion. The process of industrialization in Europe and America required the creation of millions of human components of the most primitive sort.

All of this entailed the release of great amounts of male aggressive energy. In such a situation, it was not possible to create NDDs primarily by frustrating the culturally induced aggression. Sexual anxiety became the chief agency of dis-ease. The most effective (if temporary) remedy for concupiscence is good hard work and plenty of it. Instead of masturbating the young man cuts down another tree. And when he masturbates anyway, the young man works off his guilt, gets out of himself, by cutting down two more.

To spoil the sexual feelings usually is to spoil most of the other bodily-sensory feelings. To censor inner impulse, imagination and fantasy is to reduce the possibility of empathy. Sylvester Graham and his followers not only helped create anxious, obsessive human components for the ravishment of a continent but also helped numb a young nation to what it had done to the Cherokees, the Seminoles, the Chickasaw. (In August 1830, President Andrew Jackson rode south from his Hermitage home to meet with the Chickasaw chieftains at present-day Franklin, Tennessee. "You must submit," he told them. "There is no alternative.")

The ideal nineteenth-century man remains a desensitized instrument, a disembodied construct. We cannot ignore him. He has bequeathed to us, among other antiquities, that outworn imperative that, to be a man, we must not feel, must not yield, must not weep. The imperative was once real and urgent. If the flesh-and-blood man of the nineteenth century could truly and deeply feel what he and his nation were doing to the world and to the living things in it, he could not long keep on doing it. Has anything really changed? We still rape the world and destroy life. The old ideal of manhood, far more than politics, economics or national security led us through the jungles of Indochina.

But today there is a difference. Among other changing conditions, our changing attitude towards sex frees our perceptions just enough to recognize some horrors as horrors. A ring inserted in the foreskin so that the glans cannot emerge seems a horror. Perceiving this horror, we can perceive another—the thousand miles and four thousand deaths of the Cherokee Nation's Trail of Tears, the million civilian deaths in Vietnam. Conventional wisdom suddenly becomes suspect. Military practices that skittered past our consciousness without making a ripple in all past wars begin to turn our stomachs. It hurts to feel. Awakening brings pain as well as ecstasy, and there is no sure way around the ache. Beyond the pain, only the unknown. That we have recently endured so many awakenings (with so many yet to come) is a sure sign that the Transformation is under way. Awareness destroys tradition. Awareness of Civilization's outrages heralds Civilization's end. Awareness more than any other single thing *is* the Transformation.

❧

The Victorian Age lingered in the rural South at least to the end of the 1930s, filling the pews of the Baptist and Methodist churches with shame and self-righteousness. The summer sun blazed down and stilled the morning birds. By eleven on Sunday there was only silence except for the rising and falling beat of the cicada's song, and in the better churches the better class of people were ready to begin one of the strangest rituals ever devised by the human race: There, in the intimate presence of the most powerful symbols of their God, they would practice feeling nothing. They would try to sense neither joy nor sorrow nor awe nor exaltation, but perhaps only a vague sanctimonious unease. Not for them the ranting and raving of the preacher of the colored or the poor; their gentile minister talked in a flat voice about a pale and distant Galilean who would not trouble them. Not for them the bellowed hymns; they sang beneath their breaths, stealing glances at the thin-voiced choir or at a neighbor whose voice became audible. This ritual, like so much else they endured, was designed to leech the juices of life from their bodies and beings. But neither it nor all the conditioning practices their society could devise was entirely successful.

Scattered among the congregation, like flowers in their sleeveless cotton dresses of yellow and pink and blue, are girls of eleven and twelve and thirteen. Already their bodies are becoming rigid, their mouths learning the feel of tightness. But the juices of life still are strong and rising. Their cheeks are round and glowing. The curves remain in their lips. Their unexpected breasts press against the moist cotton of their little-girl dresses. Lust rises and falls around them like the cicada's song while the minister's voice extracts only dust and dry bones from the bloodless body of Christ. And yet somewhere in every consciousness the elemental vibrancy sings the inevitability of fullness. The dissonance invites delirium. Suddenly the heat becomes unbearable. The funeral parlor fans no longer can cool the fevered faces. The inner being, denied existence, begins to swell. It grows hollow and huge, as big as the inside of the church, even bigger. And all this space is filled with the resonating, echoing sound of the cicadas, metallic and dry and enormous, continuing to swell until, with a wrenching act of the will, reality can be regained. Reality: the flutter of the fans, the tickle of a drop of sweat running down the side of the chest, the sound of the minister's voice pronouncing meaningless words: "And Jesus said unto them, 'See ye not all these things? verily I say unto you, There shall not be left here one stone upon another, that shall not be thrown down.'" Reality may mean no inner being at all, but somewhere, still resonating to the cicada's song, there is a faint high whine of madness.

❧

A time of rapid awakening to the outrages contained in conventional wisdom can be a particularly dangerous time. In normal circumstances, the culture rather effectively controls what particular fraction of existence each individual is able to bring to awareness. The rest is relegated to dreams, symbols, or rare genius. This control of awareness serves as perhaps the major stabilizing force in any society. The tightness of the control and the narrowness of individual awareness present few problems in a stable, slow-changing society beset by no significant new challenges. During periods of explosive change, however, the limitations that have been imposed on individual consciousness become serious indeed. The greatest danger lies in the fact that the awakening doesn't happen to everyone at the same time. When some people begin to see things that other people don't see, the resulting crisis may strain at every stone in the social edifice.

Within the last few years, every corner of the world has been joined together by the communications net. Every sort of human transaction has increased in speed and intensity. The opaque veil of conventional wisdom has become transparent. It has become obvious to many, especially here in the United States, that the Emperor is naked. The revelation of the secret has infuriated many more, who find security and identity only in the sleep of the senses. All of the "gaps" of the 1960s are actually only different manifestations of a consciousness gap. It is a gap between the opaque and the transparent, between the invisible and the visible. It is of such insubstantial stuff that riots and wars are made.

For hundreds of years, white people of good will could live on American shores, could lecture their children on morality, attend seminars on ethics at distinguished universities, write books on major moral issues—and never once mention what we have been doing to our black brothers. How sad it is that perceptions so often have to be shaken awake by explosions and fires. Once we are awakened, we may cry out in compassion or gird ourselves for battle against change, but it becomes extremely difficult simply to ignore reality again.

What we are seeing—dimly, incompletely—is indeed a bursting out into conscious awareness of the unseen hosts that have controlled our lives since the dawn of Civilization. Seeing is disbelieving. Some of the most awesome demons, upon becoming visible, lose their power. All we have to fear is those who do not see.

A second-grade classroom. The children are neat. Their fingernails are clean. They sit silently in orderly rows, waiting for the teacher to direct them. They speak only when spoken to, and when they do speak it is to repeat what the teacher said to them. They raise their hands to go to the bathroom.

A visitor who is unaware of the forces that control and limit us spends a few minutes watching this scene, smiles approvingly, and walks on to the next classroom. A visitor who has awakened stays longer then, unable to bear it, goes out into the hall and begins crying.

A commentator on television. He is describing a bloody battle in the jungle. Napalm. Civilian deaths. Body counts. A sequence showing badly wounded soldiers on stretchers. And all the time he remains entirely cool and collected. He speaks exactly as if he were describing a chess match.

To one who spends all the minutes of his life within the bounds of conventional wisdom, this seems a time-honored and perfectly appropriate way to describe such scenes. But there are people, many people, to whom such detachment seems weird, grotesque, stranger than science fiction.

And to some people, many people, the conventional walls between you and your brother, father, wife, lover seem equally strange and senseless. And there are many people who are finding their boundaries expanding, at last, to encompass the minorities that eventually include us all. And more people every day are becoming aware of the insane betrayal of our bodies, the numbing of our senses, our immoral and truly criminal insensitivity to others.

And then we begin to realize that all these awakenings are only a beginning.

※

What current wisdom will eventually come to be perceived as outrage? Who can tell us? The answers are, of course, that we do not know and no one can tell us. And yet it is possible to point to certain sources that are more likely than others to mislead us. The formula is actually quite simple. Concerning the significant matters of human existence, concerning the Transformation of humankind, those sources that are closest to the official seats of power, prestige and vested interest are the ones most likely to be wrong. Such sources have indeed established a certain reliability in this regard. If a highly respected official should make a judgment about some future matter of great importance, we can rather safely rule out that eventuality.

In his book *Profiles of the Future*, Arthur C. Clarke offers excellent examples of the failure of Establishment predictions in the field of science—how at the turn of the century the most distinguished scientists were almost unanimous in declaring that heavier-than-air flight was impossible; how in 1945 the civilian chief of the United States scientific war effort, Dr. Vannevar Bush, scoffed at the practicability of the intercontinental ballistic missile; how in 1956 the British Astronomer Royal, Dr. Richard van der Reit Woolley, said that "space travel is utter bilge." He cites the celebrated case of Lord Rutherford, who more than any other individual laid bare the internal structure of the atom. Until his death in 1937 Rutherford persisted in

laughing at those sensation mongers who said we might someday harness the energy locked in matter. Within five years of
his death, the first chain reaction was started in Chicago. From
this case and others, Clarke draws the lesson "that it is not the
man who knows most about a subject, and is the acknowledged
master of his field, who can give the most reliable pointers to
the future. Too great a burden of knowledge can clog the
wheels of imagination." Clarke concludes that "The real future
is not *logically* foreseeable." [11]

This conclusion has been rather well borne out by the work
of government- and industry-sponsored "think tanks" since
World War II. Using the best instruments of logic and extrapolation, these institutions have come up with excellent predictions
on obvious and trivial matters. On the larger questions, they have
often misled their clients. During a late 1969 symposium on the
future, the preeminent futurist, Herman Kahn, pointed out that
he and his colleagues had compiled a record of predictions that
were right better than 80 percent of the time. I asked him about
his record on the really important questions of peace and war,
life and death. "Oh, on those," he replied with charming can-
dor, "we've been wrong." In their 1967 book, *The Year 2000*,
Kahn and coauthor Anthony J. Wiener completely omit the
ecological crisis.

Logic and conventional wisdom have indeed proven so inadequate that even some of the more "scientific" futurists have been
questioning them. In an article entitled "The Counterintuitive
Behavior of Social Systems," Jay Forrester of the Massachusetts
Institute of Technology describes how social actions taken for
good reasons and in good conscience may produce results entirely contrary to those intended. Low income public housing,
for example, was designed to alleviate poverty. Forrester shows
how it actually cannot but increase and perpetuate poverty. He
goes on to demonstrate how other well-intentioned actions may
lead to disaster. Using complex computer projections, he argues
that short-term success in technological control of pollution will
only delay and increase the dimensions of a long-term worldwide pollution catastrophe. Even something as drastic as achieving a zero population growth rate, without a correspondingly

drastic reduction in current forms of capital investment, will only delay and exacerbate the eventual pollution catastrophe.[12] Significantly though, neither Forrester nor any other "scientific" futurists that I know of have programmed into their projections any real change in the "nature" of humankind. And yet, human transformation appears at this point to be the one element utterly essential to the survival of the race, and thus its consideration as a relevant variable is unavoidable in any study that purports to be "scientific."

Turning away for the moment from science, we might look to modern journalism, supposedly in close touch with every passing event, for guidance to the future. We would again be looking in the wrong direction. Our experiences over the past decade have revealed to us just what a poor guide journalism can be. Writing in the *Columbia Journalism Review*, Tom Wicker of *The New York Times* tells how in case after case the most respected of United States journalists failed to spot the critical issues of the times and examine the possible consequences of our actions.

> The obvious example, I think, is the failure of the American press, exemplified by the Washington bureau of *The New York Times*, of which I was in charge at the time, adequately to question the assumptions, the intelligence, the whole idea of the world—which led this country into the Vietnam War in the 1960s. It is commonplace now, when the horse has already been stolen, to examine those assumptions. But where were we at the time we might have brought an enlightened public view to bear on that question? [13]

Wicker blames much of the failure on the American journalist's heavy reliance on official sources. He feels that if this reliance continues very far into the future it will mean disaster. Institutional opinion is not to be trusted. Our institutions are currently under challenge precisely because

> they are irrelevant in many ways and are "out of touch." Life has changed, taken the ground out from

under them. . . . Therefore, you are going not only to
a self-serving source for news but to a source that
simply may not know what it's talking about. Anybody
who has been roaming the country as a reporter in the
last few years can cite examples of having gone to a
perfectly respectable institution, to a highly official
source, and taken a statement that seems to have absolute
surface validity, only to find that as events unfold it
meant nothing because it was out of touch with reality.[14]

There is also the question of focus. Existence moves in wave
patterns, waves within waves ranging from the extremely short
to the extremely long. Most journalists, because of their very
mode of working, generally focus their attention on relatively
short waves. Anxiously scanning the daily bulletins, they mistake passing fads for trends. They herald the appearance of hippies as the beginning of a new age, then prepare obituaries for
this age of their own creation when the hippies prove to be dis-
appointing. They fail to recognize the phenomenon as a tiny
ripple in a great tide.

Conventional reporting, it seems to some critics, is too primitive to cope with the complexities of the age. Perhaps, the critics
say, it should be reinforced or even largely replaced by scientific
sampling techniques. It is true the pollsters have demonstrated
that, with a few spectacular exceptions, they can predict the out-
comes of elections—that is, if the key sample is taken within a
very few days of the election itself. Polls on trends, goals and
national "moods" may also shed some light on the recent past.
In guiding us to the future, however, scientific sampling is worse
than worthless. It is misleading and, to the extent it is taken seriously, often stultifying. The opinion pollsters generally turn us
from the future by scanning only that part of the horizon from
which they got blips in the past. Their stodgy questions elicit
stodgy answers and encourage the view that we are a stodgy
people.

I cannot resist recounting a personal experience that reveals
a certain limitation of the opinion poll. In 1960 I was asked
to produce a special issue of *Look* on youth of the sixties. I

put together a team of 14 journalists. We spent quite a bit of time talking with some 350 young people in various parts of the country. We examined other indicators of change. We trusted our own feelings. In the end we realized that something new was in the air and that the nation had better get ready for a period of unprecedented turbulence among its young people. We received no support for this position from any official source, and all the other media were still talking about a Silent Generation. Nevertheless, we decided to organize the entire issue around the theme, "The Explosive Generation," and that was the headline on the cover. The issue began with these words:

> Youth everywhere is exploding into action. Members of the new generation have looked at the world their elders made. They do not like what they see. They are moving hard and fast to change it . . . social changes that once took decades are now happening overnight. But even this headlong pace is not fast enough for youth of the sixties, the war babies who at last have grown up to give voice and vehemence to a generation that has been called "silent" and "cautious." [15]

Looking back from this vantage point, it seems that only a particularly stubborn fool could fail to see the signs of upheaval among the young; our issue was filled with pictures of upheaval, stories of sit-ins and social activism. Yet it made hardly a ripple. Other periodicals went right along on noting the apathy of the young.

A year *later*, in fact, the *Saturday Evening Post* commissioned Dr. George Gallup's organization to do a scientific poll of American youth to learn the true facts about the very matters we had treated. Questions were asked of three thousand young people—a larger-than-usual sample—and Dr. Gallup himself coauthored the lengthy report built around the survey. It was entitled, "Youth—The Cool Generation," and included the following key "findings":

> Our typical youth will settle for low success rather than risk high failure. He has little spirit of adventure. . . .

> In general, the typical American youth shows few
> symptoms of frustration, and is most unlikely to rebel
> or involve himself in crusades of any kind. He likes
> himself the way he is, and he likes things as they are.
> . . . The United States has bred a generation of nice
> little boys and girls who are just what we have asked
> them to be.[16]

Opinion sampling simply cannot deal with social and human change. Even the best statistics, uninformed by a larger vision, can be dead wrong. This is especially true when people are being questioned about experiences they have not yet had or situations that do not yet exist. How many people would now say yes to the changes that are sure to accompany a transformed humanity? What percentage of our population would predict the loss of the ego structure with which we now define our very existence as separate entities? How many would vote for a new consciousness or a new way of being male or female? How many respectable parishioners would opt for a church designed for ecstasy and revels? The vote of the secret heart might surprise us, but is not available to Dr. Gallup's instruments. Conventional opinion sampling is useful only in revealing the "typical" citizen's inability to conceive of a new social and cultural paradigm. Significant change around the core of one's existence is not only inconceivable but, prima facie, threatening and frightening. Once it arrives, however, the previously unthinkable rather quickly becomes commonplace.

It would give me much pleasure here to go on in a reassuring tone. I wish I could say that the Transformation involves only developments that would satisfy present standards of humane enlightenment and good taste. All of us would perhaps prefer to go on giving our children Graham crackers and milk, trusting that moderate and reasonable measures will revivify our dead Civilization. But during times of fast technological change, predictions of the future that satisfy every present-day standard of enlightenment and good taste are not likely to prove significant. The deadness of the present is obvious. The life of the future remains outside the scope of conventional wisdom. The Amer-

ican President speaks of "negativism, defeatism, a sense of alienation" and a possible loss of "the will to live and to improve."
As a remedy he offers only "moral health" and increased economic competition with the other great powers.

But the Transformation is already under way and cannot be
blocked by opinion polls, politics, or even good taste. There
have been too many awakenings. Established institutions begin
to waver. Official sources adopt an unexpectedly tentative tone.
Unquestioning belief in all things official and established has
died. A new belief waits to be born.

No one can guarantee a hard and fast picture of the future,
for surprise is its very nature. But we can, as I have said before,
become aware of what has already changed and is changing. In
the following chapters I go on to suggest signs we may encounter on the journey towards Transformation. Yet I am aware
that my words are inadequate alongside the sense of existence
that already dwells somewhere in every heart. The essence of
the future is contained in this sense, which normally is locked
away and half forgotten. But there are certain days of freakish
weather (the chill of autumn in August, a winter thunderstorm)
when time and place play tricks on us, when old loves rise up to
mock our unresolve, when our secure faith in the impossible
shifts, leaving us no steady place on which to stand. On such a
day, when a natural disaster or a miracle seems equally likely,
the ancient everpresent imprisoned wings of belief may beat in
our breasts, summoning us back again to our wildest dreams and
darkest fears. To understand the Transformation, pay attention.

seven

Change and
Flood Change

Dogen-zenji said, "Even though it is midnight, dawn is here; even though dawn comes, it is nighttime." This kind of statement conveys the understanding transmitted from Buddha to the Patriarchs, and from the Patriarchs to Dogen, and to us. Nighttime and daytime are not different. The same thing is sometimes called nighttime, sometimes called daytime. They are one thing.

—SHUNRYU SUZUKI, ZEN MIND, BEGINNER'S MIND

THE MAJORITY of all the sculpting of the earth by rivers and streams, the creation of valleys and chasms and plains, occurs during floods. The Colorado River, for example, carves its channel in the Grand Canyon at a prodigious rate, carrying away thousands of tons of salts, clay, silt and sand every day. But the process is by no means steady. As the river's flow doubles, the load it carries increases more than four times. As it triples, the load increases from nine to twenty-seven times. During one calm October day the river carried a load of about five hundred tons past a certain checkpoint. On a day of torrential water the following June, it carried about two million tons.

The great nineteenth-century geologist Charles Lyell clearly established the continuity of geological events from the extreme past to the present, thus opening Darwin's mind to the gradual evolution of species. And it is true that all change is inexorable and never-ending. But within this relentless flow, we see many signs of flood change, climactic moments of cataclysm or unfolding. We see these signs in the earth and in the heavens, in nature and in history: A shoreline altered during a single storm, a valley inundated by lava flow. Earthquake and landslide, drought and dust storm. Stars that explode after eons of steady burning to become novae or supernovae, exploding galaxies, catastrophic gravitational collapse, and other celestial events that take place within microseconds. The instantaneous birth of the universe and that critical period some one hundred thousand years later when the photons were at last released from their prison of charged particles and all our previously opaque young universe was flooded with light. The swarming of bees, the periodic orgies of ladybugs and squid, the blossoming forth of springtime vibrancy in color, leaf, form and flesh, the sudden torrent of sunlight at dawn. Birth itself. And all those surging tides we tend to find in the historical record—the agricultural and other "revolutions," the "great men" who seem to cluster around certain points in history, the "great leaps forward" some historians suppose to have happened at about 3000 B.C., in the sixth century B.C. and the twelfth century A.D., the epic birth and death of empires or cultural movements or civilization.

Could all this be illusion? The catastrophic death and transfiguration of stars is contained in their birth. The snow-encrusted earth defines the juices of spring. Though I wait for the sun through my own dark night on this particular edge of the earth, it is always dawn, and dawn is part of nighttime. When we look more closely, some of the great turning points of history seem evolutionary rather than revolutionary; the agricultural revolution, it now appears, took several millennia. And yet we cannot shake off the report of our perceptions. Wherever a surplus of grain did develop, whether in the Middle East around 3000 B.C. or in Mesoamerica some eighteen hundred years later, what we call Civilization with its classes and castes, impressive ceremonial centers, markets and specialized vocations very quickly followed.

Perhaps we are and always shall be dealing with at least two kinds of change and two kinds of time as well: The ancient Greeks conceived *kairos*, the moments of sudden unfolding, along with *kronos*, or ordinary, steady time. Henri Bergson argued that mechanical time, or clock time, is artificial in that it is fixed by scientists through reference to simple spatial variables; all organisms actually live in *durée réelle*, or real time, in which waiting for a teapot to boil may seem an eternity. In any case, change is *observed* change, and in spite of strenuous efforts, no one has ever proved out a totally neutral, purely objective standard of observation. Perception is an essential aspect of reality. When we perceive a different world, the world becomes, literally, different. Within our perceptions, both change and flood change do exist, and it is in terms of the latter that the Transformation is unfolding.

The history of Western science provides striking examples of how drastically the most respectable perception of reality can change. In *The Structure of Scientific Revolutions*, historian of science Thomas S. Kuhn argues that, after scientific revolutions, scientists actually respond to a different world than before. They perceive and behave differently, making new assumptions, addressing themselves to new questions in new ways while totally ignoring other questions that previously may have been considered central. Scientists who choose not to live in the dominant new world are simply not considered scientists, whatever the lip service given to free and open experimentalism.

Kuhn uses the notion of *paradigm* in developing his thesis. A paradigm is a compelling model or example; thus, once you know *amo, amas, amat*, you have a good idea of how a number of Latin verbs are conjugated. A scientific paradigm is, of course, far more complex. It is also open-ended, crying out for elucidation, refinement and expansion, suggesting a seemingly endless number of experiments. As samples of the kinds of classic works that form scientific paradigms, Kuhn lists Aristotle's *Physica*, Ptolemy's *Almagest*, Newton's *Principia* and *Opticks*, Franklin's *Electricity*, Lavoisier's *Chemistry*, and Lyell's *Geology*. Each of these works triggered a scientific revolution, rendering irrelevant much that preceded it. Such specific works, Kuhn tells us, are far more effective in creating a new scientific tradition than are any of the concepts, laws and theories that may be drawn from them. In fact, some of the "rules" of any scientific tradition are never really stated but remain a part of the tacit knowledge with which every scientist proceeds.

The way a new paradigm wins out over the old is particularly fascinating. The new paradigm appears and prevails only if the old one is in a state of crisis, only when the older mode of investigation seems to be producing a series of anomalies and is running into increasing difficulties with certain key questions of the times. For instance, Ptolemaic astronomy, which was developed in the four centuries around the birth of Christ and which envisaged the earth as the center of the universe, was actually rather successful in predicting the changing positions of the heavenly bodies. Later, as discrepancies were noted, Ptolemy's successors made adjustments, which became increasingly complex and cumbersome over the centuries. Finally, as Kuhn tells us, awareness that something was wrong did come:

> By the thirteenth century Alfonso X could proclaim
> that if God had consulted him when creating the
> universe, he would have received good advice. In the
> sixteenth century, Copernicus' co-worker, Domenico da
> Novara, held that no system so cumbersome and
> inaccurate as the Ptolemaic had become could possibly
> be true of nature. And Copernicus himself wrote in the
> Preface to the *De Revolutionibus* that the astronomical
> tradition he inherited had finally created only a monster.
> By the early sixteenth century an increasing number of
> Europe's best astronomers were recognizing that the
> astronomical paradigm was failing in application to its
> own traditional problems. That recognition was
> prerequisite to Copernicus' rejection of the Ptolemaic
> paradigm and his search for a new one.[1]

A new paradigm usually does not appear upon the scene full blown. Its early formulations are generally rather crude and incomplete. It has seldom addressed itself to the broad range of problems already "solved" by its predecessor. The solutions it does present often are still far from perfect.

> Until Kepler, the Copernican theory scarcely improved
> upon the predictions of planetary position made by
> Ptolemy. When Lavoisier saw oxygen as "the air itself

entire," his new theory could cope not at all with the problems presented by the proliferation of new gases, a point that Priestley made with great success in his counterattack.[2]

No revolutionary new view of reality is accepted immediately. It may gain ground because of some dramatic and unforeseen verification—for example, the famous measurement of the anomaly in Mercury's perihelion that jibed precisely with Einstein's general relativity theory. It may be adopted by certain scientists for personal or aesthetic reasons; it is "neater," "simpler," or "more elegant" than the old. But the most important issue, according to Kuhn, is which paradigm should in the future guide research on problems that neither has yet completely solved. Victory depends upon charisma. The triumphant new paradigm seems to have the future in its bones. In the end, the decision between competing scientific paradigms, Kuhn writes, can only be made on faith.

A new paradigm, significantly, is nearly always the work of a young man or someone new to the field. After a number of years in a certain discipline, a scientist tends to be totally tied—mind, perception and all—to the prevailing paradigm. Indeed, the established leaders of the older tradition may never accept the new view of reality.

> Copernicanism made few converts for almost a century after Copernicus' death. Newton's work was not generally accepted, particularly on the Continent, for more than half a century after the *Principia* appeared. Priestley never accepted the oxygen theory, nor Lord Kelvin the electromagnetic theory, and so on.[3]

Only the death of the old guard secures the new faith. As Max Planck remarked in his *Scientific Autobiography*, "a new scientific truth does not triumph by convincing its opponents and making them see the light, but rather because its opponents eventually die, and a new generation grows up that is familiar with it."

In spite of resistance, in spite of the fact that Establishment support is not immediately forthcoming, paradigm shift gives us good examples of flood change. The historic moment comes when all that was secure seems doubtful, when the familiar suddenly seems strange. "It was as if the ground had been pulled out from under one," Einstein wrote of one such moment, "with no firm foundation to be seen anywhere, upon which one could have built." Debates are no longer guided by logic and good manners. Scientists stand on opposite sides of a consciousness gap, arguing with each other in words that take their very meaning only from the place where they are spoken. It was like that in 1543 when men called Copernicus mad for saying the earth moved. But the earth did begin to move, and soon enough all of humankind dwelled on a floating sphere that revolved in the heavens. And then the heavens themselves began to change. In the fifty years that followed Copernicus' proposal, Western astronomers first saw change in the previously immutable night sky. New stars appeared. Comets wandered at will through the space that had been reserved for the unchanging planets and stars.

> The very ease and rapidity with which astronomers saw new things when looking at old objects with old instruments may make us wish to say that, after Copernicus, astronomers lived in a different world. In any case, their research responded as though that were the case.[4]

After the controversy and upheaval of a revolution, science settles down once again to its normal course. It has its work laid out for it. Its work is mostly mopping up.

> Few people who are not actually practitioners of a mature science realize how much mop-up work of this sort a paradigm leaves to be done or quite how fascinating such work can prove in the execution. . . . Mopping-up operations are what engage most scientists throughout their careers.[5]

Between revolutions, scientists move ahead secure in their faith and fascinated by the puzzles set for them by the dominant paradigm. The central activity of what Kuhn calls normal science may be compared with puzzle solving. The desired solution generally is known in advance. The payoff lies in the way it is reached—the design of apparatus, the manipulation of variables, the particular steps that are taken. Far from encouraging major substantive novelties, normal science tends to frown at any speculation that threatens its well-defined boundaries. The textbooks of normal science are written in such a way as to minimize the fundamental cleavages that occurred during the times of paradigm shift. Kuhn sees in this a quality suggestive of Orwell's *1984*. Reading the textbooks, the science student comes to believe that he is heir to a single cumulative tradition devoted to the search for Truth. Scientific revolutions, the truly disruptive and creative moments in the history of science, tend towards invisibility in the typical text.

But the predominance, even the tyranny, of a certain paradigm is what gives science its great power. The paradigm offers the scientist a firm place to stand. It limits and focuses his field of activity. It tells him what experiments to perform and, in general, what to expect from those experiments. Without a guiding paradigm, every experiment would be of equal value, every fact would clamor for equal attention and the search for Truth would degenerate in random activity. It is not even the rightness or wrongness of a paradigm that necessarily gives it its vitality and authority. As Francis Bacon observed in the *Novum Organum*, "Truth emerges more readily from error than from confusion."

A paradigm, then. is a compelling vision of reality that sets the course and provides the impetus for the work of normal science. It assures "progress." Paradoxically, it also assures its own eventual overthrow. For, as progress continues and the methods and instruments and body of knowledge of a particular tradition of science improve and increase, that science must inevitably thrust itself into realms of reality that it cannot explain in its own terms. When that happens, the whole process—anomaly, crisis, professional vertigo and the emergence of new paradigm candidates—begins again. And then the sudden shift. "Just because it is a transition between incommensurables," Kuhn writes, "a transition between competing paradigms cannot be made a step at a time, forced by logic and neutral experience. Like the gestalt switch, it must occur all at once (though not necessarily in an instant) or not at all."

Significantly, the more effective and compelling a paradigm, the further it thrusts us into new, contradictory mysteries. The moments of *kairos* come ever faster—at least we can see it that way in science—bursting the dams that hold back change and leaving parts of the worlds of sensing and being forever altered.

eight
Civilization and Magic

—Yes, but all of the living make the mistake of drawing too sharp distinctions.
—RAINER MARIA RILKE, DUINO ELEGIES

❧

Newton was not the first of the age of reason. He was the last of the magicians, the last of the Babylonians and Sumerians, the last great mind which looked out on the visible and intellectual world with the same eyes as those who began to build our intellectual inheritance rather less than 10,000 years ago.
—JOHN MAYNARD KEYNES, NEWTON TERCENTENARY ADDRESS

WESTERN SCIENCE operates within strict if often unacknowledged boundaries. It concerns itself with the limitation and control of variables. It seeks, in its own terms, verification This discipline, these limitations, make it possible at the least for us to discuss underlying assumptions, to isolate the paradigms that shape perception and action, and to see how science itself evolves through paradigm shift.

No such clarity is possible for human affairs in general. A social system derives from a staggering number of variables, and we can rarely discover which are most important. Nor can we readily get our hands on the levers of stability or change. B. F. Skinner says that history generally makes bad experiments, and we cannot fail to note a slipshod, hit-and-miss quality in social and cultural change. There is a divine messiness about human life that protects it in the long run against the frightened dicta of a Sylvester Graham or the reductive goodwill of a social planner. Life has its own urges and only so much patience with the status quo. Sooner or later the vibrancy of existence combines in some new way that utterly confounds all plans and predictions, demonstrating perhaps that the step-by-step, logical mode of analysis is in the long run the most fruitless of all. Nevertheless, within these limitations we still may be able to perceive something like paradigm shift in the process of social and cultural evolution.

To do so, we have to step back and view a rather large time scale. The various "periods" and "ages" generally isolated out of a certain cultural lineage—Renaissance, Reformation, Enlightenment, and the like—are useful to historians. But they follow too rapidly one upon the other, overlap and blur, and thus fail to provide distinct patterns of information that rise above the background noise. The Renaissance ideal may differ from the feudal ideal, but both fall within the range that defines Civilization. By choosing to view human change in terms of what we can call anthropological time, as in Chapter 4, we may see different human beings operating under the sway of different and incommensurable paradigms, looking at each other across consciousness gaps that can be bridged only by destruction of a way of life. Thus, the hunter and gatherer exists only through total, moment-by-moment joining with the flux and flow of nature. When Smohalla cried out against the sin of agriculture, the wounding and ripping of the earth, he was not speaking of differences in food-gaining techniques but of differences in reality. Regularized farming tears not just the earth but the very fabric of existence. The primitive hunter and the tribal farmer exist in different worlds. For his part, the tribal farmer, though he wounds and tears the earth, still mediates every human transaction through the web of kinship. And he ties his religion directly to nature. The paradigm of kinship and immediate personal relationship with the supernatural is totally incommensurable with Civilization. The primacy of kinship must be destroyed for a civilized state to exist. Religion must be tied to the state rather than to nature, or simply deprived of its secular sanctions. When Civilization reaches a tribal village—for example, through the building of a road as in Joyce Cary's novel *Mr.*

Johnson—the tribal way of life is doomed. Those who cannot accept the paradigm of Civilization become the flotsam of humanity. Indians on reservations are like the outcast scientists who have never yielded to relativity and quantum theory.

Human societies, like scientific movements, cannot exist without paradigms. Without some consensual shaping, life itself would be, in William James's well-known phrase, a "blooming, buzzing confusion." We may find paradigmatic clues in a society's literature or its oral epics, in its archetypes and its choice of heroes, in its dreams and nursery rhymes. A society's paradigm may be seen most clearly of all in its myths. As anthropologist B. Malinowski has written:

> Myth fulfills in primitive culture an indispensable
> function: it expresses, enhances, and codifies belief; it
> safeguards and enforces morality; it vouches for the
> efficiency of ritual and contains practical rules for the
> guidance of man. Myth is thus a vital ingredient of human
> civilization; it is not an idle tale, but a hard-worked
> active force; it is not an intellectual explanation or an
> artistic imagery, but a pragmatic charter of primitive
> faith and moral wisdom.[1]

A myth, in fact, *is* a paradigm, pure and simple. But it is an operative paradigm only so long as it is taken as somehow true —in other words, only when it is not considered a myth.

Today, library shelves are crowded with books about the myths of almost every society discovered to have existed on this planet. These myths not only define particular societies but seem also to contain underlying material that is common to all humankind. Certain themes recur again and again. Using the fifty societies analyzed by George P. Murdock in his *World Ethnographic Survey*, anthropologist Clyde Kluckhohn finds that flood themes occur in the myths of thirty-four out of the fifty, and that some sort of catastrophe is an almost universal theme. The theme of incest occurs in thirty-nine of the societies; often it is considered a good thing, as when a brother and sister mate to form a race of people or a tribal group. The slaying of a monster shows up in thirty-seven, and sibling rivalry in thirty-two. According to Kluckhohn, the most common myths are organized around four basic stories—the creation, witchcraft, the Oedipus situation (involving some hostility between generations but often not in the classic Greek sense), and the saga of the hero (including both male and female protagonists).

Many myths seem to cut across anthropological periods. The Genesis creation myth that was useful for tribal herdsmen continued to provide a paradigm of sorts for a civilization that spread its sails and its culture around most of the globe. The myth of the hero—his call to adventure, his ordeal in strange yet somehow intimate surroundings, his moment of high reward, his difficult return to the ordinary world bearing a gift of great benefit for his people—repeats itself in nearly every type of society from Eskimo to Hindu, and resonates in every life. Each of us, as James Joyce has shown, is a Ulysses. The idea of the universal round, the cosmic cycle of destruction and rebirth, achieves eloquence and grandeur in the mythology of the Aztecs, the Stoics, the Hindus, the Jains, and the modern physicists. There obviously exist certain ultimate patterns that are sensed by all people and that will be expressed in some way by every kind of culture, whether primitive, civilized, or transformed.

What we are seeking here, however, is the particular and limited paradigm of Civilization and the incommensurables that must shift upon the arrival of a new epoch. In this search, we must keep reminding ourselves that the myths on the library shelves are, by the very fact of being there, dead or dying. They are, for the most part, no longer operative paradigms. The forces that most decisively control our lives, as Marshall McLuhan has pointed out, are "environmental," that is, pervasive and unremarkable. They are nothing that we can analyze, classify, consciously manipulate or, often, even see.

The key elements in a paradigm are generally marked by their ordinariness. It is doubtful that astronomers before Copernicus spent much time discussing the marvelous fact that the earth was a stationary platform around which all the heavenly bodies moved. And yet this assumption dominated their work. How much more the invisible paradigm of existence affects every

human life! As with the geocentric universe, the simple awareness of any controlling human paradigm may spell the beginning
of its end. When Lewis Mumford, in his recent two-volume
work *The Myth of the Machine*, brought into sharp focus one
of the controlling paradigms of the Civilized Epoch, he was
actually giving notice that the Epoch is over.

Mumford theorizes, as pointed out in Chapter 4, that the
modern megamachine had its birth at the very beginning of
Civilization, when the "divine" rulers of the great cities of the
Fertile Crescent fashioned giant mechanisms using human beings
instead of pistons and cogs. From that time until the present,
according to Mumford, men have put their greatest faith in and
perhaps sold their souls for technics, not realizing the negative
consequences that went along with the gains. Though the warnings came earlier, in Faust and Frankenstein and science fiction,
it is only recently that the monster has materialized clearly before
our eyes. The time of anomaly and crisis is indeed upon us.
What we did not realize until Mumford is how far back the
myth of mechanistic manipulation reached and how drastically
it has shaped all of the works and will of Civilization, and the
consciousness of its people.

※

A time of anomaly and crisis, and of awakening. Before long,
all the stuff of the paradigm of Civilization will take shape before our eyes, and we will be moved to outrage, laughter and
horror. And then to understanding, for it obviously could not
have been otherwise.

It started, as I have said before, with the accumulation of an
agricultural surplus, especially a surplus of grain. Those glistening seeds—the rices of the Orient, the grasses of the Middle East
and the maize of Mesoamerica—held energy in a form that is
easily measured, preserved and transported. They made possible,
indeed demanded, a reorganization of human society. Behavior
that outraged tribal consciousness became ordinary. The civilized
paradigm gathered form around the grain surplus.

The first response to the surplus was a fascinated devotion
to the manipulation of ordinary matter and energy. The pyra-

mids, temples and other works that rose throughout the new civilized states were monuments not so much to spirit as to matter itself. And this tireless manipulation and gathering together moved on from stone to territory to flesh. Living human bodies were bought and sold at the marketplace along with grain and pottery. Peoples were conquered, gathered up. Tribute was exacted. Human energy was bartered for and dealt out like tokens on a gaming table.

Fascination turned into hypnosis. It was as if the human race had spent all its years on earth in gathering together and piling up. The manipulation of matter and energy became a given: "Man is a builder and conqueror, and that's that." The only escape from materialism seemed to be reaction into asceticism. But the severest critics of matter's dominance failed to realize that "the opposite" is merely the other half of a bipolar trap. Materialism and idealism exist in dialectic tension. "Spirit" is both child and parent of "flesh." Down through the ages the noblest reactions to the civilized paradigm, whether Platonic idealism or the Mayavada school of Vedanta or early Christianity, were actually integral parts of that paradigm itself. Caught in dualism, Civilization was doomed to oscillate between materialism and reaction to materialism. We cannot begin to find the way out until we wake from the hypnosis. And then perhaps we shall see matter and spirit as one, and all moving, as all eventually must, towards Transformation. But that will not be the End, but only the Beginning of another journey, for there is not only the year 2000 (which stands as an obstacle to our vision), but also 3000 and 30000 and 30 million. Still, we shall perhaps see real change rather than just reaction in our own lifetimes, and herald the stuff of the new paradigm (which will tend towards invisibility even as we learn to see it and start to take it for granted). And it will be left for other generations to deal in their own ways with the inevitable blocks and blindnesses along that pathway.

But we are getting far ahead of our story. For now, we may simply bring to mind some of the operative folk beliefs of the old paradigm that are now emerging to our consciousness. Start with the more obvious ones:

The Myth of Growth. More is better. Bigger is better. The largest pyramid, the largest ship, the largest city, the largest empire. Thus Civilization has expressed the urge of the vibrancy to combine in ever-larger entities. But the joining of any particular manifestations of the vibrancy on any particular plane may become excessive and unbalanced. Civilization, dealing primarily in gross matter and ordinary physical energy, has at last carried the Myth of Growth to the point of anomaly and crisis. The world's largest tanker may make someone rich but its launching is a cause for alarm in the rest of humankind. The tallest building casts ominous shadows. Anomaly is surely upon us when chambers of commerce seek urgently for ways to discourage further population growth so that their city or country or state will *not* become "the largest."

The Myth of Fertility is a corollary to the Myth of Growth but has consequences of its own. All types of societies have valued fertility, and the production of numerous progeny as an aid to the state may create even more sexual pressures in Civilization. The dictum "Be ye fruitful, and multiply; bring forth abundantly in the earth, and multiply therein" comes after the Flood and helps shape the kind of society that is soon to build the Tower of Babel. When woman is cherished for the crop she produces, a rigid, bilateral definition of sex is inevitable. We think of bilateral sex as being as permanent and stable as Ptolemy's stationary earth; yet we may be sure, now that unabated procreation threatens the existence of the planet, that it is not. As will be argued in a later chapter, the whole idea of sex as we know it is doomed. The problems of woman and man cannot be solved in terms of present definitions of woman and man.

The Myth of the Limited Good. Civilized man, dealing primarily in matter and ordinary energy, is doomed to come up against the problem of short supply. And since he finds that matter and energy are limited, he comes to believe that other aspects of life—love and friendship, health, respect, security, even spiritual well-being—are also limited. Thus it seems that when one person or family or political group gains, others must necessarily lose. This view of things is particularly strong in peasant villages throughout the world. In his book on a Mexican peasant village, *Tzintzuntzan*, George M. Foster tells how mothers will go so far as to conceal the existence of new babies for as long as possible, since this "good" will cause envy. The fiesta, according to Foster, provides a socially acceptable way of getting rid of excess wealth that otherwise would threaten the stability of the village.[2] The idea of limited good is indeed a dangerous one, for it lies behind every model of human conflict. As long as humankind remains preoccupied with matter and energy, and until all people's minimum needs in this respect are satisfied, limited good will continue to pose a problem. But when the human race turns its primary attention to human transformation, it may well be that "good" can be perceived as unlimited.

The Myth of Inevitable Competition developed relatively late in the Civilized Epoch and is a corollary of the Myth of Limited Good. Along with aggression and acquisition, inevitable competition has become not only a given of the mercantile-capitalist society but also has come to define the very essence of existence for many men of our world. At a recent seminar attended by leading industrialists, I argued that competition is far from inevitable, that it is not so much an effective means for motivating behavior as for enforcing a certain class of conformity and resemblance among human components of a social machine, that, as practiced, it actually creates more losers than winners, that it encourages cheating and that by forcing those who compete to run on the same track and to follow the same set of rules it limits the human potential for uniqueness and transcendence. As I spoke I noticed a sort of anxiety on the faces of those around me. "If there is to be no competition," one of the industrialists said, "then what will life be all about?" All the recent talk about the danger of the United States becoming a "second-rate power" actually concerns the nation's ability to wage war and to dominate more than its share of the world's physical resources. When pundits speak of every movement away from aggressiveness and dominance as a possible "loss of nerve," they are speaking strictly in terms of the old view of the universe. They cannot conceive of how much nerve, courage, and imagination it will take to strike out in the direction of a new quality of existence in which neither grubbing for economic supremacy nor building extravagant armaments to guard it will consume the major part of our energy.

The Myth of Societal Unintentionality. We do not have to look to science fiction for the "group mind." Every social body has a consciousness of sorts. A society, in fact, is probably more "conscious" than are the individuals within it. The individuals are just not privy to the group consciousness. Society certainly possesses will and purpose, however veiled. Transformation entails not the *creation* of a group mind, but awareness and improvement of it.

The Myth of Separate Species. Separation and classification of the various earthly organisms provides us an interesting exercise and defines one way of looking at existence. But making these sharp distinctions blocks an even more important vision. In a very real sense, there is only one species on this planet and its name is Life on Earth. Ecologists acknowledge this fact with their discussions of the biomass. We are beginning to realize that the extinction of what we now refer to as a species is some sort of amputation within the larger species of which we are a part. Forthcoming discussions of Life on Earth can help us see past the limiting boundaries of the old paradigm.

The Myth of the Separate Ego. The idea of individuals as separate and discrete egos, pinpricks through the fine skin of existence, reached its zenith in the Western branch of Civilization. As Thomas Hobbes pointed out, "personality" or "person" derives from the Latin *persona* or mask. The voice emerging from the mask is that of cliché or archetype. The Western ego is a construct in the process of collapsing; we know now that accepting the construct means accepting eventual alienation. Increased contact with Eastern philosophy and religion weakens the Western concept of separate ego even as the process of Westernization spreads throughout the underdeveloped nations. The old paradigm struggles mightily before giving up. But it is increasingly clear that consciousness has no skin.

The Myth of the Stable Elements. Throughout the Civilized Epoch, humans have assigned a disproportionately high value to the stable elements. As Hernan Cortez told one of the first inhabitants of Mexico that he met, "The Spaniards are troubled with a disease of the heart, for which gold is the specific remedy." But gold sickness is not limited to the West. All of Civilization has left its long trail of gold and silver and diamonds and rubies and other manifestations of the vibrancy that do not readily join with others, that will outlast flesh and challenge time. Thus the Epoch reveals one of the conditions of its enslavement: its age-old, ultimately fruitless attempt to trap the stuff of the vibrancy in some permanent form (the pathetic arrogance of Ozymandias, the deathly touch of Midas). If there is a myth of true and deep futility it is not of a Sisyphus rolling his stone up a hill; more futile by far is the materialist who spends his years on earth putting something that sings in a cage, from which it always flies forth.

The Myth of Glory, Honor and Duty. That a man will suffer pain and deprivation or even give up his life for something as abstract as a flag is good evidence that a social body has intentionality. Otherwise how could it manipulate the individual to behave so strenuously and mindlessly against his own self-interest and in the interest of societal glory, honor and duty? B. F. Skinner provides the clearest picture of this process when he points out that society usually honors an individual in direct proportion to the time that elapses between action and reinforcement. (For the man who dies for glory, that time is infinite.) Every great human enterprise requires some delay of reinforcement. But for the person who has learned to flow with the rhythm of existence the delay is only apparent. Such a person lives in the always vibrant present, and the need for societal glory which is earned through delayed reinforcement becomes clearly a myth.

❦

There may be nothing surprising in the above material. My guess is that most readers already have unmasked those folk beliefs. If so, it is another sign of how far the Transformation has proceeded. There are other assumptions in the civilized paradigm that are more difficult to unmask. In listing the following I am by no means certain of accuracy or completeness. I feel sure only that those myths which our increased awareness eventually will unearth from the ruins of Civilization will seem more unlikely.

The Myth of Law. No one who lives in civilized society can expect any measure of personal security and social stability without the rule of law. But simply to assume that this will always be the case may blind us to new possibilities in social organization. We may well remind ourselves that formal law is a relatively recent development in the history of humankind, coming into being only with the rise of the first civilized states. Without policemen, judges, prisons, legal codes and lawyers, we would need a drastically altered mode of human relationship —which is a good reason for considering such an eventuality.

The Myth of Matter, Time and Space. Throughout this book are suggestions that the old consensus of matter, time and space as discrete and fixed entities is false and misleading. This is only to echo the by-now venerable concepts of relativity physics and quantum mechanics. When a more fluid feeling about the basic matrices of reality comes to our literature, our journalism and our everyday life (as it already has to our science), we'll find it much easier to deal with other aspects of the emerging paradigm.

The Myth of Illusion. Speaking from the cockpit of nineteenth-century America, Sylvester Graham stated that dreams, imagination, and even mental pictures are dangerous illusions. On the other hand, primitive societies and some early civilized societies gave more weight to dreams and visions than to waking reality. What is to be termed "illusion" as opposed to "reality" has always been a decision of the society, and has always limited the potential of the individual to participate in the fullness of the vibrancy. We may find it possible to consider *all* perceptions as having relevance, each type evoking its own appropriate response.

The Myth of Opacity. The "solid" matter of our world, as noted in Chapter 1, is opaque only to a narrow band of radiation frequencies. We may more readily break away from the old paradigm by conceiving of this stuff as far more transparent and permeable than we are now able to realize.

The Myth of the Single Body. We have already discussed the fallacy of postulating an ego that exists within the skin, separate and apart from the world. Consider now that the physical body itself as presently conceived may be only one of the possible manifestations of each human being. Though the existence of unfamiliar bodily forms and "out-of-body experiences" cannot be verified by present-day science, we would be arrogant simply to close our minds on the subject. A large literature, both ancient and modern, is devoted to the multiple body. The Hindu Upanishads describe five *koshas* or "soul-sheaths," of which the physical body is only one. Indian psychology in general has a great deal to say about the *sukshma shariria*, the so-called "subtle" or "feeling" body. Theosophical literature describes an "etheric double" which extends slightly beyond the "dense body" and sometimes leaves it. Thousands of people, many of them highly respected witnesses, have attested to their out-of-body experiences. Such experiences are a vital part of primitive existence. Science has shown us that it is literally impossible to assign a certain physical position to subatomic particles. Attempts to view the human body as having only a single, fixed manifestation may eventually come to be considered extremely naive.

The Myth of Psychic Immobility. Civilization has been, among other things, one long effort to fixate consciousness. A specific culture has come to be equated with a specific and unchanging mode of consciousness. Civilized societies program each individual to perceive, feel and be the same from early childhood to death. This means, in effect, that specific cultures must become obsolete and pass away, since consciousness does inevitably change. It also means that individual human beings, locked in single consciousness, must die in order for creative evolution to continue. The concept of psychic mobility as an essential ingredient in any truly new culture was first introduced to me by Michael Murphy in 1965. Since then I have increasingly come to see the concept as one of the most important of our times. It holds promise of societies that can change and keep changing without violent overthrow. Murphy's formulation is quite straightforward. If a person today can travel physically to many different types of places in an extremely short time, he should also be able to travel psychically. He should be able to move at will from one mode of consciousness to another, selecting the particular mode most appropriate for a particular situation. This means, for example, that he can enter a condition of oceanic awareness and merging with other beings, but that he does not have to stay there all the time. When necessary he can gain psychic distance and perspective by assuming an objective, analytical mode. One does not preclude the other. People who are comfortable in psychic travel can experiment with new personal and cultural patterns without feeling it necessary to fear and oppose others who are not in the same psychic place. As it is, there is no way of calculating how much blood has been shed because of the unexamined assumption of psychic immobility. When this myth moves from assumption to archive, we may have, among many other things, Transformation without bloodshed.

The Myth of Old Age and Death. Death is an adaptation of the vibrancy in the service of transformation. There is no inescapable physical necessity for the death of any particular organism. Extreme longevity, however, undoubtedly would have proved maladaptive, in simple Darwinian terms, for any species. What we call aging is programmed into the genes; the DNA and RNA of each cell has to go out of its way to cause the gradual dissolution of flesh and bones. Up to now, death has served as a primary mechanism of evolution, from the lower organisms up through humankind in society. We can hardly imagine a full-scale Transformation without the death of certain powerful individuals who are stuck in outworn modes of perception, feeling and being. When the time comes—as it may well be coming—that individual human organisms can truly change and go on changing in ways that now seem hardly possible, when they can create and go on creating ever-changing cultures, then death will have lost its function where human evolution is concerned. Realizing and questioning its utility, we should not be caught by surprise when we find that aging can be greatly slowed or even stopped.

❦

The paradigm of Civilization is strong and pervasive. Considering how indomitably it held sway in the nineteenth and early twentieth centuries, we may wonder at how swiftly it is now being unmasked. We might have expected Civilization with its ever-increasing manipulations of humanity and nature to have lasted for centuries longer. The earth is large and for thousands of years it endured the wars and crusades, the building and digging of civilized men, patiently transforming every scar to dust or greenery. But then in the seventeenth century human history took an unexpected turn. Within the civilized paradigm a flood change occurred, out of which emerged the magical means that have swept us, all in a rush, to Civilization's end and the dawn of Transformation.

We tend to see the change starting with the discoveries of a remarkable group of men. We call them "scientists" or "rational philosophers" now, but we have been misled by eighteenth-century bowdlerization. Actually they were astrologers and mystics, adventurers and alchemists, men who listened to the music of the spheres and took it upon themselves to solve the riddle of the universe and of God Himself.

We would probably find it difficult to enter the consciousness of those whose faces now gaze so sternly from the pages of our textbooks. We would be hard put to understand the German astrologer and numerologist who spent eight years at the beginning of the seventeenth-century torturing out the calculations that would verify his theory that the solar system is patterned after the Pythagorean solids and that planetary motion is governed by musical harmonies. Today we would call Johannes Kepler an out-and-out mystic. He believed that the planets were alive and that each somehow incorporated a guardian angel who alone could hear its music. Nevertheless, he puzzled out the melody for each of the planets, including that of the earth (a doleful "mi, fa, mi," endlessly repeated). He also came up with the three laws of planetary motion, two of which were published in his *Astronomia Nova* of 1609. (The subsequent book containing the third law is called, appropriately, *Harmonice Mundi*.)

From Kepler the mystic, we might turn our attention to a

twenty-three-year-old French soldier of fortune who had a series of revelatory dreams after a full day of concentrated meditation in Ulm, Germany, on November 19, 1619. We might scoff at the young soldier's pretensions, for René Descartes interpreted his dreams as a divine sign that he was destined to found a new science of nature based upon mathematics. But the revelation was correct and the dreams grew into Descartes' Seven Principles, starting with "extensiveness" (the fact that an object occupies space) and leading up to the Unmoved Mover, thus effectively reducing the world to its measurable qualities. Descartes maintained and reinforced the customary Western split between matter and mind. He went on to perform much of the sorcery that eventually was to drain the "scientific" world of feelings, color, taste, smell, and indeed all of the subjective qualities of existence. "Give me extension and motion," Descartes once said, "and I will construct the universe."

Kepler and Descartes along with Galileo and Copernicus and others who preceded them prepared the way for the grand synthesis that would accelerate Civilization into its final paroxysm. It is perhaps not very important for us to know exactly when and where the synthesis first took shape, but the human longing for historical particulars justifies itself by persistence alone. That longing would take us to a little English village in Lincolnshire in the year 1666. A great plague was raging in London. Because of it, Cambridge University had closed down in the fall of 1665. One of its new Bachelor of Arts, a twenty-three-year-old named Isaac Newton, had retreated to his birthplace at the Manor House of Woolsthorpe, where he would stay with his mother until the university reopened in the spring of 1667. Newton was characterized by those who knew him as fearful, suspicious and hypochondriac. He had been born prematurely on Christmas of 1642. His father, an illiterate yeoman, had died three months earlier. The infant Isaac was so small that, as his mother later told him, he could have been put in a quart mug and so frail that he had to wear a bolster around his neck to support his head. He had not been expected to live. All of his life Newton would be motivated by a desperate need for certainty, for some pervasive unifying principle that would replace his mysteriously absent father—and mother, too, for she had left him just as he turned three to live with a new husband, not to return until the husband's death, when Isaac was eleven.

Starting with the purchase of a book on astrology at a fair in 1663, Newton taught himself advanced mathematics in his early twenties. By mid-1665 he had learned virtually all there was to learn from others and had entered unexplored realms of abstraction. Seeking to penetrate the secrets of the sun, he once looked at its image in a mirror repeatedly and defiantly, and then had to shut himself in total darkness for three days in order to recover his sight. For months afterwards a spectral image of the sun returned to haunt him whenever his mind wandered to that subject.

For Newton, nothing less than the "System of the World" would do. He found the key to it in his mother's garden at Woolsthorpe in that plague year of 1666. Only one of the two versions of the famous episode—both reported from Newton's own reminiscences in his old age—includes an apple, though both have a garden. Still, the apple is a mythic fruit and is not easily banished. The eating of the Fruit of Knowledge may have foreshadowed Civilization's beginnings. The apple's fall, observed from a distance, without taste, touch or smell, may come to symbolize the beginning of Civilization's end. In any case, as Sir D'Arcy Wentworth Thompson remarked, "Newton did not shew the cause of the apple falling, but he shewed a similitude between the apple and the stars." By the time he returned to Cambridge in 1667, Newton had not only formulated and tested the inverse square law of gravity, but had laid the foundations for the great synthesis that was to dominate science for some three centuries.

This is the Newton that Civilization has chosen to remember—the Newton of universal gravitation and the nature of white light, of the calculus and the apple; Newton the lonely genius in youth, the vindictive autocrat of science in old age. But there is another Newton, considered so shameful by the eighteenth century that his existence was literally written out of the record of the times. For Isaac Newton was also an alchemist, a magician. "His deepest instincts," writes Lord Keynes, "were occult, esoteric, semantic." Up until his fiftieth year, when he suffered a severe nervous breakdown, Newton spent fully as much time and energy on alchemy as on what has come to be called his "science." Up until his death at age eighty-four he dedicated his attention to ancient chronology, prophecy and mythology— Revelations and the Book of Daniel, the precise dimensions (with their mystical overtones) of Solomon's Temple. More than a million words of this occult writing has survived. Much of the summaries have to do with an elixir or Philosopher's Stone that not only will aid in the transmutation of metals but will also invest the owner with magical powers—seeing at a great distance, forcing others to bow to one's will, gaining eternal youth. Indeed, Newton could make abstracts of material that would seem to have no possible scientific value:

> The vegetable stone is of a growing nature & works
> miraculous effects in vegetables & growing things, as in
> the nature of man and beast. The Animal is for the animal
> faculties, the Angelic for magical operations. It keeps
> mans body from corruption, & endues him with divine
> gifts & knowledge of things ["to come" is crossed out]
> by dreams & revelations. By carrying it about with him
> he feels most heavenly fragrant beravishing smells. And
> oftentimes (they say) shall see the apparition of the most
> glorious & blessed Angels. No evil spirit shall endure to
> come near the bearer thereof, nor the fire burn him.
> Dunstan calls it Angels food because a man may live a
> long time without any food by the tast of this stone.
> It is an enemy to all corruptibility in mans body. Of some
> tis called the tree of life. The tree of knowledge.[3]

Newton carried on a lively alchemical correspondence with the chemist Robert Boyle, who claimed he had a special kind of mercury that would heat up when mixed with gold. Newton's amanuensis, Humphrey Newton, tells us that in the period 1685–1690, when the *Principia* was being written, the great scientist would spend about six weeks in the spring and six in the fall, during which "the fire in the elaboratory scarcely went out," in strictly alchemical pursuits. "What his aim might be," says the

amanuensis, "I was not able to penetrate, but his pains, his dili-
gence at these times made me think he aimed at something
beyond the reach of human art and industry." We may note
that as late as in the second edition (of three) of the *Principia*,
Newton continued to maintain that all elements could be transformed into each other.

But then came the mental plunge of 1693, from which Newton never returned to alchemy or the physical sciences with any
real energy or dedication. Two and a half years after his re-
covery, in a stroke of irony that would not be accepted in the
theater, the alchemist was appointed Warden and later Master
of the Mint. In 1703 he assumed an additional office which he
held until his death twenty-four years later—the Presidency of
the Royal Society. From these positions of power he meted out
harsh justice to counterfeiters, established the gold standard, laid
waste to his scientific enemies in England and on the Continent
and, in effect, invented the eighteenth century.

Until he assumed public office, Newton was obsessively
secretive. He did not originally write for publication. His
occult writings remained hidden in a chest until after his death.
But then again, the *Principia* came to be published only through
a series of events that can best be explained as chance. The
West chose to reinforce the Newton of the *Principia*, then re-
made itself in his image. The world of alchemy would embrace
metamorphosis and ambiguity, would bring to an end the
reign of stable matter and perhaps of death itself. (*The apparition
of angels. The most heavenly fragrant beravishing smells.*) The
world of the *Principia* was a world of fixed measurements,
objective space and linear time, a world of isolated cases within
an all-encompassing System, a world without angels or smells.

But the view of Newton's theories as cool and reasonable
came only later. When first introduced, they shocked the leading scientists of the West. In Newton's day, "action at a distance"
was a disreputable concept. The prevailing view followed Descartes, who had maintained that the moon and planets were
held in orbit by the pressure of swirling vortices of invisible
atoms. Action at a distance seemed a throwback to medieval
magic. Newton's theories were more difficult for scientists of

his time to understand and accept than were Einstein's in his time.

But eventually they swept aside all opposition. The accomplishments of the third book of the *Principia* (Newton's System of the World) alone could not be denied. In this book he not only established the movements of the planets and their satellites in terms of universal gravitation, but calculated the masses of the sun, the earth, and the other planets that have satellites, figured out the ellipticity of the earth and the precession of the equinoxes, laid the foundation of the theories of the tides, established the orbits of comets, and did much more which seemed, in the words of Adam Smith, "beyond the reach of human reason and experience." Best of all, Newton dealt with forces in motion at a moment when Civilization was fascinated with such matters and created a grand model of the kind of machinery that might soon come into human hands.

Because it worked so well, because it yielded results that could be replicated again and again, the Newtonian synthesis was granted the label "science" rather than "magic." But we have a chance here to gain a different perspective. To do so, we must step out of the stream of European thought and look at the uses of magic throughout human cultures. Peter Farb provides a clear summary of the anthropological consensus on this matter when he defines the basic difference between magic and religion.

> In magic, the practitioner believes that he can directly
> affect other humans and nature, either for good or for ill, by
> performing certain steps. Magic is therefore instrumental
> —and some of these instruments are witchcraft,
> sorcery, oracles, divination, and various kinds of curing.
> Although many "religious" people do use religion for
> instrumental ends, the primary emphasis in religion is
> on broad social and cosmological relationships.[4]

As it has been practiced in its technological applications—and as it has influenced every aspect of our lives—Newtonian science is nothing if not instrumental. Perhaps Newton himself never stopped being a magician in the usual sense of the word;

late in his life he told friends that, were he younger, he might have "another shake at the moon" or "another touch at metals." In any case, the total victory of his system, the rout of all alternative approaches, did this much: It freed the West, and then all of Civilization in its wake, to devote itself totally and with single vision—mind, heart and soul—to magical manipulation.

Since Newton, in fact, civilized man has lived out most of the ancient sorcerer's dreams—sailed in the heavens, looked to the other side of the world, moved mountains and rivers, transmuted the elements, turned matter to energy, walked in the valleys of the moon, and floated in the abyss of space. And all by performing certain magical steps, by ritual, by incantation.

Perhaps one who has not been swept up in the technological rites can never truly experience the magnetic powers they possess. I remember chanting out the checklist in a World War II bomber, passing my hand like a wand over the marvelous black-faced dials, the jutting levers, the subtle knobs and switches. In those days, the red metal plates bearing the legend WARNING or CAUTION held for me all the dark and dangerous force of tribal taboos. And they still do, for my wanderings in recent years have found me the temporary inhabitant of other, more modern cockpits. Learning the feel of a jet trainer over West Germany; rolling a jet fighter in time to rock music over Cape Cod. And then by chance not long ago, two hours at the controls of a jet liner between Chicago and San Francisco on a dazzling late spring afternoon—wondering at the luxurious precision of the new automatic navigational equipment and the vibrant presence in the voice of an air controller somewhere down below as I sailed high over the snow-white Rockies. And even closer to the sacred heart of technology, a visit to the Manned Spacecraft Center in Houston. Left alone in a mock-up of the Apollo Command Capsule and then the Lunar Module, I ran through part of the checklist, threw the switches that would start my descent to a phantom moon while the on-board computer clicked off its Newtonian calculations. I emerged from each of these experiences infused with the old hypnotic sense of certainty, rededicated temporarily to the arcane rites of my youth, to the world I once thought I could never leave.

Some dreams hold us between fascination and horror. We cannot quite bring ourselves to wake up until the most dreaded eventuality plays itself out to the full. But now it is over, this dream of magical forces and motion and manipulation without touch or taste or color or smell, this dream of action at a distance, of force exerted across empty space instantaneously, however far. The dream is over. Theoretical science has long since replaced action at a distance with field theory in which things swim in and interact through intermediate fields that propagate at the finite rate of the speed of light, in which size, shape, velocity and perhaps being itself are relative. And yet we continue to pretend that we live in a fixed universe, that we can distance ourselves from others and thus from our own bodies, our selves, our God.

But not for long. Every human paradigm contains the seed of its own destruction. The Civilized Epoch might have dragged on for centuries more, but with Newton's synthesis the seed burst open. Magical manipulation of matter and gross energy, so long desired by Civilization, suddenly *worked*. It worked so wonderfully well that it moved us with unbelievable speed along the invisible lines of force of the unacknowledged paradigm to its very end. Now we begin to awaken. We *see*. The myths that have bound us become visible, popping out like new stars in a familiar evening sky. Anomalies confront us wherever we turn. All at once we realize that the planet itself is not large enough or strong enough to bear our heedless manipulations. We find ourselves bored with the moon. We turn to the infinite possibilities that lie so close at hand we had quite overlooked them. Perhaps it is not too late for us. For me.

PART TWO
❦ ❦ *Becoming*

nine

Ashes

*So when Miss Lawington told me about the cakes I thought that I
could bake them and earn enough at one time to increase the net
value of the flock the equivalent of two head. And that by saving
the eggs out one at a time, even the eggs wouldn't be costing
anything. And that week they laid so well that I not only saved out
enough eggs above what we had engaged to sell, to bake the cakes
with, I had saved enough so that the flour and the sugar and the
stove wood would not be costing anything. So I baked yesterday,
more careful than ever I baked in my life, and the cakes turned out
right well. But when we got to town this morning Miss Lawington
told me the lady had changed her mind and was not going to have
the party after all.*

—WILLIAM FAULKNER, AS I LAY DYING

❧

*Scientists believe that the earth weighs over six thousand million,
million, million tons.*

—ITEM IN "FUN FACTS," A COMIC PAGE FEATURE

NEARLY A YEAR has passed
since that first morning on Mt. Tam. It is the time of drought
again. Stones and pebbles as white as bleached bones line the
stream beds. Pale gold skeletons of grass stand in the sun, and
the rich wild smell of their drying rises like waves in the still
air. The extent of the season is measured by the deer's descent
from the mountain. Now that it is September they cross our
streets at noon, marching down the easement between my house
and my nearest neighbor's to eat the moist leaves and flowers
that are not to be found a hundred yards up the slope behind
us. There are fewer hikers now; even the well-traveled trails

around Rock Springs are almost deserted. And high above, the hawks circle for hours, rising gradually upward until they melt into the relentless burning blue.

The trails are dry and hard. In places they have turned to dust. Dust covers my boots and clings to my ankles. Dust defines the day. And in the course of a hard climb the moment comes when I can sense the desiccation of every hope, every vision. A pulse beats at my temple. The sun is an enemy. The air scorches my throat and lungs. I turn inside myself but there is no oasis, only hard angular surfaces. There is no escape, no comfort, no sleep, no healing tears. In me, around me, everywhere, the world has turned to ashes.

I cannot blame my state of being on the mountain or the season. The mountain is patient. Water still trickles here and there, and the trees are green. The season will change and soothing rain will come. But what can soothe the human race, all of us? Do tears enough exist to wash away the pain?

My world has turned to ashes and I am a hologram of my community, my people, my Civilization, a tiny fragment of all the pain and hate. Here I am:

Driving along a city street I pull into a traffic lane ahead of another car. I look into the mirror and see the driver making an obscene gesture at me. I try to laugh to myself. I had not cut him off. Why is he so angry? But there is something about the gesture (he is still making it) that chills me. It is utterly authentic. The man's clothing and his hair style and his late model car may be affectations. I imagine that his language would fail to convey his essential being. But the gesture (he is still making it) comes straight from the heart.

Later that day I am driving through a district of San Francisco that is marked by straight wide streets and sidewalks, small neat lawns and small two-story houses perfectly aligned against each other, each painted a fresh pastel color, each with its own bay window and built-in garage. This is a neighborhood of respectable, hardworking people, policemen, firemen, clerks (no colored or orientals, please), people who have bought themselves a piece of the American Dream. It is a dazzling sunny afternoon with perhaps a touch of autumn in the air. Where are the people who live here? There is no sign of life. The windows have blinds or draperies; most are shut. Here and there a car stands in a driveway or is parked at the curb. The lawns are perfectly manicured. Someone must have trimmed them. I slow my car and try to look into the windows. I can see no movement. One block passes, two. Where are the people? It is like science fiction. Maybe a deadly nerve gas has 'killed all the inhabitants in their sleep. I wonder when I will slump unconscious at the wheel. But then again, we don't have to wait for science fiction or deadly gas. Something else has banished all life from these sidewalks and lawns. The thought chills me and I am unreasonably grateful and relieved to see a flash of movement ahead. Up in the next block someone is washing his car. I hurry to get there, then slow down. The man is aware of my approach. He straightens from his chore. Water from the hose splashes off a shining hubcap as he looks at me. Our eyes meet. I manage a small smile and then a friendly wave with an absolute minimum of content or significance. His suspicion changes to outright hostility and his mouth twists down with a silent curse as he turns back to his task. The force of his reaction hits me like a blow in the stomach. Still, I think I understand his position. *I've worked hard. I have my house and my car. We have a clean neighborhood. I keep my nose clean. Now let's don't have any trouble. Nothing weird, nothing different. No trouble, do you get me? No trouble.*

It is the same, really, in the first class sections of the airlines that fly from coast to coast, transporting the bodies of the nation's managers and professionals. Over the past fifteen years, in addition to all my other travels, I have spent thousands of hours flying back and forth between San Francisco and New York, averaging some twelve or more round trips a year. I almost always fly on the same airline, having discovered after much experimentation that it is, as its advertisements once claimed, the most professional. Which means that it has learned to operate coolly and efficiently, with a minimum of emotion and trouble, and that the people who fly in its first class section— almost all of them organization men on expense accounts—are the most practiced robots.

We robots enter the cabin encased in suits of lifeless hue, carrying our neat attaché cases. There is no fluster as we take our seats and fasten our seat belts. We nod with carefully measured smiles to the robot who will be sitting next to us as we sail across the continent. We know there will be little or no conversation, perhaps only a few pleasantries as the meal is served. Even before takeoff, most of us open our attaché cases and lift out the manila folders containing the sheets of paper that justify our existence: projections, analyses, feasibility plans, sales campaigns.

The stewardesses on this airline are older than those on the others, and maybe not quite as pretty. But there is wisdom and compassion in their eyes. They know our secret and they will take good care of us. They move quietly along the deeply carpeted aisles and do not disturb the concentration that numbs our pain and memory. They offer us the smile of the kind but efficient nurse in the critical ward. When we start to tire of our work, they are there with their drugs in chilled glasses so that we will not have a moment to remember existence. For they know our secret. They know that we are dead, that our work is maintenance work, that our journey is meaningless.

On a 747 flight the senior stewardess, a friend from previous trips, asks if I would like to see their new galley. We get into an elevator barely large enough for the two of us. It descends with a shudder. We enter a narrow refrigerated room in the belly of the plane. The light is cold and wan. When I stand up my head hits the ceiling. "None of the girls are as tall as you," my friend says with a laugh. On either side of the room large drawers fit flush into the wall. All the meals are in these drawers. One of the stewardesses stays in the room during mealtimes and passes the meals up a dumbwaiter. The drawers look large enough to hold human bodies. "My God," I say, "did you ever stop to think that this is just like a morgue?" My friend laughs uneasily. "Please don't let the girls hear you saying that. Some of them are already scared to work down here." It is a morgue.

There will be no dancing in the aisles of the first class section of my favorite airline as long as Civilization lingers. Or if there is, it will be handled in a "professional" manner. Once a few years back I flew from New York to San Francisco feeling a joy and exuberance I could barely restrain. I had been involved in a project that had seemed unlikely if not impossible of success and yet had succeeded beyond my highest expectations. It was one of those moments when all things, including dancing in the aisles, seem possible. My companions on the flight were a man in his thirties and a woman in her early twenties, both good friends. Not long after takeoff the three of us managed to squeeze into the two seats on the left of the aisle. As the plane rose, we seemed to rise much higher. We were completely oblivious of the other passengers. We talked about the incredible weeks just passed and the more incredible possibilities of the future. Our voices rose. We hugged and kissed each other with passion and belief. We wept tears of joy. About two-thirds of the way through the flight we became aware of the other passengers. Surely they had been shocked and outraged by our behavior. But no, it was all exactly the same. The robots applied themselves to their paperwork. The stewardesses moved efficiently along the aisles. Their smiles revealed no change of attitude or emotion as their glances met ours. It was as if we had been encased in clear plastic so that our energy could in no way infect the other passengers or otherwise influence the functioning of the cabin. The airline, after all, is professional. And so the flight ended and we came to earth. A month later, I joined the robots again. *No trouble.*

And so we pass our lives away, always really knowing better, knowing in some part of our being that we are serving death in a dead civilization. And this death in life, this Gift, is what we pass on to our children—that is the bitterest realization of all. Some time ago, while doing an article on schooling, I made a note on yellow legal-sized paper and marked it with a large star. It never appeared in print, for it did not particularly apply to the subject matter of my story. Now it returns to haunt me. I remember sitting on the floor in a dark corner of a big-city classroom listening to two nine-year-old girls talking about their fathers, whom they had recently lost through divorce. "I never did see my father," one of them said in that matter-of-fact way that children have of describing the most shattering events. "He was always behind a newspaper. When he was eating he was behind a newspaper with a spoon going in and out. Or he was behind a book. And sometimes he was asleep behind a newspaper. And all I knew about him was that he had white fingernails."

A year later I heard from her teacher that this girl had drowned. She had been swimming in a lake and had been trapped under a raft. Or at least that was the supposition. But it is not the pathos, the divorce and death, in this story that heaps ashes on my world. It is simply the fact that whatever life we have has been so numbed that we do not even experience the pain of it, much less the joy. We know the color of our father's fingernails but we do not dare look into the hurt that he hides behind his newspaper. We live as robots, provided with automatic cutoffs against the rise of any feeling that might open us up to the vast reservoir of hurt we carry with us always. We are so numbed, so inured to feelings that the creators of current movies and television dramas must resort to the most extreme tactics to make any sort of impression on us—the shotgun blast in the face, the thud of a pistol butt on the back of the neck. So horror and terror and torture become staples in our family fare, rated "G," safe for children, perhaps their safest way of learning not to feel.

These G-rated movies flicker before me during my transcontinental flights. I try to resist them, but sometimes I put on my earphones and watch. There was one Western in which, for the life of me, I could not tell which of the two protagonists was the hero; both seemed equally villainous. The final battle takes place far out in the desert. After a display of every conceivable brutality, one of the hero-villains gets the other down and holds him at gunpoint. Then, quite casually, he shoots him through both elbows and both knees. The victim, writhing on the dry earth, begs the victor to kill him. The victor returns his pistol to its holster. Without emotion, he turns and walks away, leaving his opponent to die a slow, horrible death in the desert. And over this scene, to the sweep of violins, against the golden light of the desert sky, there appear the words "The End."

For the next few hundred miles of the flight, I fantasized appropriate punishments for all the men responsible for that film, none better than condemning each of them to the fate they had shown us so clearly. But then I realized that the scene had barely touched most of the viewers. I remembered that, under the present conditions of life, producers of "entertainment" feel they must drop blockbusters just to make us feel a tremor. And there the tragedy lies.

But our numbness to feelings only exacerbates and prolongs the bitter ache of our greed. The commercial appeals to this greed grow ever more urgent and ingenious, rattling through the day and the night on radio and television, appearing ever more blatantly on every available printed surface. "You only go around once in life," one of these appeals warns us. "So grab for all the gusto you can." The accompanying image is of a group of jut-jawed, tense-muscled men endlessly sailing a schooner from port to port. The gusto they are grabbing for seems to be contained in cans of beer that they throw to each other with hard, choppy motions whenever possible.

This series of commercials is archetypal. In a society that effectively bans feeling, only grabbing is left. And how we grab! The last cry in the final parody of democracy may be, "I'm getting mine, buddy." The clearest definition of freedom without vision is the freedom to grab. We grab for money, grab for property, grab for prestige, grab for leisure, grab for scenery, grab for a larger office, grab for culture, grab for love, grab for orgasm. Nothing is more pathetic, and illustrative, than two "lovers" locked in a frantic, savage struggle for their separate orgasms. I am not referring here to something hypothetical, something that "one" does, but of the times when I have been caught up in such a struggle—muscles tight as piano wires, jaws clenched, thrusting unfeelingly, unflowingly. And there are moments when I open my eyes and become an observer, and then I am filled with pity and alarm for my partner's plight, her contorted face, the desperation of her body. And there is really only one thing to do at such a moment and that is to stop the struggle, to soothe, and to weep. But that is not appropriate behavior for robots. We go on grabbing for gusto.

And so I walk the streets, aware of the pervasive ugliness of the people in this most fortunate nation, the lines of hurt and anxiety and greed around their eyes and mouths, the imbalance of their walk, the deformation of their bodies. Oh no, it is not genetic. Civilization has twisted and scarred those bodies as surely as it has damaged and tortured the face of the planet. And I consider the subtle hate that often underlies the most casual interchange. And the specific karma we have built up in this country by our specific treatment of blacks and Indians and orientals, the result of which we now suffer and will go on suffering. And the self-righteous hostility among some of those who march for peace ("Peace On You," one of the signs reads). And the bristling animosity in some who would loose their "love" on the world. And the physical and psychic garbage in the dwelling places of some who proclaim the new life styles. And the elitism and divisiveness among the theorists and activists who would create a reformed culture. And the growing intransigence of those who would maintain the old culture. And the impersonal greed of the giant corporations and unions and governing bureaucracies. And the weight of the past, the ponderous, ever-pressing, immovable weight, as heavy as the earth itself.

We do not have to evoke war or starving children in Calcutta or plagues or political oppression to justify the feeling Hindus call *vairagya*, in which all seems meaningless and everything is ashes. We have merely to listen to the rhythms of the commonplace. Sometimes at night I tune my eight-band radio receiver to the frequencies that deal with the maintenance of the society —police calls, taxis and tow trucks being dispatched, construction companies and repair crews sending for reinforcements and supplies, airplanes being directed to various traffic corridors. But nothing is really happening. No one is really going anywhere. Tomorrow night it will be the same, all summed up in that doleful Sanskrit word *samsara*, the endless round of birth and death.

If numbness offers no real sanctuary, awakening promises shock and vertigo. Added to the Gift that Civilization has bequeathed us is the intolerable pain of the gap between what we could be and what we are. We all feel that now, but some fail to recognize it for what it is, and try to find something or someone to use as a scapegoat for what exists in them. I am under no illusions. When I curse the old culture, I curse that culture in me. When I hope for Transformation, I hope that I may be transformed. And sometimes it is hard to hope.

What would happen if we all felt, truly felt, for ourselves and all the others? In the science fiction classic *Childhood's End*, Arthur C. Clarke envisions a time when the Overlords come down to earth and prepare it for the next stage in human evolution. Before evolution can take place, the world must be reformed and improved. Such cruelties as bullfighting, for instance, must be ended. The Overlords warn the people involved to stop this sport, but they refuse. The next Sunday a spaceship appears over the biggest bullring in Madrid. When the first pic is thrust into the bull's shoulder, a piercing scream rises from the audience, for the Overlords had caused every person there to feel the pain exactly as the bull felt it. There was no more bullfighting.

What if such a thing were possible today? What if each of us could share the feelings of all humanity, simultaneously and with full force? First there would be a terrible and prolonged scream of pain. And then something far more awesome: a shock of recognition. *We would realize that we had already felt it.* Somewhere within us, however veiled, all of us *know*. This knowing pervades our being. Unacknowledged and struggling for release, the common consciousness of humanity exhausts our energies and numbs our perceptions. Experienced to the full, it would bring clarity.

And with clarity there would be tears. After the scream of pain, after the shock of recognition, all the world would weep, not just for the needless torture, but for the moments squandered, the beauty overlooked, the potential unrealized. The world would weep for the words unspoken, the painful confrontations eternally postponed, the fathers fallen with their secrets locked in their dying hearts; for all the walls between us that we have not pulled down. Feeling this and far more for which no words exist, all the world would weep (for a week?

for a month?) until the last tears had soaked into the earth. And in this flow humanity would know at last the true meaning of the Flood, the universal and saving catastrophe which is not the end but the beginning of the world.

And after the flood of tears—we know this too—there is joy, the simple, matter-of-fact joy of existence. The tears of loss would turn to tears of joy. For beyond the pain, beyond all the man-made walls, there is always the elemental vibrancy. To attain contact with it, pure and clean, seems a miracle. Once attained, as Suzuki Roshi tells his students, it is nothing special. It is existence. It is the sheerest, most miraculous ecstasy. It is nothing special.

I remember now—it was here on Mt. Tam on one of those sunny, hazy late January days of false spring between the winter rains—coming upon a ladybug orgy on this same trail. Millions of bright orange ladybugs were gathered in great swarming clumps. The bushes around the trail were heavy with them; they fell from the tips of branches like raindrops after a thunderstorm. I kneeled beside one of the seething balls of life and placed my hands on it. The sensation—a most delicate yet powerful vibration—was unlike anything I had felt before. It was as if these radiant particles of existence were making a model of all joining, all affirmation. They transmitted their energy to me. Even after I continued up the trail my hands felt lighter and more alive. It was nothing special.

But now, in the heat of September on the same trail, the memory of all that joining irritates. To one who has lost the rhythm of existence, as I have on this trail, the very thought of anything spontaneous and pulsing serves only to tease the raw nerve ends. The ridge is another five hundred feet in elevation above me. A half mile down on the other side there is a spring that flows cool and clean all year. Getting to the spring, however, is no cure for this despair. There is only the climb itself, the difficult journey against the weight of the earth. I continue climbing, putting one foot before the other, up a steep dry slope armored with manzanita and buckthorn. The trail is dust and sharp rocks. The sun seems more cruel than ever. Pain is part of existence, nothing special; awareness of existence includes awareness of pain. I turn all my attention to the desolation somewhere near the center of me. I pursue it resolutely, willing now to experience it to the full. If all my hopes are delusions, let me know it in the clearest detail. If I am to live in the desert of no-love beneath the endless eye of time, let me feel it without compromise. If everything is ashes, let me experience ashes. For a moment I find it hard to breathe. But if it is hard to breathe, so be it.

In this acceptance I feel a certain lightness, the beginning of a flow. I am climbing a little faster. It seems I am sweating copiously. The hard dry desolation comes back in waves. I find I can stay with these waves. The physical ache of my legs and chest is a part of this steep slope with its thorny bushes, its dust and heat, a part of the rains to come and all the seasons of the future and past. And so it happens that when I accept the dryness and the heat and the desolation for what it is, a part of existence, I am connected gently to the earth again. I am suddenly aware of how thirsty I am, and at the same time aware that I am free of the weight of the world. For I know now with my being what physicists have long known: This planet does not weigh six thousand million, million, million tons. It does not weigh an ounce. It floats without effort, lighter than a feather, along a perfect curve of space-time. And our moon is there on soft summer nights to remind us how gently we may fly, how solid and centered and yet weightless we may be, how natural it is for all things in the universe to glide free and easy along those pure and perfect curves. And the stars and sun are there night and day to remind us that all things change. For every one of them is destined for transformation. Only through a trick of perception do we see them as unchanging. They exist, all of them, in a state of becoming and what they will eventually be is beyond our conceiving.

The last few steps ascend precipitously to the roadbed that runs along the ridge. I climb up almost effortlessly, cross the road, and open my senses one more time to the superb vista that stretches out to the north—the dark green wooded valleys, the chain of deep blue lakes in the valleys, the bare golden hills, all repeated for as far as I can see. I will sit here for a while, then go down to the spring. I have not forgotten all the dark forces that oppose and impede the Transformation. But I have remembered what we already know.

We are evolutionary creatures. Like our ancestors in the late Devonian Period some 400 million years ago, we have just pulled ourselves out of the waters in which we have lived for millennia. The first thing we notice is the water itself, Civilization. While we were in it, we had no way of knowing how it shaped our existence. Now we are beginning to understand. But we are not yet ready to look directly at the new life waiting for us on the land of Transformation. It hurts our eyes. And perhaps it is better that we not know all at once how much we must endure and change before we are comfortable there. Still, as we keep looking at the water from which we have emerged, we cannot help seeing gleaming reflections of the time and place we have entered.

ten

Gleamings on the Water

The future is beyond knowing, but the present is beyond belief. We make so much noise with technology that we cannot discover that the stargate is in our foreheads. But the time has come; the revelation has already occurred, and the guardian seers have seen the lightning strike the darkness we call reality. And now we sleep in the brief interval between the lightning and the thunder.
—WILLIAM IRWIN THOMPSON, AT THE EDGE OF HISTORY

❧

When I come down from the mountain
I am Marley's Ghost
Sleepless among wandering trees.
—ELLEN LEONARD, FROM A NOTEBOOK OF LYRICS PRESENTED ME
ON THE OCCASION OF HER TWENTY-FOURTH BIRTHDAY

SCIENCE FICTION constitutes the most matter-of-fact report now available on recent human developments. The revelation of the new age has indeed already occurred. The knowledge of it is ours whenever we stop suppressing it, the knowledge ancient and novel that destroys the civilized paradigm.

We may start with a modest example. The oldest joke among hunters and fishermen has to do with the prodigious size, energy and majesty of the one that got away. The fish in the water seems to have qualities that simply disappear in the fish lying on the deck. A friend who is a banker, a man given to precise quantification, recently told me about catching a scorpion for his son. "When I first saw it in its wild state under a rock, this

163

scorpion looked very large and powerful. It had a sort of presence about it. When I saw it in the jar a few moments later, it was entirely different. It was smaller, much smaller, and weak. No presence. I knew it was just illusion, but somehow I couldn't get over the feeling that I was looking at a different scorpion." My friend discredited himself. Rulers and calipers, after all, do not lie.

Or do they? We may have arrived at the point where we can seriously examine the possibility that the object in my friend's jar was, literally, a different scorpion. The dominant scientific paradigm already grants that all particles and collections of particles possess electromagnetic and gravitational fields that interact to some extent with all other fields. We have also come around to the notion that these fields, as well as an object's other qualities (mass, shape, time frame), change, literally, for different observers. Let us now conjecture that living things— that is, certain kinds of collections of vibrancy—also possess fields. These biofields are more complex and various than electromagnetic fields, but no less real. They, too, change for different observers and yet are integral parts of the living things they emanate from and exist with. When such a field is drastically altered, the living thing is also drastically altered and may be said to become a different entity.

The ethologist's concept of territoriality would be an over-simplification in this context, but it does show how biofields work in three-dimensional space. A photographer with a telescopic lens approaches a heron feeding at the edge of a marsh. When he comes closer than, say, sixty meters, the heron takes to the air, flies farther away, and resumes its feeding. If the photographer approaches again over the same kind of terrain under similar conditions, the heron will again let him reach a distance of approximately sixty meters before taking off. An ethologist might say the bird's territory is being invaded. But we can say more simply that the photographer touched the heron.

Recently, I visited a zoo and approached within five or six feet of a creature identified as a heron. It was confined with other marsh and water birds in an aviary made of chain-link fencing. This creature stood motionless, dispirited, seemingly unaware of my approach. Remembering the herons I have observed through cameras or binoculars in the wild, I could say without hesitation that this bird was no heron. It was a "heron," a sort of façade, a pitiable representation of what is left when a certain type of wild creature's biofield has been drastically distorted. In the same way, we mislead our children when we give them the impression that the large striped cat pacing back and forth in its cage is a tiger. It is clearly not a tiger. It is a "tiger." It has lost its biofield. To one who sees with transformed eyes, in fact, a zoo is a hideous, obscene place, and this includes those that have replaced cages with "open" environments that parody the wild environment. No wonder a zoo attracts cruelty and vandalism—the young teenage boys who throw rocks at the "lions," the old men who offer food on long sticks to the "elephants" so that they must strain every muscle to reach it.

Perhaps the basic, unacknowledged purpose of every zoo is to distort our children's perceptions, to show them that living things can be ripped from their biofields and held, still "alive," behind bars and fences and moats. The children are thus further prepared for what Civilization, through a more complex series of manipulations, is going to do to them. It is interesting to note that zoos are prominently featured in those societies that mask their almost paranoid anxieties behind powerful machines of war —the Aztecs, the Assyrians, the Romans, the modern megastates. These societies must possess some buried knowledge that a living creature cannot exist without its field. In a zoo it may go on breathing and digesting. It may grow larger, with a more perfect coat, than its wild counterpart. It may even be tricked into reproducing. But it continues to exist only as a symbol of our decreed blindness. The situation is different with domestic animals, which require humans and the works of humans in their environments. Domestication may be viewed, in fact, as a series of genetic manipulations of biofields.

The biofields of human beings are far more complex and variable than those of the other animals. In terms of three-dimensional space, these fields are extremely flexible. Anthropologist Edward T. Hall provides a wide range of data on humans' spatial fields in his book, *The Hidden Dimension*. The human biofield, however, is not limited to the spatial. It extends to psychic space, to time and to dimensions in space-time that we are only now beginning to be aware of. I must stress once more that I am not being figurative. I am speaking of fields that are finally available to human perception, as clear and direct as the words on this page.

As it is now, our perception of biofields comes up against the sternest censorship. Thought control, the kind we imagine for ourselves in the most frightening fiction, is already a reality. Indeed, thought control is the most pervasive fact in our existence, and possibly always will be. The most crucial function of the human central nervous system is rejection. Around 100,000 separate bits of information start towards our brain every second. If all of it arrived, we would go instantly mad. A number of neural mechanisms, particularly the reticular formation in the brainstem, act to screen out all but a small fraction of this information—that which is needed for bodily survival plus that which is decreed as relevant by a particular society. *We cannot overestimate the quality and quantity of the perceptual material which could reach our conscious awareness, but does not.* A major portion of what we call education is devoted to training our screening devices. To insure the continuation of Civilization, we are taught to screen out perception of our own biofields and the biofields of others as early and as completely as possible. It generally takes quite a jolt to open up our perceptions to this aspect of our existence.

In recent years, the use of psychedelic agents has provided just that jolt for a number of people. I once participated in an experiment testing the effects of one of these agents in creative problem solving. This was in 1966, before the national panic about psychedelics had reached its heights. Responsible leaders had not yet totally abandoned these powerful chemicals to the counter-culture; the experiment, wonder of wonders, was partially financed by government funds. Our mission was to imagine the future. Near the beginning of the seven-hour taped discussion, one of the other three participants, Paul Fusco, had a vivid perception of his biofield. It appeared to him as a colorless plasma extending all around him. One of the experimenters inadvertently stepped into this plasma; Fusco informed him that "part of me is all over your shoe." "I know," he told us, "I *know* that you're in my plasma. But that's all right."

"This may be what it's all about," he said later. "Maybe if this could happen every day, you know, that I would be sitting here with my wife, and then she would leave and I'd say, 'Oh my God, something very important is happening,' because I'd really *feel* her pulling away from me. And when part of me would get stuck on somebody's shoes, I'd want to know where it was going. I'd want to keep track of it. If this could happen every day, maybe we'd have a different world."

Countless other people have had similar perceptions under the psychedelic impact. There are other ways to gain awareness of the biofield, ways that entail systematic, disciplined retraining of the perceptual system. I had the good fortune of entering one such discipline at the time I began writing this book. *Aikido* is the newest and perhaps most subtle of the Japanese martial arts. My teacher, Robert Nadeau, had been a student and teacher of judo, karate, and other of the arts for many years, then had studied for two and a half years in Tokyo at the *dojo* of Master Morihei Uyeshiba, the founder of aikido. I entered the training enthusiastically, attracted primarily by the prospect of a regular physical workout during a period of concentrated reading and writing. From the beginning, however, the "physical" merged with the "spiritual." My training in this art has shown me, among many other things, that the biofield is palpable, practical and, indeed, nothing special.

As a martial art, aikido is purely defensive, teaching no aggressive moves whatever. It is, in Uyeshiba's words, "not a technique to fight with or defeat the enemy. It is the way to reconcile the world and make human beings one family." Competition between participants (as is common in the other martial arts) might create discord and would certainly require a limiting set of rules; therefore it is strictly prohibited. Aikido's spirit, according to Uyeshiba, "is that of loving attack and that of peaceful reconciliation." Practice of the art entails one or more students attacking another, who responds with one of several thousand basic techniques and variations—wristlocks, throws, pins, or simply avoidance of the attack. Knowledge of the specific physical techniques, however, is less important than understanding of the essential principles, summed up as *centering* and *blending.*

In teaching these principles Robert Nadeau, who is more concerned with what he calls "energy awareness" than are most aikido teachers, in no way denies what we call the physical body. He insists, however, that we gain awareness of other manifestations of our presence, of the flow of energy throughout our bodies and the energy fields that we create around us. Through various exercises, Nadeau teaches us to change the quality, quantity and direction of this energy. We learn, for example, to balance the flow of our own energy so that it is smooth and evenly distributed rather than locked (as it is in so many of us) in our eyes or head or chest. This sort of energy balance is an important part of the centering process, during which we learn to move, all of a piece, from the *hara,* an energy center just below the navel. Once centered, we learn to meet any incoming attack, not by opposing it, force against force, but by blending precisely with it. Blending generally entails a graceful circular movement that looks like a dance. If the student successfully blends with the incoming energy and remains centered, he may then deal with the attacker in any number of ways. The circular movement often positions the defender so that momentarily he is seeing everything just as the attacker sees it. Looking at the situation *from the attacker's viewpoint,* the defender can act with a minimum of force to bring matters back into the harmony and balance that is a natural condition of existence.

The point of all this in terms of biofields is that to blend with incoming energy, you must be able somehow to sense the quality, direction and force of that energy. Simply looking at it with ordinary eyes is not good enough. Masters of the art, in fact, often deal with the attacks of a half-dozen or more people. Thus, Nadeau spends a great deal of time training his students to sense impending attacks behind their backs, or to identify, with eyes closed, the *quality* of energy directed towards them. In addition to sensing and identifying the biofields of other class members, students practice extending and contracting their own fields and changing the quality of the energy.

Some of the energy-awareness exercises yield results that might be considered, in terms of the old paradigm, esoteric or occult. But from another point of view, they are quite ordinary. The wonder is that our extraordinary civilization has managed to block perceptions and capabilities that are so useful and obvious. In one of our exercises we form a circle and place our outstretched hands, fingers extended, near the center of the circle. By increasing the radiance and intensity of this collective energy field and by paying close attention, most of us can soon perceive softly glowing streamers connecting the fingers of the participants. It is interesting to sense the flux and flow of the streamers, to note which people are connected and how intensely the streamers flow.

Most of us, after some fifteen months' training, have learned to sense a whole range of previously veiled information about ourselves and others. I would guess that the primary condition of this learning is simply that we have discovered an environment that grants us permission to have such perceptions. Most social or educational environments in our present culture would exercise the most strenuous, if covert, censorship in these matters. This censorship continues to exist in the face of psychological studies showing that perception cannot be understood in terms of single, separate senses, and that perception is a function of learning—that is, the total life experience of the organism.

Precivilized cultures were not nearly so rigid in perceptual matters as is ours. Postcivilized cultures, as will be seen later, cannot afford to be. In his remarkable book *A Separate Reality*, anthropologist Carlos Castaneda describes perceptual abilities of a present-day Yaqui Indian shaman named Don Juan. There are, according to Don Juan, two basic ways of perceiving reality. One he calls "looking"—simply perceiving the world in its usually accepted forms. The other way, attained only after years of disciplined effort, he calls "*seeing*." For a "man of knowledge" who can *see*, the world is a startling place. Humans appear as luminous beings made up of something like fibers of light that rotate from front to back, creating the shape of an egg. A special set of long, tentacle-like fibers comes out of the area of the body near the navel and is particularly important. "Sorcerers act towards people," Don Juan tells Castaneda, "in accordance to the way they *see* their tentacles. Weak persons have very short, almost invisible fibers; strong persons have bright, long ones. . . . You can tell from the fibers if a person is healthy, or if he is sick, or if he is mean, or kind, or treacherous." A sorcerer can use his own tentacles to reach out and influence objects and people. Castaneda witnesses a spectacular feat of balance by a sorcerer named Don Genero, who uses his tentacles to pull himself across a waterfall in defiance of the laws of ordinary gravity. "When you *see*," Don Juan says, "there are no longer familiar features in the world. Everything is new. Everything has never happened before. The world is incredible." [1]

Compared to *seeing*, my poor attempts at perception and manipulation of the biofield are rudimentary indeed. And yet I have experienced many things that add resonance to my reading of Castaneda. Skepticism becomes less of a knee-jerk response. I watch films taken of Master Uyeshiba when he was in his eighties with new appreciation. I begin to understand how this little old man could repeatedly throw and pin three powerful young attackers. What once might have seemed magic or trickery takes its place among other pieces of newly perceived reality.

Energy-awareness training in aikido is especially helpful to those of us who have grown up skeptical and blind. It makes it possible for us to check out most of our new perceptions in the unfamiliar realms of energy fields and higher awareness in terms that are familiar to all of us. If a student resorts to physical force alone in performing a certain wristlock, he or she may be able to bring a strong attacker down, but only with a great deal of muscular strain. If on the other hand the student follows the recommended aikido practice of sending energy out the arm, through the hand and over the opponent's wrist like a waterfall that flows from the fingers down towards the center of the earth, the opponent goes down like a shot without the use of any perceptible physical effort. The difference is truly striking. There are times when I, even as a novice, am able to perceive the lines of force in the biofield of an oncoming attacker and somehow, with a motion that takes feeling rather than thought, align my field precisely with his (which may be one way of being momentarily aligned with the universe). Whenever this happens, the attacker is thrown through the air with what seems to be no effort on my part. It is as if my arms and hands are simply following a motion that is already happening.

At such moments it appears obvious that some sort of universal harmony does exist and that it is tantalizingly close. All things *already are happening.* One small step over an invisible line will get us there, to the place where everything flows and neither effort nor waiting can be. When these delightful moments come, the thrower is not separate from the thrown. We blend in a single motion, a small ripple in the endless sea of existence.

Nor are these moments restricted to the class periods. There can be the same sort of awareness in every daily situation. Walking can become an exercise in blending with the motion and stillness, the fields, of all surrounding objects. Every human interaction can partake of the essence of being. Each chore can be totally involving. Under these conditions, what we call "boredom" is impossible.

We realize on such occasions how much of our time we spend merely waiting, how our existence is dominated by its insistence on climax, by its reliance upon the "great moment" and upon what we have been led to think of as "greatness" itself. To the person who *sees,* as Don Juan points out, life is filled to the brim. How then, if this is so, can we spend even an instant *waiting?* What are we waiting for? The concept of "waiting" does not spring from being. It is a culturally conditioned judgment.

Perhaps even "matter" is a judgment, something we have created perceptually out of the vibrancy so that, like children, we may have it to play with. The plaything (taken as *separate from* the rest of existence) has become dangerous. Now, just in time, we can glimpse adventures in which we do not have to pile up great hoards of matter to make ourselves large, in which we do not have to build an empire or make a war to prove ourselves great, in which we do not have to burn ever-increasing quantities of fuel to raise our "standard of living," in which we may need no spaceships to journey to the stars.

We are terrified of the potentialities in ordinary objects and events. We may, in fact, spend much of our apprenticeship for the new life learning to bear the terror of the ordinary. We may learn to realize that every tree and stone and hill and cloud is vividly alive, that all our friends exist as focal points in shimmering, ever-changing fields of being with which we continually interact. We may already agree with Astronaut Edgar D. Mitchell, who feels sure that intelligent life exists elsewhere in the universe, "more than likely in our own galaxy," and believes human beings will make contact with that life. But some of us will need an unfamiliar kind of courage even to consider the kind of space travel that this man, who holds a Ph.D. from MIT and has walked on the moon, has in mind. "I'm not so sure that you need the space program for that," Mitchell writes. "This may be extremely far out and hypothetical, but if the phenomenon of astral projection has any validity whatsoever, it might be a perfectly valid form of intergalactic travel, and a lot safer probably than space flight." [2]

There are indeed strange murmurings within the temples of science and technology. Astrophysicists are playing with new perceptual toys that follow nicely from relative theory but shake the civilized paradigm to the root. With growing excitement they spin out formulas showing the necessity for black holes in space that can crush matter out of existence in a split second or perhaps momentarily join ours to another universe. These almost unthinkable phenomena can suck "matter" and even light into them, never to escape, and yet can theoretically transfer their energy of rotation to something outside them through the medium of space-time itself. And though the space program has seemed firmly leashed to government public relations and Newtonian mechanics, orthodoxy is by no means certain even there. Operations officers I have met in Houston speak guardedly of mystical feelings that surround the enterprise. And at a state dinner, my oldest daughter, seated next to the first man to step on the moon, shared a small but not inconsiderable revelation. After the autograph seekers had been satisfied and the dinner served, the two of them entered into a conversation in which she argued for the value of including poets on space trips and he responded with the expectable arguments against such inclusion. A moment came, however, when the field between them suddenly changed, and Neil Armstrong said quietly: "I want to tell you one thing. When I first looked back and saw the earth there in space, something happened to me." And then, in a lower, more intense voice: *"I'll never be the same."*

However flat their voices may sound to us, however coolly they may hew to their sometimes robot-like duties, those men who have seen the earth floating in the heavens can never be the same. Nor can any of us who have shared their perceptions. Even the television pictures from space suggest that the realms of science fiction exist not on the moon but on this shining blue and white globe. The mythic world is here and now. This is the magic planet.

It is all magic. Civilization long ago cast a spell over humankind, dulling human senses to what is most vivid and fascinating, infecting them with a dis-ease so pervasive that it has come to be assumed as part of the given. Newtonian science made the spell even more powerful by providing effective mechanical means for achieving most of the ancient dreams of magical will and manipulation. But the Newtonian magic was so strong that it has proved its own undoing, spinning us out past the perceptual limits set by Civilization itself. It has created a surplus of information just as powerful and potentially disruptive as was the surplus of grain that destroyed tribal life and triggered the birth of Civilization.

And now information whirls around this globe with unprecedented speed and in incredible quantities. Ancient wisdom and new ideas beat about our heads, confusing us, but also disrupting the sleep of our senses. Information gained from spaceships helps us understand that we may need no spaceships. Information about electromagnetic fields blends with information from an esoteric oriental discipline to help us sense the fields of life and being in which we all exist. The information surplus creates unlikely juxtapositions. Images of Bushmen hunting fade into images of space flight. The words of William Blake and B. F. Skinner come at us from the same television channel—two uncompromising theorists, one saying that mental things are alone real, the other saying that even self-aware consciousness is a construct.

We begin to understand—vaguely, incompletely—that *all* things are real. It is only a small step from there to the awesome realization of our ultimate power to select a universe of our choice from an infinite number of possible universes. We need look no further for a lifetime filled to the brim. As Don Juan says, "our lot is to learn and to be hurled into inconceivable new worlds."

The terror of the ordinary chills us, paralyzes our perceptions, prevents that little motion needed to step into a more intense reality. We fear, perhaps more than anything else, to give up our neuroses, our discontents, our dis-eases. Simply to be at ease fills us with fear. We rush for the sanctuary of our sickness, the safety of the morning news, the stock market, the pennant race. We reach for chemical drugs or the more powerful drug of consumerism. We plunge into the forgetfulness of "education" and "culture," then go on trying to change everything except ourselves.

But a glimpse through unscaled eyes invites another glimpse. Overcoming our terror, we may at last be able to see ourselves in a grain of sand or a leaf or our lover's face. We may realize that we need not seek connection, for we are already connected to all existence. The convict in solitary, the dread enemy in the Asian jungles are clearly *us*. We interact not only with a specific other person (as commonly supposed) or with a father or mother figure (as the Freudians would have it) or even with a generic Other, but also with what we call the Self projected on the Other. We meet ourselves around every corner of time.

Whether we will it or not, we are in the very business of recreating the world at every new instant. In the realization of this act we may find a new freedom—to explore, to experience, to be. We may choose to live in an ever-changing universe where figures from other worlds (which are this world) break out into our consciousness, as vivid as those translucent, seaborne figures in Turner's "Ulysses Deriding Polyphemus." We may choose to alter time, or to become one with a friend or a tree, or even to see the earth itself becoming transparent, glistening in ever brighter colors at every level of transparency.

Here, conventional limitations simply do not apply. It is clear that in such a universe there would be no need whatever for us to lust after bigger cars or bigger buildings or faster physical travel or "power." Thus we can at last foresee an end to that heedless, desperate hoarding of matter and burning of energy with which we now divert our attention from the fascination of ordinary reality.

eleven
Beyond Incest

The precautions taken against thieves who open trunks, search bags, or ransack cabinets, consist in securing with cords and fastening with bolts and locks. This is what the world calls wit. But a big thief comes along and carries off the cabinet on his shoulders, with box and bag, and runs away with them. His only fear is that the cords and locks should not be strong enough! Therefore, does not what the world used to call wit simply amount to saving up for the strong thief? And I venture to state that nothing of that which the world calls wit is otherwise than saving up for big thieves; and nothing of that which the world calls sage wisdom is other than hoarding up for robbers.

—CHUANGTSE, THE SAYINGS OF CHUANGTSE

TO ENCOURAGE unrealistic expectations or offer hope of change without pain is obviously irresponsible. The Transformation entails enormous difficulties and a great deal of pain as well as joy. But to disavow hope, to settle for expectations that are far lower than our present capabilities (much less our potential) is perhaps even more irresponsible. Here in the United States we may come to see that our current national goals are difficult to attain—perhaps unattainable —*precisely because we have set them too low.*

Our ameliorative goals (the reduction of poverty, crime, pollution, racism, disease and the like) are customarily conceived in such a timid, piecemeal manner as to stultify rather than excite. And our positive goals (generally adding up to the freedom to consume more and compete more) so clearly run against our real needs that every failure may appear as a blessing.

If the Transformation involves changes in human perceiving, feeling and being, it also involves changes in the society at large.

Institutions and human consciousness obviously reflect each other; one cannot long maintain a new shape without some kind of shift in the other. Suggestions for changes in human consciousness do not automatically produce step-by-step action programs for social reform. Specific tactics are best left flexible in any case, so as to flow with the inevitable surprises of time and the vibrancy. Nor does a new human paradigm come equipped with the gift of prophecy. The future will be determined, not only by the force of the Transformation, but by the force against it. (If institutional resistance to change continues at its present level or increases, the outcome could be ominous indeed.) But a vision of the Transformation does imply certain overriding "goals" that can guide day-by-day social action. The vision may prove to be large enough and bold enough to lift the human spirit and mobilize the energy needed for difficult and unusual enterprises.

Conventional wisdom is not to be brushed aside without careful consideration. We must pay all due respect to customs and taboos that have stood the test of thousands of years. But it seems inevitable that a transformed vision will take us beyond custom and taboo to imagine a life worthy of the capacities we now waste and misdirect.

Take the current crisis in our prisons. Here it is obvious that conventional wisdom is bankrupt, that the most "practical" men have proven impractical. More than one billion dollars a year is being spent to imprison an average of 350,000 sentenced prisoners plus an unknown number of people "awaiting sentence." Fully 95 percent of these will eventually be released. Far from being rehabilitated, the vast majority will emerge from prison as more skillful and determined criminals—cordoned off from many social benefits, bitter, heedful only not to get caught next time. In spite of their increased skill, more than 40 percent will find themselves in prison again.

There is no clear idea, even, of what prison is for. If it is simply for punishment, it should be a fairly unpleasant place. According to behavioral theory, the punishment should start out at full force as quickly as possible after the crime is committed and should be severe from the inception. But to carry out such punishment would do violence to our system of constitutional safeguards as well as to our sense of humane justice. Then again, prisons may be considered necessary simply to protect society from people with dangerous tendencies. But since almost all these people are released, generally with even more dangerous tendencies, the present system is less than adequate here. And long term preventive detention runs, once more, against our sense of humane justice. Rehabilitation is the official function of most of our prisons. But it is not working and may never work so long as it is associated with the punishment of detention. This is especially true now that so many inmates consider themselves political prisoners of a system they despise. They simply do not accept rehabilitation.

Trapped in the old paradigm, penologists are hard put to effect any change whatever in prison practices. To get tougher would create additional resentment among prisoners and increase already explosive tensions. And yet to give in to demands and initiate step-by-step reforms towards humanizing prisons might have even more disastrous consequences. It is well known (reinforcement theory is useful here) that to make small, sequential concessions to the discontented only inflames discontent and increases demands.

How much better it would be if penologists could seize the initiative from the dissidents through a series of bold, imaginative and sweeping reform measures. This might be possible were the penologists guided and bolstered by a large vision. But vision comes slowly to one stuck within a system. One of the major biofields in which the penologist lives includes prisons and prisoners (just as the policeman's or criminologist's biofield includes criminals). The penologist may imagine more modern prisons, more humane prisons, prisons without bars, halfway houses, work-release programs, weekend furloughs, and all manner of truly humane rehabilitation programs. But it would be extremely difficult for him to take seriously, *as the central, motivating, guiding force for all his actions,* the ultimate vision of a society without prisons, without prisoners—indeed, a society without criminals.

And yet this is the compelling vision that emerges naturally from the new human paradigm. To one whose field of existence has expanded to encompass more than his immediate surroundings, Eugene V. Debs's statement that "while there is a soul in prison, I am not free" becomes a matter, not just of thought and "practicality," but also of feeling and being. It becomes clear that people locked in prisons, and animals in zoos, reflect something fearful locked up inside ourselves. Criminals are an essential part of our society and of each of us. Criminality is inextricably bound up with Civilization. If the Transformation involves relinquishing what is criminal and freeing what is locked up within ourselves, it also involves emptying our prisons.

This does not mean emptying the prisons in a day or a year, but it does mean seriously planning for and working towards that eventuality. The goal of a society without prisons provides the motivation and guidance for action now largely lacking. It also forces us to imagine a society in which prisons would not be needed, and thus to look with new eyes at the conditions in today's society that create, indeed demand, criminals and prisoners and jails.

Seeking explanations for criminal behavior, the eyes of the old paradigm turn to "human nature" or to the dark and dirty corners of our society. The "human nature" copout was discussed in Chapter 5 and elsewhere in this book. As for the commonly held belief that crime is caused by the social problems of the ghetto, of poor schools, inadequate housing, lack of jobs, and the like, it is true that victims of these social conditions are more likely to land in jail than would otherwise be the case. We must probe deeper, however, for the root cause of crime. The more fortunate, middle-class citizen has access to the reinforcement system approved by the society. He does not necessarily obey its laws, but knows how to use laws for his own benefit. The less fortunate citizen is not able to use society's legal system for his own purposes. But he is driven by the same biological needs and motivated towards the same measures of success as is the fortunate citizen. Even if he engages in illegal acts, in fact, he is most often operating well within the basic behavior pattern inculcated, valued, and glorified by the culture.

Successful citizen and criminal alike have learned in a thou-

sand overt and covert ways to value competition and individualism, aggression and acquisition. I am not speaking here of competition as a seeking after perfection for its own sake or as
devoting intense efforts towards a worthy goal. I am speaking
of the more familiar brand of competition which generally
entails pressing the rules to the limit, getting away with whatever
you can without being caught at it. Individualism here means
considering yourself a separate, basically isolated creature that
thrives and survives mostly through separate effort. There is
nothing noble about this individualism, which so often leads
to those familiar moral imperatives: "What's in it for me?" and
"I'm getting mine, buddy." In this framework, unions, corporations, and associations become group egos, devoted primarily
to "getting mine."

Competition and individualism, aggression and acquisition:
It would be rare indeed to spend four straight hours observing
a classroom, a playground, a sports event or a television screen
without seeing these values glorified to the full. If varsity
and professional competitive sports build character, it is character fit for a criminal. Having helped build this character,
our sports may provide a relatively safe and socially approved
outlet for otherwise criminal impulses. They provide it, that
is, for the few who are good enough to participate. For the
rest, they offer vicarious thrills and a clear-cut model of behavior.

In professional football, the current preoccupation of millions
of American males, we can see social approval of criminal-type
behavior carried to a poetic extreme. There is no gainsaying the
epic intensity of a good pro contest. Where else in the culture
are men called upon for such mighty efforts, such courage and
will in the face of adversity? The march of those teams up and
down the gridiron sounds the horn call of famous military campaigns of the past, Leonidas at Thermopylae, the surge of empire. In many ways, this sport is truly beautiful. I address myself
to football not because I am repelled but because I am fascinated.
I can appreciate the skill and finesse involved in every play.
But this skill and finesse is built upon a solid base of force,
violence and physical brutality. The most skillful play is for

nothing if the opposing team is more "physical"—a euphemism for brutal and dirty. Hardly a play goes by without some infraction of the rules, especially in the center of the line, the "pit," where biting, gouging, clapping hands over an opponent's earholes, and elbowing his throat are commonplace.

According to the rules, no holding is allowed for the team on the offense. A certain amount of offensive holding, however, is necessary to compensate for the defensive freedom of movement. The players know this, the coaches know it, and the officials know it. Therefore, whether a player is penalized depends upon how sneakily he commits the infraction. And this is true not just for offensive holding. All over the field, players who are driven to desperation by the overriding need for victory at all costs are getting away with whatever they can, restrained only by the ever-present policemen in the striped suits. This is accompanied by much pointing the finger of accusation at opposing players and doing everything possible to make it appear that *they* are breaking the rules. Can you imagine a player walking up to an official after a play and saying, "You may not have noticed it, but I clipped Johnson on that last play"? The fact that such a notion seems ridiculous gives you a pretty good idea of how much and what kind of character is built by highly competitive sports.

Actually, most fans are very well aware of one of the game's key aspects. It is best summed up in that aching desire, shared by players and spectators alike, to smash and disable the opposing quarterback. A fifteen-yard roughing-the-passer penalty seems a small price to pay for the removal of this key adversary. I have before me a copy of the tabloid *Pro Football Weekly*, a favorite of hard-core fans. On the front page is a picture of one quarterback about to be struck down by a charging lineman and a picture of another quarterback, obviously in great pain, walking off the field on crutches. The captions tell the story:

GET THE QB! Hunt is on in NFL action and prey is
the quarterback.
Above: Bengal's Ken Andersen unloads
under hard Packer charge.

Victim of Ram "hunters," Bear QB
Jack Concannon, leaves field for rest of
season.[1]

The obvious appeal to sadism is bad enough. But the adversary arrangement between the forces of law and order on one side and the demand for victory at all costs on the other is even more pervasive and insidious. The officials are there to keep you in line. You are there to get away with everything you can on the way to glorious victory. Try to imagine what would happen if the officials should get together before a certain game and agree secretly not to call any personal fouls. How many minutes would pass before the all-out brawl that is implicit in every play? The officials make football possible. Remove the officials and you would have to think up another game, one not based on the intent to break rules.

Football's popularity may seem to prove the inevitable appeal of aggression, violence and hot competition. But there are other reasons why we are able to spend a vibrant Sunday afternoon slumped before a television set. We have been separated from the immediacies of existence, offered no education whatever in the arts of ecstasy, and denied even a vocabulary of consciousness. Like the players marooned there on that rectangle, we are hemmed in by artificial boundaries and restrained by officials who do not trust us, thus assuring that we shall be untrustworthy. We are driven to smash others out of our way in order to cross a meaningless goal and achieve an empty victory. Then and only then we can stand and cheer and proclaim to the world that we have really lived.

There are other rewards. The game is delayed so that the rich desserts of competition can be dangled before the eyes of the millions sitting near their television sets—the sleek sedans gliding across meadows of electronically enriched violins, the whoosh and whine of the jet sweeping you away to God knows where with the silky-voiced stewardess promising you God knows what, the electrically powered hedge clipper that will allow the football fan's hand and arm muscles to remain flaccid as he manicures the shrubbery around his suburban dream house.

The danger in these commercials lies in the fact that they are actually seen. They are seen in the ghetto as well as in the suburbs. The rewards are made clear just as the game is made clear, not only in televised sports events but in the great majority of all the programs, so many of which achieve suspense, characterization and denouement only at the point of the gun. The ghetto resident sees and he understands. He also understands the tired, halfhearted, pleading slogans thrust on him by a worried society. "Earn, baby, earn" somehow lacks the ring of the cry from which it was taken, "Burn, baby, burn." He suspects that if he is "good," that if he continues with his officially sanctioned brainwashing, stamped and sealed with a high school diploma, he may eventually drive a delivery truck rather than shine shoes. He also knows, unless social and personal attitudes change, that he will probably never earn his fair share of the goods and goodies dancing on the screen. And nowhere on the horizon can he find officially sanctioned delights of the senses and perceptions that might make the television commercials seem simply irrelevant. He may count himself lucky, in fact, if twelve full years of schooling offer him as much as fifteen minutes' worth of learning about the intrinsic rewards of being. But the high, brief thrill of "winning out," of "getting away with it," is clear. The extrinsic rewards of a consumer society are clear. Not to prove his "manhood" would be, in fact, un-American. The wonder is that we have so few candidates for prison.

This nation has no monopoly on criminality. Every civilized state has its share. In America, however, the intimate relationship between Civilization and criminality has become visible as never before. Moreover, the current crisis in crime and punishment may help force us towards the new perceptions that are prerequisite to reform.

Some psychologists have recommended a kind of benign brainwashing for those with criminal tendencies. But new perceptions are ultimately far more effective than any such crude and stopgap measures. True reform will begin when we all perceive clearly that we are being relentlessly brainwashed *towards* criminality, that it is largely what our society values *most* that lies at the root of criminal behavior. Then, at least, we would know what to hope for. We would not hope for violent, highly competitive sports to be banned; such a step would bring force against force and would in no way exemplify the blending and flowing that can best serve the Transformation. But we would find hope in the first elected official who would not actively glorify competition and violence. We would find great hope indeed in the President who would refuse to throw out the first ball of the season in favor of some more constructive activity. We would be cheered by news of every Police Athletic League or other organization supposedly devoted to law and order that would renounce the teaching of violence and "winning" to deprived children. We would support every department of physical education that would replace hot competition with such sports as gymnastics, tumbling, dance and creative new forms of athletics that would teach the varied joys of the body and senses. We would be very pleased to get more news of the young pro football dropouts who currently are gathering together to formulate a new mode of play that would preserve the exuberance and the intricate beauties of the sport without the brutality, cheating and exploitation.

We would indeed find hope in much that already is happening. We would be encouraged by every public or corporate decision that involves renunciation of bigness, growth and high energy consumption. The 1971 vote against development of a United States supersonic transport, even if later overturned, must stand as one of the most significant decisions since the Pyramid Age, a historic affirmation of human values over the insatiable demands of more-and-faster. We would share the early hopes of the ecology movement and would not be overly disheartened by the opposition it is bound to generate for some years to come. We would be pleased but not lulled into easy optimism by every harbinger of shift in outmoded basic values, especially in the younger generation. We would cheer the death of the Horatio Alger myth and the devaluation of the corporate ladder as a measure of success. We would encourage every abandonment of conspicuous consumption and every attempt at a life style that is both modest and elegant.

The vision of a transformed society would encourage us to get on with the matter of emptying the prisons. Equally important, starting to empty the prisons would help force us into a vision of a transformed society. Most of the necessary information already is available. We know, for example, that there is a rather clear relationship between the number of laws and policemen on one hand and the number of criminal offenses on the other. Which causes the other is not entirely clear.' But it is certainly reasonable to support the reformers who have suggested elimination of all laws against nonvictim behavior—gambling, drunkenness, vagrancy, drug usage, sex deviancy, and the like—which alone would reduce the number of arrests by nearly half. In the short run, this measure would help clear courtrooms and prisons and make possible a reduction in the number of correctional personnel. In the long run, it would constitute a first step towards a society in which there are no policemen and in which legal sanctions (an expedient of Civilization, not an inevitable condition of human life) are replaced by the long-forgotten web of kin-ness and community

The direction of prison reform—that is, towards local community responsibility—already is becoming apparent. The 1971 Kelgord Report on California Corrections, for example, recommends that communities or counties be rewarded with state subsidies whenever they worked out alternatives to sending people to prison, and that they be penalized by paying most of the costs for those they did send to prison. Among the suggested alternatives are improved probation services, local "open" institutions from which offenders would go forth for daily work and education in the community, and local "closed" institutions in which inmates could serve no more than six months, during which time they would interact with volunteers from the community who would come into the institution. All this assumes shorter sentences and a significant reduction in the California prison population.

The Kelgord report, considered bold by penologists, is indeed a good start, but only that. A transformed consciousness brings the realization that we are something more than our brothers' keepers, that in sharing their consciousness and their culture we share their crimes. In this light, a greater measure of urgency would seem appropriate—for example, the early release of large numbers of inmates and the transfer of their responsibility to small volunteer groups that would meet three nights or so a week in the volunteers' homes. Since institutionalization is quite expensive, the money saved would make it possible to pay the volunteers rather well for their time. Some of these volunteers would be recent graduates from prison; research evidence from a variety of sources shows that ex-convicts in charge of rehabilitation programs have a better rehabilitative record in working with convicts than have correction officers and other specialists. Each group would be made up of about five offenders and five volunteers. Professional guidance would be provided, where needed, on a rotating basis. But the main responsibility would lie within the group itself. Interaction would be intense. Both offenders and volunteers would reveal their on-going activities and their feelings, and would join in a mutual search for better modes of life. The offenders would bear an absolute responsibility to attend every meeting. The volunteers would be required to report any absence immediately to a correctional authority.

This idea, I must emphasize, is no hard-and-fast recommendation. I present it primarily to trigger creative planning in others. My main point, as I have said before, is that prison population can be reduced more quickly than we might think possible and that we can eventually live in a society that has neither prisons nor crime. It seems obvious that, even by present-day standards, the United States prison population is twice as big as it should be. Therefore, we might well move with all deliberate speed to cut it in half. Further deadlines could be set. For example, we might hope that by 1985 the prison population be reduced to one-fourth its present size in proportion to total population; that by the year 2000 it be down to around 12 percent; and that by 2020, nearly fifty years from now, it be practically zero. This assumes, of course, that by that date child rearing, school, sports, and indeed all manner of human interaction will have been significantly altered.

❦

The Transformation eventually will touch all that is human. It is possible that within fifty years many present-day fields, specialties, institutions will barely be recognizable or will no longer exist as such. It is not my purpose here to provide a compendium of institutional change; I believe such prediction to be impossible. All I can do is suggest a few possible signposts on a journey that is uncertain at every given point but inevitable in the whole.

❧

Politics. We can read the grotesque condition of our dying Civilization in the political arena almost as unmistakably as on the gridiron. I have written elsewhere that doing the things now deemed necessary to achieve high office makes a man unworthy of that office.[2] The candidate schemes, manipulates, lies, veils his true sentiments, appeals to friendship and loyalty for ulterior ends. Upon taking office, he assures himself, he will change. That he rarely if ever does is becoming clear to increasing numbers of voters. What has been termed the Credibility Gap has widened to include not just the politician's words but his very being. We begin to disbelieve the existence of the human being behind the campaign poster. It is probably a testimonial to our awakening perceptions that those smiling faces look more and more like Halloween masks.

The coming years may well bring about reforms in political structure. The Center for the Study of Democratic Institutions, for example, has been working for several years on a tentative new national Constitution. But the first omen of a transformed politics may simply be the emergence of a new breed of political candidate. Some, in fact, already have been elected to state and local offices. Such a politician is dedicated to a kind of openness and honesty that is quite inconceivable to the traditional office seeker. He is clear and aboveboard, not just in verbal statements, but in the deeper matters of feeling, sensing and being. This may seem quite traditional, but actually, in this culture, just to get in touch with real feeling is a radical act. The new politician recognizes that whether he wills it or not he is an exemplar and that the way he leads his life will affect the electorate. He may take it as one of his functions to articulate a new social vision and to help guide his constituency through the difficulties and joys of social and personal change.

The election of large numbers of this breed—not really so unlikely in view of the growing public revulsion against traditional politicians—could create a more significant and lasting political revolution than could a new Constitution. It might also result in real changes *within* formal political structures.

To illustrate, the idea of inevitable winners and equally inevitable losers may be rather easily modified. The pervasive debate-adversary mode of politics cracks reality down the middle. It is as if every issue must have two sides and every decision must leave a disgruntled minority, with its members muttering, "Just wait until next time." But hardly any question really has only two sides. When legislative or administrative bodies give up the sole notion of victory, they may also avoid the inevitability of defeat. Assuming some sort of eventual agreement, the members would not debate but would explore possibilities. They would make every effort to avoid complete defeat for any faction. This would mean moving towards pluralistic decisions in many cases. Sociologist Herbert Gans points out that, contrary to present practice, we can provide minority groups with maximum choice: "Instead of forcing three minorities to shoehorn themselves into a majority in favor of policy A, let's provide three policies, A, B and C, and let people choose their own best alternative." Such diversity is not always possible, but it applies more often than we might imagine.

The Transformation may also bring changes in the politician's attitude towards power. Though we often hear the traditional warnings against its corrosive effects, political power of the most outrageous stripe still evokes widespread fascination and admiration. The cult of the present-day, overblown United States Presidency, for example, includes many journalists and scholars who should know better. The grasp for more and more power results not just from the increasing size and complexity of our society but also from increasing fear and personal emptiness among the men involved. Modern Western man, essentially alone against the world and deprived of the natural satisfactions of the body and senses, is especially susceptible to the desire for external dominance over others. Political scientist Harold Lasswell argues that the power seeker "pursues power as a means of compensation against deprivation. *Power is expected to overcome low estimates of the self.*"

Our Founding Fathers, well aware of human frailty, turned their best efforts to the humane restraint of power. Several of the framers of our Constitution, notably Benjamin Franklin, went so far as to favor a council at the head of our government rather than a single executive officer. Franklin, with remarkable foresight, feared that an individual President might prove "fond of war" or that he might get sick while in office. Franklin was voted down (the young republic had George Washington waiting in the wings), and so we have our latter-day, individualized President, a man who controls more deadly power than any king or emperor, a man glamourized for his seat at "the lonely pinnacle of power," glorified for making such statements as "The buck stops here," nurtured by crisis, melodramatic in his "command decisions"—and utterly ravaged by the power he has spent a lifetime seeking. The Presidency sets the style for every other public office, and in every legislative and administrative hall you can smell the decay of humanity as the predators and scavengers gather. Whether he is a United States senator or an assemblyman in a small state, the politician's eyes glint towards something *not here*. So long as he is holding the floor—making speeches, manipulating people or blocs of people, establishing positions—he is likely to be charming, dynamic, and possibly charismatic. But when the situation turns to dialogue, to the candid interchange of thoughts and feelings, the great man begins to fade before your eyes. He becomes restless, preoccupied. Time drags. Each new moment seems to weary him.

The desire for surplus power, the capability to dominate as many people and as many things as possible, is at its height in our society. It is also diminishing. The two tendencies exist simultaneously on either side of a consciousness gap. The new breed of politician may emerge from those who are less deprived personally and thus have less need for dominance. The new politician will seek new power relationships. Already the President, and most other elected officials as well, operates as a member of a group. (He is, of course, more likely to call it a "team.") But the group remains in the shadows, leaving all the dangerous pressures of power on the President's frail and fading humanity. Simply by making it public, by making it clear just how and with whom power is shared, a President would be taking a first step towards what later may be formalized as a true Group Presidency, with merged consciousness. Whatever his office, the politician and the political groups of the Transformation will do everything they can to share, not amass, political and personal power. That would be revolution enough.

Revolution in the conventional sense is, in fact, an aspect of Civilization, not of Transformation. Surely we have seen enough of those armed overthrows that replace one set of bosses with another set that holds a different doctrine but possesses the same consciousness, the same mode of personal being. Without transformation of the person, there is only the endless chain of injustice and revenge for injustice. The new politician, with his or her being as well as with actions, helps break the chain.

❧

Old Age. The plight of our "senior citizens" (and the condescension in that term) provides not only a preview of our future but a glimpse into our present. A society that values its individuals chiefly as components in the social machinery finds little to value when their efficiency as components wanes. In T George Harris's words, "As life drains away, only the neuroses remain." We look for neither wisdom nor joy in these discarded components, these walking neuroses, and we try to forget that what remains in them at the end of life also lies at the core of those of us who are younger, beneath all the motion and grabbing. The guardians of the dead civilization value "senior citizens," but only to the extent of their conservatism. Convincing old people that their enemies are hippies, black militants and others who criticize the established order is a neat trick indeed. Actually, the enemies of the old—inflation fueled by military spending, misleading merchandising, poor craftsmanship, planned obsolescence, impersonal and expensive medical care and the general depersonalization of human relations—are the enemies of other minority groups. But the old tend to go on voting their resentments rather than their own best interests. And we shun them, fearing to look fullface into our own dis-ease. We give them television and card games and bingo and, if they have stored away enough of the money they grabbed for, golf and escorted tours. And at the retirement communities the hearses slip in and out again during the hours between midnight and dawn so that the used-up bodies, at last, may be disposed of without anyone's noticing.

Such a shameful ending to life would be unthinkable in a fully transformed culture. Where the central values of existence are intrinsic rather than extrinsic, where being itself is admired, people would tend to grow wise with age. Where true learning (that is, *change*) is encouraged from earliest childhood, people would tend to be lifelong learners. Where the radiance of existence is not systematically dimmed through all the days and nights of our life, people would tend to become ever more radiant. We would grow old and bright. When the paraphernalia of daily existence became less important, when we could shed job, family responsibilities, mortgages and schedules like old skins, then only the glow of our inner vibrancy would remain. Young people would come near us, even on our deathbeds, to experience that pure glow and learn, in Blake's words, to bear the beams of love on this earth. And if these possibilities should seem unrealistic and impractical, I can only suggest you visit a senior citizens center or an old-age nursing home to see exactly where realistic measures and practical men have taken us.

Even now, in this world-between-worlds, we might expect something better at age sixty-five than the society sees fit to grant us. Why shouldn't we be sanctioned to become the glorious clowns of our communities? Why shouldn't we experiment with sexual variations, if that is our long-suppressed desire? Why shouldn't we, after being stuck for all these years in a single, alienating consciousness, engage in meditation and yoga and every manner of consciousness-changing activity? If there is a legitimate use for the psychedelic drugs, it is surely for the very old, so that even after a lifetime of brainwashing each of us may at last glimpse the infinite worlds that lie just outside the prison compound. As for me, transformed or not, I would like to be known in my final years as a singer and a dancer, a lover of children and picnics.

Journalists and scholars have commonly looked towards the young for evidence of social change. In coming years they had better turn to the old, to see if the change is real and lasting.

※

Drugs. The increase in drug usage in the United States may be seen as a symptom of a society in transition, a society in which the old values are dead and the new values are still unclear. But it is, in my view, a creature of Civilization, not of the Transformation. Drugs, even the "best" of them, eventually dull our senses and emotions and help us forget existence. Every drug, used long enough, is a downer. Cigarettes constrict the blood vessels, prevent the flow of feeling. Each challenge we meet, each moment of tension, provides us a heightened opportunity for growth and change. But the smoker passes it up. He reaches for his pack of cigarettes. His feelings are dulled and he does not have to deal with the tension. It remains there within him in the form of acid in the digestive system, spastic colon, surplus hormones in the blood, spasmed muscles, thickened lining of the vessels. The body becomes a sink of undischarged emotions. Medical researchers keep looking for specific chemical agents in tobacco smoke to account for each of the many ills it causes. They are not yet fully aware that nothing is deadlier than unexpressed feelings.

In a civilized component, feelings *must* be bottled up. Drugs help. Alcohol is a perfect drug of Civilization. It starts out by dilating the vessels and depressing some of the higher functions of the brain cortex, allowing a brief flight of relaxation and exhilaration, a certain sense of power and omniscience. Quickly, however, it brings its own punishment, demonstrating that you can't get away with pleasure. The liver is stunned, the brain dulled. Soon the continuing drinker feels less rather than more. Like the smoker, he is unable to deal with and discharge significant emotions. The hangover that follows is a precision instrument of civilized consciousness, a sort of condensed version of all the neuroses/diseases/discontents—the throbbing head, the ache behind the eyes, the nausea, the repulsion to all sensory experience, the vague anxiety, the pervasive sense of guilt. The hangover sufferer shrinks in disgust from his own body and being. What is there for him to do (unless he slips over into alcoholism) except to plunge himself back into his work, seeking expiation in robot-like busy-ness, repenting of joy, forgetting existence? Crime and punishment. A civilized morality play performed again and again in the theater of his body. No wonder Civilization can tolerate and even encourage a great deal of heavy drinking. The individuals lost to alcoholism are more than compensated for by the components saved from joy.

Most of the other drugs have the same ultimate function (reducing the connection between the individual psyche and the environment that lies within and without the skin) and the same ultimate effect (allowing undischarged emotions to build up and stagnate). Whether barbiturate, tranquilizer or psychic energizer, whatever the physiological mechanism, whatever the initial effect, the end result is the same. In the case of the hard narcotics, the opium derivatives, the user degenerates into the most rudimentary of components, dedicated to the repetitive and seemingly endless task of obtaining and administering the narcotic. Addiction is not only a sign of failure within the social organism but also a form of individual suicide, a cutting off of the self from the rest of the vibrancy.

Psychedelics present a special case. Occasional use of the mild psychedelic marijuana often appears to enhance perception, which is one reason the established order fears it. Continued heavy use, however, has the same dulling, deadening effect noted in the other drugs. The more powerful psychedelics—LSD, psilocybin, mescaline, and the like—could conceivably find a limited place in a transformed culture. As in some primitive cultures, these agents might be administered during certain significant ceremonies, rites of passage, to help shake up the perceptions. Such ceremonies would be sanctioned and participated in by family, friends, and other respected members of the community. This obviously would bear no resemblance to most current drug usage. A fifteen-year-old popping a pill and going off to the amusement park is such a waste and a perversion that it even makes the term "drug abuse" seem less prissy and punitive than usual. To be more precise, current drug usage is not just a waste and a perversion, it is an indictment of the lack of love and connectedness that characterizes this culture.

The initial, dazzling insights triggered by the psychedelics undoubtedly helped many people envisage alternatives to civilized consciousness. But the continued, careless use of the psychedelics, no less than other drugs, can only delay the Transformation. Without some larger human vision, LSD soon becomes as empty as competitive corporate striving. Actually, a transformed consciousness requires no drug whatever. Multitudinous, prismatic levels of consciousness are with us all the time, hidden behind, in William James's words, the filmiest of screens. I have enjoyed more startling perceptions through love, nature, aikido training, and group experiences than through psychedelics. Where heightened perceptions are sanctioned and reinforced by an effective social group, a drug generally can only get in the way of such perceptions.

A reduction in drug usage as we now know it may well be one of the signposts on the way towards Transformation. The drug problem will probably fade along with Civilization. But it will not fade because of friendly warnings and dire punishments by the established order. Recent television commercials against "drug abuse" offer young people a nondrug way of (in the words of the commercials) "turning on," and offer, for instance, defensive back Willie Brown of the Oakland Raiders as exemplar. Brown's way of turning on turns out to be intercepting a pass and running about eighty yards for a touchdown before tens of thousands of cheering fans. The commercial does not make clear how many young people can avail themselves of this alternative to drugs. Effective alternatives do exist, but they do not involve winning out over others.

The best alternative to drugs lies simply in not turning off young people in the first place.

None of this is to be read as a hard-line argument for total abstinence. We were born in Civilization. Sometimes Civilization's relentless pressures demand an easy amelioration. But we should be aware of what we are avoiding or delaying, even with a glass of good white wine: pain, yes, but also the best chance to be wide awake and fully alive, the best chance to try for one more precarious foothold on the climb towards the Transformation.

❧

Race. Even before the coming of Civilization, human beings had developed us-versus-them as a mechanism of social cohesion and control. Group prejudice probably predated racial prejudice. But now race stands out in high definition, a symbol of our hates and fears, a metaphor of the centrifugal forces that oppose joining and ecstasy. To the mind of Civilization, racial prejudice appears as a problem, an obstacle to change. It may also be viewed as an opportunity, as one of the most direct, if painful and abrasive, routes towards Transformation. The United States, in fact, has moved further into the Transformation than other countries partially because of its large black population—the crisis it has created, the behavior and consciousness it has changed.

Each time a person of one race confronts one of another, he may consider it an opportunity for self-examination. The loathing, rage, frustration, anxiety and guilt normally lodged deep within rise to the surface, tend to focus on the member of the other race. In 1967, Dr. Price Cobbs and I led the first marathon racial confrontation group. Since then, I have co-led several more; Dr. Cobbs, a black psychiatrist, has gone on to lead or supervise some three hundred racial confrontations and has carried out follow-up studies on the people involved. Cobbs and his colleagues have found no white without prejudice, no black without anger, and no person entirely free of self-deception. Race provides a powerful searchlight. It penetrates to the dark core of the civilized sickness. It illuminates individual neuroses. It makes obscure dialectics as sharp and clear as black and white. If the opportunity for confrontation is taken, what was hidden begins to become visible. What was numbed begins to hurt. The oppressed can turn his anger upon his oppressor rather than in-

195

ward to poison himself. The oppressor can express his guilt and fear of retaliation. He can recognize, through the oppressed, the spontaneity, the joy, even the ability to perceive reality that he has had to hide somewhere in the sterile suburb of his senses. Through pain and recognition, the most profound learning—that is, significant human change—can take place. In breaking through the many barriers made explicit by race, you break through all barriers to some extent.

It must be said, however, that it rarely happens this openly and directly in this society, for it requires communication on the level of emotions as well as intellect and is impeded by the pervasive rationalization usually practiced by obvious racist and liberal alike. And yet here in America—bit by bit, willy-nilly—the learning has been taking place. Unfortunately, perceptions sometimes are awakened only by explosions and fires, for the cry of the heart cannot reach those who sleep as if drugged. And it is sad that laws are needed to insure simple consideration and courtesy. I once asked Martin Luther King, Jr., if laws could change the human heart. "Laws can't change men's hearts," he told me, "but they can change men's behavior. When the behavior changes, the hearts may follow." It may seem a matter of regret that the awakening of perceptions so often increases the expression of prejudice. But feelings must be expressed in some way before they can be dealt with. The mere presence of large and increasingly vocal minorities in this country moves us towards change. Through the rage and fear and confusion, a music of Transformation is rising, blending European, African, Latin-American and Oriental in a peculiarly American way. Sometimes you can even hear it on Musak.

A bold and imaginative national leadership with a vision of human transformation could help speed the process. Just to give an example: If every high school and college in the nation spent the first month of next term doing nothing but confronting the matter of race, the amount of learning would far exceed anything now generally considered possible. What is more, the nation would be joined, at last, in a sense of common purpose that does not involve war and killing. Tremendous difficulties are involved in all plans of this scope and daring. Perhaps such things are simply impossible. But we will never know until we find leaders with vision enough to propose them seriously.

❦

Man and Woman. The two sexes are here on earth to remind us night and day of how living breathing things, no less than planets and suns, are drawn to join. The particular curve of a neck or bicep or breast that can set off a particular delight is also a notation in a grander equation, signifying that all duality is temporary. The joining of female and male becomes a parable of the continual re-creation of existence—the moments of our life bursting out of the void like a thunderclap or a sigh. Through all the centuries of repression, sex has provided a lifeline to ecstasy, making possible those hot, half-helpless Victorian daydreams ("The laughing leaves of the trees divide,/And screen from seeing and leave in sight/The god pursuing, the maiden hid"), and even surviving the plastic nudes of the magazine foldouts. Sex—the word itself probably derives from the Latin verb *secare*, "to cut or sever"—may seem to highlight separateness. But, optimally, man and woman, taken together, help us to perceive the distance between what we are and what we could be. Sex provides our poor eyes a safe glimpse of the ultimate unity, still too bright for us to bear.

And yet, in the Transformation, we shall probably relinquish "man" and "woman," those caricatures of sexuality that have developed during the reign of Civilization. The proponents of Women's Liberation are right. The traditional construct of man as hard, unfeeling, aggressive and conceptualizing, and woman as soft, yielding, nurturing and intuitive, insults male as well as female. Many of the reformers recognize that "liberation" will mean something quite different for both. Unfortunately, however, much of the society's reward system still works on the basis of competition, aggression and unfeelingness, and we are sometimes presented with the sad spectacle of "liberated" women becoming more like present-day males. Women today are even making inroads into the crime field, once an almost exclusive male territory; since 1960, the number of arrests of women has increased at a rate three times that of men.

Transcending our present, limiting sex roles may seem almost impossible, but it is no more difficult than simply living with our mates for as long as seven straight days with any assurance of harmony and personal growth. The problem of the man-woman relationship, about which so much has been theorized and so little understood, continues to resist rational solution. For most people, long-term marriage involves walling off one sensitive area after another and doing all that is possible to numb those areas of feeling that cannot be entirely walled off. Opening these areas, becoming sensitive to what was numb, provides an always painful and often joyful period of renewal and learning. But long-term openness and encounter also seem to have their limits, escalating rapidly until there are not hours enough in the day to reveal all the increasingly subtle and finally esoteric resentments and difficulties involved in living together in Civilization.

We may at last have to admit that there is no satisfactory answer to the man-woman puzzle in the present paradigm. The answer most likely lies somewhere beyond "man" and "woman." This means just what it says. It means dispensing with what now seems most indispensable. It means peeling off layer after layer of the man-ness and woman-ness wrapped around us by Civilization until we discover the essential humanity at the core. What, then, will we have lost?

In our distant past, our life in the wilds may have required lasting pair-bonding to assure care for our slow-maturing young. Agriculture increased the need for fast breeding and large families. Now these tendencies work against us, creating overpopulation and a tight little vacuum-packed family. We need fewer children and bigger, less well-defined families. We need groups of friends and neighbors who are willing and able to share the strongest feelings, to share responsibility for all the children in the group.

During the Civilized Epoch with its wars and empires and physical frontiers, we needed men who would not yield, would not feel, would not weep. But it has turned out that we have no more Vietnams or Lake Eries to spare for the John Wayne-type male.

In a world of work and human components, we needed to hold erotic impulses on a short leash, thus helping to create the dis-ease so necessary for the central tasks of Civilization. But now this work is coming to an end and we must learn to play.

In a world of no "men" and no "women," everything will be erotic and what is erotic will not necessarily be sexual in any way we now recognize as such. The "polymorphous perversity" described by Freud and recently given differing but equally brilliant explications by Herbert Marcuse and Norman O. Brown is perverse only to certain civilized sensibilities. To many people, directing the erotic impulse only towards members of the opposite sex at certain times, under certain conditions, with certain parts of the body and in certain physical positions seems perverse indeed. Though the true gravity between male and female will continue to guide us as the clearest objectification of this impulse in human form, we may yet become aware of that fine yearning of all-that-is for all-that-is. We may learn to blend what we now consider physical and spiritual love so that there remains between the two no final distinction. This promises neither more nor less of what we now term "sexual" acts. It does mean that such acts will be both more important and less fraught with tension. Eternal delight, after all, is nothing special. The end of "man" and "woman" opens the way for the eventual creation of a family as wide as all humankind, that can weep together, laugh together, and share the common ecstasy.

In such a family, what is not incestuous? Indeed, the incest taboo as we in the West have come to know it provides a good example of our blindness and confusion on sexual matters. We have been led to assume that this taboo is universal, whereas, in fact, some societies (for example, the Hopis of North America, the Nuers of Africa, the Caribs of the Caribbean, and Lugbaras of the South Seas) have no formal sanctions against incest, while in some others (notably in Persia and Egypt) incestuous marriage was widely practiced. In Egypt, sibling incest became so common that by the second century A.D. two-thirds of the citizens of Arsinoë indulged in it; the words *brother* and *sister* in Egyptian poetry have the meaning of lover and beloved. Mythology both East and West is filled with cases of propitious incest, and there is an earlier version of the Oedipus story in which the hero goes unpunished. In our own direct mythic lineage, Adam and Eve's children must have been incestuous to have populated the world.

Western theorists have never agreed upon the reasons behind the taboo. In 1940, Lord Raglan compiled a list of seventeen well-known theories for explaining the prohibitions against incest. (Examples: "Because such marriages are sterile.—Pope Gregory I." "Because marriages within the family would be without love.—Luther." "Because such marriages would lead to excessive love within the family.—Aristotle, Saint Chrysostom.") All the reasons offered are incomplete or wrong, including the argument that offspring of such relationships are likely to be weak in mind or body. Inbreeding is not necessarily deleterious. And even if you would extrapolate from animal to human, the prohibition against it cannot be said to come from our biological roots; in all of man's animal ancestry, only the Canadian goose and possibly the rhesus monkey are known to avoid inbreeding. Some societies encourage marriage between close cousins while others, including our own, prohibit marriage with certain in-laws and step-relatives. The taboo is thus by no means tied to blood kinship.

The most compelling explanation for the evolution of the taboo in primitive times has to do with a quite practical concern. Exogamy—that is, "marrying out"—is the best and generally the only way a primitive bandsman or tribesman has of forging alliances and obtaining extra hands for the hunt or the harvest. *Not* to marry out would be madness and possibly suicide. The taboo is thus firmly grounded in a reality of primitive life.

In a civilized state, however, marrying out of the "tribe" is rarely possible except in the case of the ruling class, and there it often has served the same function as in primitive societies. And yet, as Civilization has advanced, the taboo against incest has survived and increased in severity. It is true that, in the simplest Freudian terms, mother-son incest would threaten the stability of the family ruled by an authoritarian father. And other sex relationships would probably exacerbate the jealousy and discord within the sort of family we are familiar with. But none of this explains the continual widening of the definition of incest to include, for example, laws in fifteen of our states against marriage with the wife's step-granddaughter. Nor does it account for the severity of the penalties for incest in civilized society.

Here in the West, where the incest taboo is at its very strongest, we may be able to view it primarily as one of the more powerful mechanisms for inculcating dis-ease. The inevitable elemental yearning to come close, to fondle, to join is vitiated from the start. In many families, the "dangerous" areas of a child's body are never touched, never mentioned. It is as if they do not exist. Where there could be sweetness there is something dead, or sometimes a painful knifeblade of lust rising out of emptiness. The normal longing for mother, sister, brother, father is coated over with shame. How, then, can any longing ever after achieve innocence? And yet the taboo is violated again and again. Accurate statistics on this matter are hard to come by, but it is clear that incest is far more common in our "advanced" society than we have been led to believe.

The flowering of the Transformation will probably bring with it a progressive erosion of the incest taboo. This does not mean the advent of brother-sister marriages; marriage will not be the dominant factor in the new sexuality. The conventional incest taboos may fall quietly, almost unnoticed. As humanity comes closer to a true unity, a unity of being no less than of politics, sexual barriers will simply be ignored. The exogamy of the Transformation will not involve marrying-out to other "tribes" but reaching-out to all beings, to members of other races and language groups, to previously excluded age and sex groups, and even to members of the immediate family. The sexual "act" will not be defined as separate from the rest of life. All of life will become erotic and what is erotic will become commonplace. Recognizing that all bodies are part of the same field, ultimately one, we shall not hesitate to touch what is really ourselves. Someday, perhaps tomorrow, we shall think of human individuals scurrying through life avoiding every significant touching, even eye contact, as being grotesque and terribly sad. We shall emerge from "man" and "woman," those cocoons spun by five thousand years of Civilization, spread new wings, and begin life as human beings at last.

※

War. Civilization is impossible without major war. Because of nuclear weapons, major war is impossible. Ergo, Civilization is impossible.

The syllogism may leave room for argument. But do not leave it quickly.

We cannot talk about the end of war without first singing its praises. That war is a necessary element in civilized society, a prime organizing device of the state, need not be argued here. (Among other books, *Report from Iron Mountain*, purporting to be the proceedings of a high-level secret strategy meeting, makes an ironic and chilling exposition of the many social and cultural functions served by civilized warfare.[3]) War is a social necessity. It is also something more. For a citizenry numbed of sense and deprived of emotion, war provides a blessed opportunity to hope, to fear, to exult, to suffer—for God's sake—to *feel.* When the war alarms go out, young men and old are drawn to the stirring of a lost memory. *What is it I've forgotten? Ah, now I remember. My own existence.* The real promise of war is not that we may gain some glorious prize but that we may lose everything. Our lives, our honor. Our flag in the mud, our city in ashes, our women raped. In what other circumstances can we truly do our best, give our all for friends, for others we do not know, for a noble cause?

And without war how can we have those epic movies? (Beneath his helmet, John Wayne's eyes are slits. His mouth is a slit. "Gentlemen, we didn't come all this way to sit on our tails. We're movin' up that road. Tonight.") Without war, the memory of war and the anticipation of war, a good third of our literature would lose its meaning entirely. The obligatory pre-battle scene (the common soldiers solemn-faced, grasping their relics, talking of home; the officers heavy with decision, quietly philosophical) is hardly a cinematic invention. The script is etched in our brain, going back in our direct lineage through

Shakespeare at least to Homer. It is not something we can easily relinquish.

In war Civilization thrives. Sometimes, in fact, the numbness of dis-ease is scrubbed away and we exist for a moment in the clean vibrancy, not just during the great battles but all around the edges of danger. I landed in my first combat zone, a staging area in New Guinea, at twilight of a spring·day in 1945 after what then seemed an epic flight across the Pacific. The friend who had flown with me and I were disoriented from lack of sleep and the strangeness of the surroundings: the devastated tropical landscape, the peculiar cast of the soldiers' skin, turned bright yellow by an antimalaria drug. Darkness came suddenly, before we had received our tent assignment. Struggling with all our luggage, we started searching for one tent among hundreds on a plateau lit only by scattered gasoline lanterns. Suddenly, there was a jangling of triangles, an alarm signal. All the lights were extinguished. We dropped our luggage and were swept up in a crowd of men running through the darkness. The situation struck us as hysterically funny. We managed to ask why we were running and where we were going. Someone said, "To the cliff." Repeating, "To the cliff!" we ran on, stumbling, laughing, gasping for breath. By the time we reached our destination, I had lost my friend. Helped by someone I could not see, I managed to grope my way over the rounded top of the cliff and onto a natural platform a few feet down. I cannot recall ever having experienced so dark a night; the cloud cover must have been thousands of feet thick. Down below I could make out only the faintest ghostly images of the surf, but the sound of it rose clearly and soothingly, soon joined by the murmur of voices on either side.

I discovered I was sharing a sort of crevice in the edge of the cliff with one other person. He explained that a serious bombing raid was not likely. We were probably being harassed by "Washing Machine Charlie," a single Japanese plane that would circle high overhead to disturb our sleep. We would probably be there an hour or so. My hilarity had quite subsided. I was relaxed but wide awake. There was room to sit, so I made myself comfortable and settled into the experience—the aliveness of the earth, the roll of the surf, the splendid darkness, the gentle talk floating in the dark air. My companion began telling me of his life in a midwestern city. I could not see him, but his voice seemed to convey an unfamiliar power and sense of presence. He was married and had two young daughters. He had been working as a night watchman, trying to pay his way through school. There was never enough money. He explained to me what it was like not being able to buy his wife and daughters what they needed. A sort of rhythm developed and his words entered me like music. Memory is selective and perhaps faulty, but I now hear him saying things that were prophetic. I had no way of knowing then—I was an unmarried, inexperienced twenty-one—that much of what he talked about would someday have immediate meaning for me: how much he missed telling his little girls goodnight, the smell of their hair and the feel of their arms around his neck, his sexual difficulties with his wife, his fear that she was being unfaithful to him while he was so many thousand miles, so helpless, away from her. The situation became almost unbearably intimate. I began to feel I knew this unseen stranger better than anyone I had ever met. The all-clear sounded, and we separated. I never saw his face. He remains a disembodied voice representing the intense connectedness that is rarely available as the days and nights of peace slip past us.

I went on to fly missions that were neither as dramatic nor dangerous as I had been led to hope for. I felt no particular enmity or aggressiveness towards "the enemy." I made and deepened friendships that still survive. When squadron mates were shot down, I joined in the rush to take possession of their unused shaving cream and hair tonic. Never before or since have I slept so soundly or dreamed so pleasantly as during the one month I flew twenty-two strafing missions and amassed nearly a hundred hours of combat time.

For most of those involved, of course, war is hardly so painless. Flying is a removal from dirt and blood. In the end, war is always ugly and dirty and painful and obscene. But we tend to forget that for a majority of people in a nation a great war has usually provided a heightening of experience, a punctuation mark of drama in a lifetime of routine numbness, an occasion for renewing our epic sense.

The Vietnam War has been different. It has become a powerful antidote to glory and perhaps an inoculation against war itself, coming just at a time of widespread awakening of consciousness in this country. The length and futility of this misadventure has helped focus our attention on the ugliness. We may also find a sign of some human transformation, some increase in our sensitivity, in the fact that certain practices not so much condoned as simply ignored in previous conflicts now rise to outrage us. And the sensibility that perceives a war correspondent's detachment as grotesque is by no means a conventional civilized sensibility.

But in spite of the inoculation provided by Vietnam, in spite of increasing national sensitivity to war's horrors, in spite of the fact that all-out war is now "impossible," war and the threat of war continue to hang over our lives. War takes precedence over domestic problems for underdeveloped nations in which millions starve to death every year. War remains as a major option for our own national leaders, supported by an enormous establishment that commands vast resources of money, material, energy and information. These men have tough-minded, practical objections to peacefulness. What would happen, they ask, if we let our guard down and the *others* didn't? They argue that if we do not continue urging our young men, in effect, towards criminal behavior, then those *other* yellow-black-brown-red criminals will come over in hordes and destroy us. Their fear is not entirely paranoid. We would be fooling ourselves to discount aggressive impulses in other civilized states. But it is clear that our own aggressiveness does much to fan the flames.

If a deeply felt, positive will towards peacefulness were present in our national leadership, this nation—master of the most powerful machine of destruction in the history of the planet—could do much to end war. It could make its will known to the world through the usual diplomatic, treaty-making channels. In addition, it could act unilaterally through various imaginative and dramatic means. Not the least of these would be treating every move towards disarmament—dismantling a major foreign base, closing an ABM site, retiring a warship—as an occasion for celebration. These celebrations would be truly festive events, to which representatives of all nations would be invited, accompanied by music and dancing and the best of the arts, described to all the world through every possible medium of communications. The moral force of such celebrations, if a true expression of our own leadership, would be considerable.

Unfortunately, such occasions would seem funerals rather than festivals to far too many of the men who lead us. To help end war, our leaders would have to *want* to give up war, to give up their esoteric underground war rooms, their secret briefings, their hands on the pulse of destructive power, the possibility of great sacrifice and great achievement through violence, and the attendant renewal of their sense of existence. We must face it. Within the framework of Civilization and in the light of our present unambitious, uninspiring goals, there is nothing to take war's place. Pro football is not the moral equivalent of war, even if the President himself can call the plays.

Opposing war by writing letters, signing petitions, voting for the present breed of peace candidates, engaging in marches, and committing civil disobedience can be quite useful. But it is doubtful that a momentous surge towards true peacefulness can occur until some great enterprise not involving war becomes clear to us. The transformation of the social order into new forms and the commensurate transformation of human beings into what amounts to a higher species certainly constitute such an enterprise. The tingling sense of aliveness that would be sanctioned and inculcated by a transformed society would make it unnecessary for us to remember existence through the memory, anticipation or actuality of battle. And the sweeping reforms implied in the search for a new human nature would make war seem less than epic. To empty our prisons, create a new education and a new politics, end racism, provide a decent minimum living standard for every inhabitant, open the possibilities of meaning and joy for old people, make every city a festival and the entire country a garden is, for a start, enough to engage our energy and aspiration, our enormous unused capability.

※

Energy and Information. We who live on this planet have been granted vast amounts of energy from the sun, and a bit more from the tides and the lingering heat within the earth. In addition, we have at last mastered the alchemy that extracts energy directly from matter. How we use and influence all this energy ultimately defines our society and our selves. We have only to open our eyes—an act requiring no small courage in this case—to realize that we are nearing a great turning point in the way we manipulate energy. This alone promises social and human transformation. At no other point in this writing am I so tempted to drop everything and devote the years of study that this subject demands for a full and expert treatment. But, we cannot expect experts who have spent long years developing a single specialty to initiate discussions of the intricate linkup between, say, electric power and the human soul.

Electricity indeed may serve us as a starting point in understanding the human crisis that is upon us. Since the beginning of the decade we have been treated to full-page advertisements proclaiming the fact that Americans will double their consumption of electric power in the next ten years, and that the producers of such power must double their production to meet the demand. The tone is dogmatic. Nothing is said about the desirability of the doubling. It is presented as an inevitable fact of our existence.

Let us accept the message of the advertisements and carry it further. It is probably true that the United States will generate as much electricity during the next ten years as it has previously generated in all its history. If this awesome growth rate continues —and much of our economy is based on its doing just that—the same thing will happen the *next* ten years, and so on. For the sake of argument, let's assume that technology solves the problems of air and water pollution. Let's also stretch our imagination and assume that the power plants of the future will be located far out to sea, so that the waste heat of nuclear reaction or fossil fuel burning can be disposed of (for a while anyway) in the surrounding ocean. When the electricity is consumed here on the mainland, however, it will turn into heat in any case. Bearing all this in mind, let's see what would happen if the message in the ads continued to be the same, decade after decade. According to electrical engineer Claude M. Summers:

> In 1970 the U.S. consumed 1,550 billion kilowatt hours of electricity. If this were degraded into heat (which it was) and distributed evenly over the total land area of the U.S. (which it was not), the energy released per square foot would be .017 watt. At the present doubling rate electric-power consumption is being multiplied by a factor of 10 every 33 years. Ninety-nine years from now, after only 10 more doubling periods, the rate of heat release will be 17 watts per square foot, or only slightly less than the 18 or 19 watts per square foot that the U.S. receives from the sun, averaged around the clock.[4]

Obviously we cannot bear the heat of approximately two suns shining upon us. We must and shall change our pattern of power production and consumption long before such a cataclysm overtakes us. The above case, as a matter of fact, is strictly hypothetical, since technical factors will stop electric power doubling, probably before A.D. 2000. But it clearly illustrates the ultimate weakness in any human order based on endless expansion in the realms of physical energy. There are other restraints that will be felt much sooner; catastrophes may grow from air or water pollution or from radiation accidents. And we have not yet even considered the problem of waste heat, the disposal of which already requires 10 percent of America's rivers and streams.

The most promising technological alternatives to overheating the world now seem to lie in the development of invariant energy systems; that is, generators that absorb as much of the sun's energy as they release, thus adding no heat to the earth. Such systems might involve harnessing the wind (which is ultimately created by solar energy) or collecting the sun's radiant energy directly. The latter could entail covering large areas of our land surface with solar heat collectors. If, for example, all the sunlight falling on 14 percent of our western deserts were efficiently collected, it could produce the additional electricity needed, according to present projections, between now and 1990. But no such system has yet been developed, and even the most ideal invariant system now on the horizon would soon fall behind the demands of the current doubling rate. Converting to energy systems that somehow bypassed electricity would not solve the problem; heat would still be released in doing the kind of work our present culture deems useful.

I am unwilling to discount the most startling scientific or technological breakthroughs, even to the creation of antigravity or antiheat devices. And I feel that we shall undoubtedly find uses for modes of energy unmeasurable on present-day scientific instruments. Such breakthroughs, however, would have their own startling effects on human consciousness and would probably render much of our current culture obsolete. The point I am making is that unless we find ways around the most basic physical laws (the Second Law of Thermodynamics, for example) our expansionist way of life, dealing as it does primarily with physical matter and heat energy, is utterly doomed. The Thermal Barrier stands beyond the full-page ads, beyond the ever-rising lines on the economic charts, beyond all the talk of ever-increasing competition with other nations. Whether or not we envisage human transformation, we must start thinking differently about energy.

The flow of energy in a human society is regulated by information. Information is also energy, if only a fraction of that which it regulates. It takes only a tiny bit of energy for a Pharaoh to order a pyramid built. But the information in that order controls vast amounts of energy. The same thing is true when you supply information, via the starter and throttle, that sets your car in motion.

We may go a step further and look upon energy of any sort as information. The equation describing the transformation of energy from order to disorder (entropy) in terms of heat is quite similar to the equation describing the transformation of what we perceive as information to "noise." Only human consciousness can supply the terms of these transformations, and it is in terms of consciousness that the entire system becomes one.

The intimate relationship, the ultimate oneness, of matter and energy has been well established. The oneness of energy and information becomes clearer every day. The equations describing the oneness of all this with human consciousness remain to be formulated. Perhaps we can find clues in the type of information we call money.

Money as a symbol of commercial value developed, as we have seen in Chapter 4, when societies expanded beyond the bounds of blood or totemic kinship. Thus it first served as a substitute for kin-ness, *kindness*. Even now we note that money and kin do not mix smoothly; financial dealings with immediate family members often take on a painful emotional tone that is rare outside the family. Money helped join larger and larger, increasingly impersonal social groups. Serving to span time and space, it came to be fashioned from the most changeless metals. Coins of silver and gold are unlike flesh and blood and breath. The grave does not corrupt them. They spill forth after centuries to remind us of the shining dreams of Pharaohs and Zapotec chieftains.

For thousands of years, money was exchanged primarily for material goods. Until around the middle of the seventeenth century, labor was generally not for sale; work was regulated by tradition or command. The medieval craftsman made shoes because his father made shoes. The serf tilled the soil at his owner's behest. Money measured energy only indirectly. The association of money with stable matter reached a climax in the sixteenth and seventeenth centuries when the Bullionists measured national wealth almost entirely in terms of the amount of precious metals on hand. But gold was too ponderous for the free-swinging capitalist market economy that rose up in the eighteenth century.

Since then, money has gradually become a direct measure of energy as well as matter. The exploitation of fossil fuel, the development of the steam engine, the internal combustion engine, the jet engine and the rocket have demonstrated the magical powers of fire. In the United States, energy consumption has multiplied some thirty times since 1850, when wood supplied more than 90 percent of the energy we consumed. The usual piecemeal financial indicators of the 1930s were inadequate to measure the state of prosperity in the industrial nations that controlled all this energy. In 1941, the American economist Simon Kuznets published his huge study, *National Income and Its Composition 1919 to 1938*, out of which came the concept of Gross National Product. The GNP, essentially a statement of the market value of a nation's production of goods and services over a one-year period, soon became the favorite instrument for measuring the level of economic well-being. It is a measure of activity. *It tells us nothing about the desirability or quality of the activity.* Since the GNP correlates rather well with energy consumption, we may perceive it as a measure of national heat.

According to the GNP, when material things deteriorate quickly, are junked or destroyed, our prosperity may seem to increase. A. W. Clausen, president of The Bank of America, points out that almost any natural calamity can create a GNP bonanza. "An earthquake like the one in Los Angeles in 1971 can wipe out millions of dollars of physical assets. Yet, because labor is paid and materials purchased to rebuild the community, the result is a GNP rise even though the renovation may never be able to match the assets destroyed." [5] The United States heroin trade, involving the theft, "redistribution," and replacement of billions of dollars' worth of goods a year, is an excellent tonic for the Gross National Product. Up until the time of the Vietnam debacle, war or the threat of war also served to fatten the GNP, which has always displayed a strange yearning for the destruction of things. Indeed, some of the most closely watched financial indicators of our time—the Dow Jones Average, for example—have only a tenuous connection with material things. They have a much closer connection to people's anticipations about what sections of our economy are heating up. Present-day money not only links itself mainly to energy, but also specializes in high-entropy energy, that is, energy that entails the release of large amounts of heat.

Actually, money can serve as information either about the

creation of things or the destruction of things. Money can measure anything we want it to measure. If a social consensus exists, a person can be paid for the beauty of his aura. Already, as Alvin Toffler has pointed out, people are willing to pay money not just for manufactured goods or even ordinary services but for "experiences." The GNP itself reveals anomalies. The overall growth rate in the United States seems to be slowing down, in spite of those projections of ever-doubling power consumption. And as early as 1965 a full 34 percent of the GNP consisted of educational or informational activities. That percentage is steadily rising. As the Transformation proceeds, it is likely that money will continue to transfer its allegiance from gross burning to the low-entropy energy of human consciousness. A human being who lives in elegant simplicity, sitting in the meditation position, enjoying a condition of *satori*, represents low-entropy energy in the extreme. For large numbers of people to engage in such activities would not involve a renunciation of all technology (a common mistake of some radical futurists), but a refinement of technology towards simplicity and economy. It would not involve bypassing money, but broadening and clarifying the nature of the stuff measured by money until at last money and human consciousness coexist in balanced harmony.

Just as that which money measures is becoming less material, money itself is tending towards etherialization. Heavy metal has become paper. And now paper is rapidly being converted to dancing electrons moving at the speed of light through the wires and airways and computers of the planet. The electronic money of a cashless society is hardly something a rich man can take to his grave. Even more transient than flesh and blood and breath, it resembles nothing so much as consciousness itself. If this new money can float free of its lingering ritual relationship with metal, if it can realize a new affinity for low-entropy energy rather than smoke and fire, if it can pulse freely across all the world, not becoming dammed up in the overdeveloped nations only, then it may well become a powerful medium indeed for linking the planet in a common consciousness.

There is reason to hope that money akin to consciousness cannot long mediate the destruction of consciousness. Indeed, the present economic paradigm is shot through with anomalies that can only foreshadow its death. While people go hungry in cold buildings, the economy keeps its heat up by spewing out retractable headlights, electric can openers, and packages worth more than the commodity they contain—items that must be sold whether or not people want or need them. Extravagant air conditioning keeps power plants operating at high polluting levels. The high pollution creates further demand for air conditioning.

Wasteful consumption is mirrored in wasteful thought and action. Human particles bounce from place to place in a sort of Brownian motion just to keep the heat level high. Even so, the system begins to fail. Inflation continues along with recession and rising unemployment. How can this be in a competitive market? The secret is already out. The hardheaded men who proclaim competition as a religion actually engage in less and less of it every day. They conspire, in many conscious and unconscious ways, to hold prices up, to expand production even in the absence of any real increase in demand. They do not serve demand. They serve dis-ease. They conceive no other way to occupy their years on earth. They fear to look at the figures on their own charts. They hold their tongues when a self-styled free-enterprise, conservative President opts for wage and price controls.

The economy can probably be heated up a few more times. But the end of our present way of dealing with energy and information is in sight now. Economists and engineers, entrepreneurs and state socialists alike failed to foresee the pollution crisis, much less the Thermal Barrier that stands like a guardian angel against our depredations of the flesh and spirit. Those exponential curves of "inevitable" growth may change their direction sooner than we now imagine, inscribing graceful "S" forms on the economic charts. This "S-ing out," this ending of growth for its own sake, will be fiercely resisted, for it signals the end of a way of life. The same men who must believe that criminality is inevitable must believe that endless economic growth is inevitable. To those who have never tasted the joys of intrinsic being, any limits on production and consumption must be threatening. Just at the time that competition is dying out, we hear the most passionate glorification of competition. Just as exponential growth ends, we hear it justified in the most reasonable and indeed humane arguments: "We must have growth to fight poverty, to create jobs. Pollution be damned."

In terms of the old economic paradigm the argument is correct, but only in the short view. The problem remains. We cannot long continue to expand our energy consumption in the United States at anywhere near the present rate. Yet we cannot now make any major move towards a lower per-capita consumption without severe economic dislocation. *Severe economic dislocation is thus inevitable*. Here is a situation that calls for biting the bullet in the best John Wayne tradition. The courageous and responsible leader will articulate the forbidden truth. He will inform the electorate that the economic paradigm based on endless growth and full employment *in the old sense* is doomed, that we must find new ways of distributing energy and also new ways of thinking about energy. We must summon all our ingenuity to reduce consumption and waste. We must go beyond ingenuity, calling upon our best sense of common consciousness and human concern, to take those steps that will guarantee a modest subsistence for every person, regardless of job status. Doing this with a stable GNP will undoubtedly mean a significant reduction of external living standards for those who are now among the "favored."

But the current quality of life with its frantic consumption, hectic movement, pollution and dis-ease may seem a small loss indeed against the rewards of a new, fully awakened existence. Here I must stress that I am not calling for an economy or a psychology of scarcity. The realms of intrinsic experience are endless and the riches to be found there are practically without limit. No adventurer could hope for more. Once the new joys are known to large numbers of people, the inevitable economic dislocation ahead of us may be taken as the opportunity for a humane relocation of our priorities and a re-definition of abundance.

Our present taxing system, for example, encourages every activity that thrusts us towards a catastrophic breakdown. It rewards, among other things, large families, impersonal incorporation, business expansion, fast fossil fuel exploitation, rapid depreciation, waste, loss and movement across the face of the earth. In addition, it creates a large, complex, expansive bureaucracy that is itself paradigmatic of the society it helps perpetuate. It invites legalistic resistance, petty cheating and outright fraud. A new economic paradigm will involve a simple, fair tax system tuned to a new way of life.

Such a system might continue to tax incomes at approximately the same percentage rate now prescribed, but would remove practically every single exception presently granted. It would reduce the tax on property and on all stable matter. It would raise additional revenue by means of a transactional heat tax. According to this plan, every monetary transaction would be taxed at the point of transaction. The tax would be scaled to reflect the prorated amount of heat released by the activity involved in the transaction. For example, when a steel manufacturer buys iron ore, the price includes a tax on the heat released during the mining and transportation of the ore. The ore producer collects the tax and pays it to the government. When a car manufacturer buys steel, the price includes a tax on the amount of heat released in the production and transportation of the steel. When a car dealer buys a finished car, the price includes a tax on the amount of heat released in the manufacture and transportation of the car. When a consumer buys a car, the price includes a tax on the amount of heat released in the process of selling the car. The car's purchase price, of course, reflects the preceding taxes indirectly. Though the heat tax on each transaction would be relatively small, the total tax on a large automobile would be quite high.

In a quite different case, when an individual pays for a music lesson, the price includes the amount of heat released by this activity—obviously very little. If the lesson were a private transaction between individuals, no tax would be collected. Transacactions involving secondhand goods would be, for the most part, tax exempt. Power sources—gas, electricity, coal—would be highly taxed.

The transactional heat tax would best be collected at a national level, since heat release is a national (actually worldwide) problem, and since many transactions cross state lines. It would involve some form of revenue sharing with state and local governments. The exponential heat scale would not apply to necessities such as food and essential services, nor would it preclude additional penalties on specific pollution-creating activities.

Such a tax plan would encourage efficiency and simplicity in manufacturing, marketing and distribution, since every middleman, every step along the way, would involve an additional tax, and since inefficiency of any sort almost always shows up eventually in the form of heat. Indeed, by taxing heat itself we would be encouraging the development and use of low-entropy energy akin to consciousness in its purest state. An armor-plated, oversized, overpowered automobile would be taxed repeatedly and heavily as it came into being. A training course in the enhancement of consciousness would be taxed hardly at all.

Like all other tax plans, this one contains many difficulties. Working them out could be a redeeming activity. The national heat-release inventory needed for this plan eventually will have to be done in any case.

Some of those who call for a transformed consciousness seem to believe that we can bypass money completely. Perhaps this will someday be possible. But even if what we now call money were junked, some analogous medium of information would be required to mediate the transactions of the society. The money-information system of this planet holds a potential for sublime order that we had best not overlook. It would probably take a visitor from another world to remind us of the beauty and grand sweep of the money system as it already exists.

The Transformation promises a more highly organized society than does Civilization and thus requires not less but more communication. Rather than bypassing money, a transformed society may well expand and reform the transactions money mediates and add to it the element of kin-ness that it has lacked throughout the Civilized Epoch. Money may eventually provide for us a single, well-modulated scale for consciousness, information, energy and matter based upon their ultimate oneness. And then, wonder of wonders, every monetary transaction may become an act of love and transformation.

The Transformation will not, cannot, be without a technology. We shall have food, shelter, clothing, communications, transportation, and inner and outer space programs. But we cannot have purposeful inefficiency and waste, nòr can we afford to spend the bulk of our federal revenues for "defense." We may be moving into an era of retrenchment in terms of burning, hoarding and wasting. But we may also foresee an era of affluence in terms of existence. The human urge for exploration and development will turn from physical growth and energy consumption to areas which (lacking an adequate vocabulary) we now call mystical. Along with the development of electrical energy, we can develop the energy associated with our bodies and beings that the Hindus call *kundalini*. Along with jet and rocket flight, we can seek to fly, as Edgar Mitchell and Charles Lindbergh have suggested, by means of something akin to astral projection.

Recognizing that we are in the process of transforming ourselves into a higher species, we can focus our best efforts on this historic and all-absorbing goal. We shall need instrumentalities already developing in such diverse fields as biology, biophysics and bio-feedback; in education, psychology and astrophysics. It seems certain that in this enterprise philosophy and religion will be revivified and return to their central places in our lives. No field of endeavor can long remain untouched. We may even look forward to a modern literature, a drama and a cinema based not entirely on degradation, alienation and despair. The death of Civilization is a large event, having its own dynamics and inevitabilities. The transformation of humanity into a new species is even larger.

❦

But all of this draws too sharp distinctions. Now that most of us are totally dependent on others, many others, not only for luxuries and fuel and electricity, but also for food and water and pure air itself, how can we go on pretending we are not sisters and brothers, one consciousness, one flesh? And how can we suppose that all which exists, tree and stone and book and star, is not also one and somehow alive?

We exist as the unfolding of a flower, heedless and unaware of our source. We perceive in space and time alone, separated from God only by our inability to perceive that which we are. We sleep unquietly. But the awakening will come, in pain and in joy.

twelve

The Pain and Joy of the Change

When I came home: on the abyss of the five senses, where a flat sided steep frowns over the present world, I saw a mighty Devil folded in black clouds, hovering on the sides of the rock: with corroding fires he wrote the following sentence now perceived by the minds of men, & read by them on earth:

How do you know but ev'ry Bird that cuts the airy way, Is an immense world of delight, clos'd by your senses five?

—WILLIAM BLAKE, THE MARRIAGE OF HEAVEN AND HELT

☙

"We've eliminated grades and compulsory attendance and exams and the kids can go play Ping-pong any time they want to. So my question is, Why doesn't our school have ecstasy?"

—QUESTION FROM THE FLOOR DURING LECTURE ON EDUCATION

IN THE mid- and late- 1960s, the dissatisfaction with education that often smolders just beneath the surface of American national consciousness erupted once again. For a few brief years, outrage and hope were blended in equal proportions. A number of critics wrote passionately of the anachronistic, inefficient situation in the typical classroom, where one teacher presents information to twenty-five or more children at the same rate, affording them little opportunity for response. The generally drab and repressive atmosphere in the schools was described as stifling emotional and intellectual development. The emphasis on testing, grading, units, courses and required attendance was characterized as antithetical to the spirit of learning. At the same time, innovative educational environments began springing up in storefronts, old churches and townhouses, or on the campuses of established institutions. Many of these "free schools" still are thriving, while new ones continue to appear. The movement towards a less repressive, more fluid, more joyful education has also touched many teachers and administrators within the system, who have quietly modified their practices. The most significant changes wrought by the movement are those you never hear about.

And yet it must be said that many experimental schools have failed with a swiftness and impact that shocked their founders, while some of them have merely traded one sort of drabness for another. Such failures must be viewed as part of the evolutionary process. Before the emergence of the first successful air-breathing organism, many millions died gasping for oxygen in the mud. The first successful airplane was preceded by thousands of fruitless dreams and hundred of crashes. The very fact that the desire for social and cultural change rises again and again in the face of a high failure rate is evidence of the evolutionary urge that resides in existence itself.

We bear the responsibility, however, to reduce the failure rate as much as is possible within the power of consciousness and will. There are lessons in the failures of some innovative schools that we can perhaps apply to other aspects of social and cultural change.

Many of the founders of these schools were not at first aware of the difficulties involved. They did not appreciate the complex interlocking life support system that had been developed over the years by ongoing educational institutions. A number of imaginative and seemingly promising experiments ran up against insurmountable obstacles that are best expressed in institutional terms: zoning restrictions, fire code compliance, heating systems, student and faculty procurement, personnel practices, funding. It also turned out that most children, themselves products of the old methods, attitudes, assumptions and perceptions, could not move automatically from repression to ecstasy. Dis-ease-producing child rearing and school practices do indeed create dis-eased children. These children may express a desire for freedom and joy and yet be at a complete loss when presented the "opportunity" for freedom and joy.

Indeed, purely negative reform leads rather reliably to failure and disillusionment. The assumption behind negative reform goes like this: There are bad, repressive things in the traditional school, things such as exams, grades, group instruction, fixed seating and the like. All we really have to do is remove the bad things and then ecstatic education will flourish. But this is obviously and demonstrably untrue. Such things as exams and grades, no matter how oppressive, inefficient and antithetical to learning, do provide the glue and bailing wire that holds the old structure together. To remove them, it is necessary to put something in their place. Any attempt to create an environment with no reinforcement system at all can only lead to the growth of a hidden reinforcement system, dangerous because unacknowledged and unexamined. Some of those who attempt negative reform in education are motivated partly by a repulsion towards such aspects of the society at large as its obsession with cleanliness, punctuality and precision. Thus they consciously or unconsciously reinforce children towards dirtiness, tardiness and sloppiness. Disliking authority in any form, they covertly encourage rebelliousness and are surprised when the rebelliousness turns back against them. Their schools often become unpleasant places where children wander around wondering what not to do next.

In my book *Education and Ecstasy*, published in 1968, I imagined a school of the year 2001. Admittedly visionary, it was based entirely on positive change. The learning environments I described were designed to elicit intense and highly interactive behavior. The students were free to move at will from place to place, not just in reaction to traditional restrictiveness, but as a necessary condition for an improved educational environment. The school was created around a futuristic technology and social atmosphere. I hoped that my fantasy of the year 2001 would inspire readers to create their own educational reforms with the tools currently available. The several thousand letters I have received in response to the book reveal much inspiration, much frustration, and more than a few convincing accounts of success.

There is no question but that the success stories involve positive, not negative, reform. This agrees with firsthand observations and reports from other sources.

The quest for a new education, moreover, seems to have much in common with the quest for new organizational modes, new living patterns, new religions, and even new consciousness. All this social experimentation may be viewed as merely a symptom of the deeper transforming forces that underlie the entire culture. Free schools and communes affect the society at large rather less decisively than do the pervasive, almost invisible changes in its technology, economics and communications. Still, social experimentation stands out in high definition and does contain a certain amount of significant information, which may lead to the following generalizations.

Social experimentation requires intense effort. People who assume they will find an easier life in a free school or a commune are quickly disillusioned. Insofar as output of human energy and imagination is concerned, it is much easier to coast along with the momentum of the traditional culture, no matter how oppressive or limiting. People are quite unaware of how closely they are controlled by cultural conditioning—day by day, moment by moment—until they try changing basic patterns of relating and being. Undoing the unacknowledged brainwashing of the traditional culture requires efforts that often appear to conventional perceptions as brainwashing. The fact is, brainwashing is pervasive. Just as all the circuits in the brain are always filled, so too all the possible circuits available for social control are always filled. Changing personal or social patterns requires not just clearing out old circuits but adding something to take the place of the old material. This is exhausting, painful, and often discouraging work. It comes down to an ancient paradox often noted by those who have addressed themselves to the question of Enlightenment (itself a way out of the pervasive social hypnosis). Enlightenment cannot be forced; it is achieved only by finding the true flow of existence and going with it. And yet, finding and going with this flow requires the greatest dedication and hard work. The "condition of complete simplicity," T. S. Eliot reminds us, costs "not less than everything." The whole idea of great effort combined with total surrender to the eternal present is unfamiliar to the Western mind. Still, it offers guidance to every social reformer. A well-known educator, a hero of university reform in the 1930s and 1940s, once confessed to me that he had not read *Education and Ecstasy* because of the title. "Education," he told me sternly, "is hard work." If he had taken the trouble to read the book, he might have discovered enough work to fill another distinguished career. Ecstasy is hard work. Ecstasy is easy. There is no way around the paradox.

Social experimentation requires increased discipline and structure. That a traditional classroom represents a high order of discipline and structure is pure illusion. Students sitting silently in rigid rows while a teacher talks may represent a condition of expedient convenience for teachers and administrators, but that's about all. Little subject-matter learning is taking place at any given time, and the chance to practice responsibility is negligible. Order exists only on the surface of things; there is chaos beneath. A carefully structured free learning environment, on the other hand, offers the opportunity for a high efficiency of learning. The physical movement of students from one experience to another may appear chaotic to unaccustomed eyes, but where the learning experiences have been made attractive and interactive, the student has a chance to learn and practice responsibility *all the time.*

If the rigid traditional classroom represents one kind of disorder, there is also the other extreme, summed up in the dogma "When a child is ready to study a frog, then he will study a frog; it's up to the child." This omits the fact that a frog exists only in a context. A child will not be "ready" to study a frog until the frog is made available in a context the child can understand and enjoy. Arranging this context—which entails blending and interacting with the child—is the task of the innovative educator. In fulfilling it, he will deal with method and structure. He will create a discipline.

That very word now has an aversive ring because it has so often come down to us in crude and authoritarian applications, and because it has so rarely served a compelling vision. But no great work, neither a masterpiece of art nor a transformed society, is possible without discipline. The discipline of the artist is part of the joy of the creative process. Men have walked on the moon because of a compelling vision, but also because of close attention to detail. Those with a vision of a larger human change can't afford to forget that something as awesome as the Transformation begins with the way you stand and walk and breathe. The Zen strategy of seeing equal "religious" significance in every aspect of life, not holding ceremonial meditation to be any more or less crucial than eating or sweeping or building a wall, could well inform all who experiment with new life styles. Many a commune that began with the most grandiose spiritual aims has broken apart because of troubles having to do with getting dishes washed and toilets cleaned. The reformer must deal with such matters. He must help create an improved discipline that avoids the rigidity and authoritarianism of the old. Dishes and toilets are, after all, part of the Transformation.

Social experimentation requires patience. The restlessness and impatience of the West reaches an extreme in America. That is one of the reasons why Americans have arrived earlier than anyone else at the *Ultima Thule* of the civilized journey, a place from which there is no return, only the farther journey into the Transformation. But impatience is a threat to the social experiments that spring from the transforming impulse. This impatience is inflamed by our current definition of "the news." Our omnivorous news media are afflicted with a raging and insatiable hunger for large-scale trends. They thus tend to "discover" such trends at the slightest provocation and quickly build them up to disproportionate size and importance. This leads to unrealistic expectations that are dashed as the media go on to the next thing, belittling what they once heralded.

In 1958 I ran into a delightful low-key subculture along upper Grant Avenue in San Francisco composed of poets, jazz musicians and colorful drifters named "beatniks" by columnist Herb Caen. Not knowing better at the time, I produced a picture story on the beatniks, one of the first to appear in a national magazine. Within two weeks of the publication of the story, the Gray Line sightseeing busses were cruising upper Grant Avenue every night, followed soon afterwards by television crews and reporters from all over the world. The less than two hundred regulars who made the Grant Avenue scene were transmogrified into a worldwide "movement." One young man who appeared on the title page of the story became (or somehow already was) a true archetype; his dark cap and pullover sweater, dark glasses, mustache, pointed beard and flat expression created a costume of alienation for countless young people and informed countless cartoonists and illustrators over the years.

The media did their work. Within a few short months the subculture was utterly destroyed by the influx of imitators, tourists, motorcycle toughs, and by the continuing media raids. Beatniks who had prided themselves on their existential coolness began playing up to the cameras and collecting press clippings. Hysteria and violence descended on previously peaceful bars and coffeehouses, bringing bad vibrations and policemen. Nine years later the same sort of thing was to happen, with far more disastrous results, in the Haight-Ashbury district on the other side of the city.

In another case, one of the first and most promising educational experiments of the decade was started at San Francisco State College in 1965. The Experimental College there, again, received much favorable national publicity, which contributed greatly to its later difficulties. James Nixon, one of the founders of the experiment, describes what he calls the "media effect" in metaphorical terms: "News goes out in concentric waves that spread all over the country, then reverse themselves and rush back in to smash you." The problem lies not just in the resultant influx of ill-starred seekers nor even in the overinflated expectations created in the society at large but in the aberrant reinforcement system that corrupts those who receive the publicity. Favorable publicity may help performers sell tickets or politicians get votes, but for most people and organizations it offers only an illusion of power. This is especially true for a social experiment, generally a tentative, fragile thing, often involving only a small number of people. When it is overinflated or oversimplified in the media, cognitive dissonance is likely to arise. Too frequently, the experimenters begin to respond to the publicity rather than to the task at hand. Unfavorable publicity has its obvious ill effects but is probably less damaging in the long run than disproportionate favorable notice.

The media are easily bored. To trigger yet another story on the same subject, experimenters must resort to statements or behaviors that are novel, bizarre or outrageous on an ever-increasing scale. The movement towards Black Power started as a valid and probably necessary social experiment. It made big headlines. The headlines gave the impression of importance and power. Several young black leaders, perhaps not realizing how they were being led on, competed to *keep* getting headlines. The leader who made the most inflammatory public statement received the heaviest type and the most prime time on television. Good solid organizational work and real social change caused not even a blip in the media. I am convinced, having known some of the Black Power spokesmen before the media escalation began, that those brilliant, attractive young men were stretched far beyond their original intentions by the insidious and insatiable demands of "the news."

At this time I know of two substantial and rather successful social experiments that have not yet received national publicity. The founder of one of them recently called on me for advice on how to approach the national media. He pointed out that his organization was fulfilling a real need in a period of social transition, and that it would be good for other people across the nation to hear of the work so that they could form similar organizations. I told him that publicity would come soon enough, and that when he received requests for media coverage he could not in good conscience deny them. Meanwhile, I suggested, why not consider every month, every day, every hour without national publicity as golden? During this period his organization could continue to mature and explore simply for the joy and satisfaction of the work itself. It could test out and, if necessary, discard new ideas and new modes of operation without their being locked into the national consciousness in oversimplified form. It could grow strong and sure of itself in preparation for the eventual onslaught of the media effect. As for spreading the word, there is a sort of national underground that operates some months or years ahead of the media anyway. The word, really, can't be contained for long.

This should not be read as a condemnation of the media per se. That they are so restless, so eager to swallow up new ideas, helps keep this nation in a creative flux and helps insure it against the dominance of a single dogma. The process of co-opting, despite the dire warnings of the radicals, does work both ways; the nation at large is changed, if ever so slightly, every time it absorbs and corrupts a radical idea or movement. And perhaps it is just as well that every time a New Left or the like comes along it neither prevails nor maintains its "ideological purity." The traditional American resistance to pure ideology will certainly do nothing to slow the Transformation, which exists beyond all ideological considerations. The media may destroy specific social experiments and yet spread abroad the impulse within them. In recent years, isolated farm families in North Dakota and southern Alabama have been confronted with many concepts and human possibilities they had never dreamed of. Even in resisting, they have been changed.

The media offer social experimenters a choice. They can burn brightly on the pyre of publicity, thus calling attention to their cause, or they can work quietly and modestly over a period of years to make those small incremental changes that become significant over a lifetime. I suspect that a majority of the teachers and administrators fired for their efforts against the status quo in schooling could still be carrying on their innovations, even at an increased rate, if they had been willing to do so without proselytizing others and without receiving publicity for themselves. A period of social change needs both types of experimenters, the martyrs and the quiet ones. But both need to temper their efforts with patience, to cultivate a sense of destiny that can perceive the larger waves beneath the ripples, and the tide beneath the waves.

To do so requires the joining together of people of more than one age group. More than a few social experiments have failed because the participants in these experiments have all been young. For example, in 1969, hundreds of ecology action groups sprang up around the United States. For three or four months the groups were pervaded by a sense of excitement, activity and imminent change. Ecology marches, cleanups and recycling programs were featured on television, in newspapers and magazines. Six months later, however, the media were no longer responding to every ecology press release and, to the surprise of many young people, pollution had not been significantly slowed, much less stopped. Many of the groups disbanded. "The Establishment is hopeless," the young leader of one group in northern California said. "It can't be changed. We're splitting to Canada to start a commune." That anyone could dream a problem with such deep and complex roots as ecological rape would yield to a six-months-long campaign is proof of the need for perspective and patience.

The social experiment best suited for survival in this era will include people of varying ages. A twenty-year-old has invaluable force and enthusiasm, but is likely to look upon six months as a long, long time. The years flow differently for older people, especially those who have weathered past campaigns. Anyone interested in substantive and lasting change in social systems or human consciousness had best not think in periods any shorter than five years. That is how long Cesar Chavez worked in the fields of southern California before he could claim a single real victory. But the victories did come. What is more, his National Farm Workers' Association has created and is continuing to create basic change in society and consciousness.

Five years, however, is just a beginning, and a lifetime is short. In a single human life, the best ally of patience is awareness. In awareness there is no waiting. Regardless of the comings and goings of a thousand social experiments, the Transformation proceeds. Its existence is known to all who are aware. Awareness, as I have said before, *is* the Transformation.

Social experimentation entails pain as well as joy. Arthur Janov's book *The Primal Scream* suffers from its unfortunate claim that it is the one and only "cure" for neurosis and from its rather naive dismissal of all other ways of change. It is enormously popular, I feel, mainly because so many people immediately recognize the truth of Janov's major thesis: We are stuck in lifelong, stultifying neuroses because we are unable and unwilling to face and deal with and fully experience the acute pain that precedes personal change. Though Janov hammers away at this point, it is not his alone. Freud knew a great deal about the uses of pain. Most of the newest ways of change—Gestalt, encounter, Rolfing—involve some significant movement towards pain as the surest route to new awakenings. Every neurosis/ disease/discontent serves as a homeostatic device to maintain us in our dulled, druglike condition. It also conceals and protects itself, being extremely sensitive to any threat to its own existence. When the dis-ease mechanism recognizes any action or attitude that might constitute such a threat, it immediately sends out messages to us in the form of pain, telling us urgently to avoid that which would free us. The best practitioners of Gestalt, encounter, Rolfing and the like pursue pain as the best clue to the hiding place of the dis-ease. Participants in group work are reminded again and again to say or do the things that seem most painful to them if they really want to change. When Rolfers discover a certain muscle that is particularly painful to pressure, they have good reason to suspect that the location, tension and function of that muscle holds information as to the particular dis-ease that maintains the neurotic stasis. Pain is both the clue and the way out.

Every one of us was born in Civilization. We live in Civilization, brainwashed, dis-eased, conditioned to competitive hostility and aggression. Thus, any social experiment in this era must, to survive, involve ways of facing and dealing with the pain of the change. A classic case of an experiment which completely ignored this problem, which indeed tried every possible shortcut towards pleasure, is that of the hippie movement which arose in the mid-1960s. This experiment suffered from all the mistakes outlined in this chapter. It assumed change would be easy. It rejected discipline and structure. It was made up almost entirely of very young people. And it experienced all the corrosive effects of overinflation in the media. Most of all, however, it failed and failed disastrously because it made no real provisions for dealing with pain.

Now that the wreckage is so clearly visible—the boarded-up storefronts and dirty sidewalks along Haight Street in San Francisco, the epidemics of hepatitis and VD, the dazzling acid visions turned to heroin despair, the open hostility on the faces of the survivors of what was called the "Love Generation"—it has become as fashionable to condemn the movement out of hand as it once was to praise it uncritically. Both judgments are wrong. The impulse towards unity and ecstasy from which the hippies sprang will break out again and again in one form or the other, no matter what efforts are exerted to contain it. To deny the power and beauty of the movement's beginnings is to falsify history.

Indeed there was a time before the media came, a few brief months from late 1965 through the summer of 1966, when all in life that had been gray and two-dimensional seemed to explode into unexpected color and depth, rich with new smells and sounds and the imminence of miracles. Almost overnight a new culture was born with its own dress and art styles, its own music, its rituals and incense and bells. It is true that beautiful young women dressed in joyful swirls of color would give you flowers as you walked by. And it is true that for a while the crime rate in the Haight-Ashbury district (with the exception of drug arrests) dropped to an amazingly low figure. My young daughters, then aged six and two, would wander happily through those exotic surroundings, when we visited the district, and there was no thought for their safety. Every Saturday afternoon free rock concerts materialized as if by magic in Golden Gate Park. While we waited for the bands (some of which later became so successful that they were unavailable at any price) the anticipatory rustle of tambourines seemed to evoke a mythic presentiment of transcendence. And there were moments in the wash of color and sound and flashing lights at the original Fillmore Auditorium when the world did seem to tilt and all the dancers merge into a single consciousness.

But then the media came. By early 1967 all of the new culture that could be transported by paper and print and wire and air-waves was being spread throughout the world to be diluted, absorbed and co-opted—and to some extent to change perceptions almost everywhere. In June of 1967 the wave rushed back in to destroy the Haight-Ashbury. The "Summer of Love" brought to San Francisco tens of thousands of teenagers with flowers in their hair and dazed looks on their faces, seeking something they could neither name nor recognize. They found a measure of transcendance, but they also found chaos, clogged toilets, and a rapidly deteriorating drug scene. The culture simply could not handle the influx, physically or psychically.

Even without the media effect, however, the hippie movement in its original form was doomed. The impulse towards love and understanding was quite real, but so was the hostility and confusion that inevitably lingered underneath. The one was acknowledged. The other was not. Hippies could verbalize their love for all people, could renounce material gain, could give flowers to policemen, could say they saw only beauty in everything, and could then deny any negative feelings—*but only for so long*. Such a radical change in behavior and being does not come easily. It involves relinquishing basic patterns of competitiveness, acquisitiveness and aggression and creating positive new patterns to take their place. This means undergoing a great deal of pain. Most of the hippies' energy and awareness, in aikido terms, was concentrated in their heads. They simply assumed that if they could change their heads they could bypass effort and discipline and, most of all, that they could escape pain. Drugs were to be the means of escape. Used in the beginning supposedly to cleanse the doors of perception, drugs came to be used simply to hold back the ever-increasing pain. And, as is appropriate in a technological society, when one drug was no longer effective, there was another, more powerful one to take its place.

Here we cannot avoid some kind of connection between the war in Vietnam and the hippie movement. The escalation of our forces and modes of warfare in Southeast Asia shows a remarkable parallel with the escalation of drug usage in the Haight-Ashbury district of San Francisco and in hippie communities elsewhere. When the demon in the jungle (and in ourselves) would not go away, we refused for several years to face the pain of a great national change of consciousness. Instead, we sent more troops and guns and planes, and thought up increasingly bizarre techniques for eradicating what would not be eradicated: defoliation, electronic snoopers along trails, area bombing from high altitudes, low-altitude jungle busting, infrared nightfighting, search and destroy missions. Similarly and simultaneously, when marijuana could no longer kill the pain and LSD only made nightmares of the unexpressed hostility more vivid, the Haight-Ashbury went on to speed, then STP, then LSD or STP mixed with speed, then uppers and downers, then speed straight-lined, and finally (as in Vietnam) heroin.

The escalation failed. The hippie movement may be said to have had its My Lai in the Altamont rock concert tragedy in 1969, in numerous individual psychic disasters, and in the rise of scattered Satanic cults which employ the hippie idiom to celebrate values diametrically opposite to those celebrated by the original Haight-Ashbury culture. Some critics cite these ominous developments as reason to fear the ecstatic impulse itself. They should not overlook a far more ominous case in point. The Third Reich arose as a result of the Treaty of Versailles—as a result, that is, of incredibly stupid, shortsighted and vindictive actions by several highly civilized nations. But it cannot be denied that it arose initially in the guise of an impulse towards joy and mystical union.

There is truly reason to fear this impulse, for it contains within it the ultimate powers of creation and destruction. Harnessed to a destructive cause, it can wreak devastation and horror. Given over to evil *or* to good, it is not to be denied. This transforming force eventually breaks the most carefully tied bonds of empire, bursts asunder the heaviest confining walls, smashes every monument to a way of being that would last forever. At the very heart of our modern problem is not the fact that evil or inexperienced people turn to ecstasy, but that people of experience and goodwill, trapped and crippled by civilized dis-ease, keep refusing to ally themselves with the potent transforming force of the ecstatic impulse. That "The best lack all conviction, while the worst / Are full of passionate intensity" is not so much an indictment of passionate intensity as of lack of conviction. The time has surely come for the best to embrace the passionate intensity of existence and transformation. The time has surely come for women and men of humor and intelligence and compassion to accept the fact that life involves evolution, and to join their skill and energy, not just to polite social and political reform, but to the awesome journey into a higher state of being. The time has surely come for our leaders to apply all they know about structure and discipline and focused effort to something more than maintaining a dying and deadening civilization; for executives and board members of established institutions to seize the initiative of radical change, beginning with the painful and finally joyful process of changing themselves.

When a great culture dies in a vacuum with nothing to take its place, chaos is almost sure to ensue. Today, there is a sense of a vacuum in that aspect of the present we call future, drawing us towards something we simply cannot conceive. The vacuum will be filled. If humor and intelligence and compassion are to have a hand in filling it, there is little time to waste. There is little time for the painstaking work of creating a new politics, a new education, a new culture that starts with what is best in the old—leaving off dominance and greed and narrow individualism but not respect for the personal nor appetite for exploration; following joy but not fearing pain. Social experiments such as Esalen *Institute* and Synanon and the Zen Mountain Center, that have survived and even thrived since the early 1960s, have evolved systematic ways for dealing with the pain that accompanies change. The far more difficult enterprise of helping change the society at large still faces us. Wherever that change appears to be easy and painless, it is probably neither significant nor lasting. The leader who denies the pain of change is fooling his followers or, what is worse, himself.

❧

With each passing day it becomes clearer that we cannot maintain our present course much longer. The computer projections of Jay W. Forrester cited in Chapter 6 have inspired further predictions of doom, including one book, *The Limits of Growth*,[1] that has stirred up a worldwide controversy. Certain caveats should be attached to Forrester's work. It should *not* be read as a precise prediction of the future. It suffers the defect common to all straight-line extrapolations; that is, the omission of the unexpected. But the cultural politics and noisy debates swirling around the Forrester controversy should not obscure the crucial, undeniable point: To continue our present mode of life under the present set of assumptions can lead only to major catastrophe, perhaps involving, as Forrester and others suggest, the death of a majority of the human race.

Indeed, the cold-blooded cosmic gambler, observing the events on earth from a detached vantage point in space, would be hard put to give even odds on our reaching the year 2030 without some worldwide upheaval. And when we look around us at the smoldering hostility, resentment and bitterness even in this "favored" land, at the shocking inequities here and abroad, at the buildup of armed might and industrial heat throughout the world, the cosmic gambler with his even odds begins to seem optimistic.

There is also the matter of cultural inertia. Civilized men look at themselves as "progressive" and view the superstitions and taboo structures of primitive peoples as preventing them from embracing new ways of life—which is simply one more indication of our lack of perspective and self-knowledge. When white settlers prohibited tribal conflict and provided a market for native manioc flour in the Amazon jungles, the Mundurucu tribes made the shift from patrilineal to matrilineal social organization, about as sweeping a change as can be imagined, *in a period of fifty years*. And it is well known that the coming of the horse to North America resulted in the birth of a vivid new Plains Indian culture in a matter of a very few generations. Only now are we beginning to realize the obduracy of our own superstitions, our myths. Added to this is the very size and complexity of our culture, the sinuous and often invisible interweavings among our many vested interests, most of them based solidly on the "What's in it for me?" ethic. When Charles E. Wilson, Defense Secretary in the Eisenhower administration, said that what is good for the U.S.A. is good for General Motors, he was simply making an accurate assessment of the situation in terms of the old paradigm. That it is difficult to imagine an America without a General Motors is a measure of our built-in inertia, our unacknowledged resistance to change. And yet, every fact points to the conclusion that by the year 2030 there will *not* be a General Motors in anything near its present form. There may be an entity by the same name, but it will be dedicated to providing transportation of the most efficient, most functional, least polluting type (which may not include private automobiles). It will be concerned with economic and technological balance (which may involve contraction rather than growth). The very idea of beating out Ford will seem an anachronism. And the people who work there will derive their greater satisfactions from modes of cooperation and merging and psychic movement that are now barely imaginable. This GM of the future may seem improbable, but any GM at all will be impossible if we continue on the present course.

In these fading days of Civilization, we do not hear our political leaders telling us of the inevitable difficulties we face and the dislocations that are coming. We do not hear them revealing to us their perfectly understandable doubts and fears. Instead we hear weary debaters trying to make us believe—whatever we may think, whatever they may feel—that they are always, always *right*. That we can continue to listen and give even the most minimal credence to their plastic pronouncements shows, again, how this culture resists change.

And in the final lingering madness of the old paradigm, we find a nation terribly concerned about the reading and mathematics achievement scores of elementary schoolchildren, yet not even considering a curriculum including those skills of transformation that are absolutely necessary for our mere survival. In fact, there is an outcry and a shrinking back when something as mild and inoffensive and indeed inadequate as "sensitivity training" is mentioned at a PTA meeting. Reading and figuring are undoubtedly important (and, were it not for the culturally induced anxiety and dis-ease of our children, extremely easy to learn). But exercises in fundamental states of being, in something as basic as sensitivity to and union with others, in something as simple as merging identity with that of a tree (a familiar exercise in Tibetan mysticism), are far more important.

The most powerful resistance, however, resides deep in each of us. We fear to relinquish our neuroses, our discontents, our diseases. More than anything else, we fear any significant personal movement towards that which would save us and our world. For it is only in that unfamiliar, always newborn, ever vibrant sense of pure being that we can comprehend an alternative to warfare, competition, endless expansion, and lifelong grabbing.

The odds against peaceful transformation are truly less than sanguine. But I am not a cold-blooded cosmic gambler. Life has always confounded the odds. I know that the Transformation is possible because it is already so well under way. We must program a change in human nature into our computer model of the future. This change—silent, subtle, difficult to perceive—proceeds and spreads around the world. If the channels of communication (in money as well as news) can remain open and continue to become more responsive, the world will probably not have to wait for transformation by catastrophe. What seems more likely is a series of less-than-global disasters. Communicated swiftly, clearly, throughout the world, these disasters may well lend credibility to the nature and the scope of the changes required. Even so, we must face the fact that the messages may not be correctly interpreted at the outset. It is possible to imagine that when the first ten thousand die as a result of a smog attack, the established leaders will respond merely by instituting more effective smog alert procedures rather than by getting on with the business of helping the human race evolve into what amounts to a new species.

But this new species *will* evolve. And there is some reason to hope that it will take neither catastrophe nor disaster to reduce resistance to its birth. For those who are willing to overcome fear and learn through pain, there is the delight of high adventure in store, travels of the spirit, festivals of accomplishment in realms now hidden from our senses. What was once impalpable now summons us to dismantle the walls between ourselves and our sisters and brothers, to dissolve the distinctions between flesh and spirit, to transcend the present limits of time and matter, to find, at last, not wealth or power but the ecstasy (so long forgotten) of commonplace, unconditional being. *For the atom's soul is nothing but energy. Spirit blazes in the dullest clay. The life of every woman or man—the heart of it—is pure and holy joy.*

And after all the journeying, all the pain and joy, we may discover that the Transformation was difficult to grasp, not because it was so far away but because it was so very near. To find the immense world of delight is, in the end, to come home again, where it always was.

thirteen

A Crystal on the Mountain

There is always a Body beyond our little body, arms to hold us, new eyes to see, a larger being waiting here closer than our physical skin. There is a deeper self that thrives on the craziness of this teeming world, that sees every breakdown as an opening to the original crazy shimmering dance, to the eternal explosion of the sun in the night, to the floating worlds all around.

—Michael Murphy, golf in the kingdom

AWARENESS of the Transformation comes to us like the rustle of a distant tambourine. We awaken in a darkened room with a sense of some sort of visitation. The next morning the world has changed. It is like breathing a different kind of air beneath another sky. But the visitation was nothing special, only the return of some aspect of our own true selves, lost and long forgotten in the sleep of Civilization.

Awareness *is* the Transformation and there is no force that can stop it. Revolutions, riots, strikes and subversion are not required to bring the old order down. It is only necessary that enough people—having established the requisite discipline and order, having faced the pain of change—can bring themselves to accept the intrinsic delight of existence. The most radical act of this age is perhaps to experience four straight days of joy, without anxiety or guilt or regret. Civilization cannot survive very many such days.

❧

It is midnight of the first full moon after the autumnal equinox. An old man stands on a rocky prominence near the east peak of the sacred mountain. He is dressed in battered work shoes, faded khakis and a shabby parka. Above his head he holds a crystal about the size of a soccer ball. His head is flung back so that his eyes and the crystal and the moon are perfectly aligned.

Earlier in the evening this man, the last shaman of the tribe of Indians that once lived on the mountain's slopes, drove south to the mountain from the little town where he makes a living doing odd jobs in the white man's world. He parked his old pickup truck at the end of a dirt road that runs about halfway up the mountain, took out a shovel, and climbed to the crystal's hiding place. He followed no trail, only his sure sense of where it would have to be.

The shaman dug the crystal from the ground, placed it in a gunnysack, and returned to the truck. He drove then to the ocean on the other side of the mountain. He parked near a lonely stretch of beach. He unbuttoned two buttons of his parka and slipped the crystal inside. Cradling it there, he walked out into the moonlit water where it ebbed and flowed among rugged rocks.

He washed the crystal thoroughly, then, holding it carefully in both hands, approached one of the projecting rocks. Chanting softly, he struck the crystal on the rock four times, each time with increasing force. It was a perilous operation. The shaman knew he had to strike hard enough to jar loose any demon that might be clinging to the crystal. But if he struck too hard the crystal would break, which would bring the world to an end. He was not absolutely sure that would happen. He did know, however, that if the crystal broke he would die in an instant.

The shaman drove back to the mountain and climbed to the prominence. He waited there for the moon to mount to the zenith, then raised the crystal above his head. A faint pulse from the sun, reflecting off the moon, resonated at the precise frequency of the crystal and entered the shaman's very being. He fell into a trance and was transported to the circumference of that sphere where physical distance yields its domain, where past, present and future touch.

At the same time three other men, also shamans of near-extinct tribes, raised their crystals to the moon. They too were standing on sacred mountains. The mountains were many miles apart, the four corners of a great square on this earth. In an instant the four men were joined into a single being. There was in each of them an awareness of all aspects of all of them, aspects we might express as facial expression or smell or sense of humor or essence. But none of this was experienced as separate. No face was separate from another, and "face" was not separate from smell or sound or being. In this joining the great vision of change within the changeless unfolded again.

The shaman was so filled that there was no space left for regret or exaltation. He had seen it before. Those who came before him had seen it. He was an old man. He would probably not see it again on this plane of existence. But that was all right, for it *is:* The passing away of his people's way of life. The coming of the white men. The passing away of their way of life. The coming of something different, long awaited. Was it a way his people might have hoped for? He was not sure. But that is not a question he would ask, for the end may precede the beginning, and beneath every conceivable sky it is always now.

The shaman stands there in my memory, a moonlit statue against the cloudless night.

Notes

CHAPTER 1. A MORNING ON MT. TAM

1. Sri Aurobindo, *The Life Divine* (New York, 1949), pp. 761, 880.
2. Leo Tolstoy, *Anna Karenina*, trans. by Joel Carmichael (New York, 1960), pp. 267–268. (PB)
3. *Ibid.*, p. 269

CHAPTER 3. AN INTRODUCTION TO MASS MURDER

1. Dorothy Lee, *Freedom and Culture* (Englewood Cliffs, N.J., 1959), p. 90.
2. Thomas Berger, *Little Big Man* (New York, 1964), pp. 213–214.
3. Jean Piaget, *The Child's Conception of the World* (New York, 1965), p. 117.
4. Melvin Laird, *A House Divided* (Chicago, 1962).
5. Marcus Annaeus Lucanus, *The Civil War*, trans. by J. D. Huff (New York, 1928), pp. 131, 143–151.

CHAPTER 4. HUNTERS AND FARMERS

1. Peter Farb, *Man's Rise to Civilization* (New York, 1968), p. 36.
2. Laurens van der Post, *The Lost World of the Kalihari* (New York, 1958), pp. 243–244.
3. Alvin W. Gouldner and Richard A. Petersen, *Notes on Technology and the Moral Order* (Indianapolis, 1962), p. 38.
4. James Mooney, "The Ghost-Dance Religion and the Sioux Outbreak of 1890," in the *Annual Report of the Bureau of American Ethnology*, XIV, 2 (Washington, 1896), p. 721.
5. George B. Leonard, *Education and Ecstasy* (New York, 1968), pp. 87–100.

CONCORDANCE REFERENCES. The information for the concordance on page 47 was drawn from a number of sources. There are, however, standard references to introduce the reader to the work of each scholar we discuss. Needless to say, in some cases the concordance is not identical to the cited work, since it was constructed from a composite of several of the author's publications.

Lewis Henry Morgan, *Ancient Society* (New York, 1877).

Elman Service, *Primitive Social Organization: An Evolutionary Perspective* (New York, 1962).

Julian H. Steward, *Theory of Culture Change* (Urbana, Ill., 1955).

Morton H. Fried, *The Evolution of Political Society: An Essay in Political Anthropology* (New York, 1967).

Yehudi A. Cohen, *Man in Adaptation*, 2 vols. (Chicago, 1968).

Leslie A. White, *The Evolution of Culture: The Development of Civilization to the Fall of Rome* (New York, 1959).

Richard K. Beardsley and others, "Functional and Evolutionary Implications of Community Patterning," in *Seminars in Archeology: 1955*, Robert Wachope and others, eds. (Salt Lake City, 1956).

Philip L. Wagner, *The Human Use of the Earth* (Glencoe, Ill., 1960).

For Marx, the basic reference is a little-known volume: Karl Marx, *Pre-Capitalist Economic Formations* (New York, 1965), original ms. written in 1857-58.

Later, Engels redid this schema to conform more closely to the work of Lewis H. Morgan in: Friedrich Engels, *The Origin of the Family, Private Property and the State;* in the light of researches of Lewis H. Morgan (New York, 1942), originally published in 1884.

In his Preface to the First Edition, Engels states: "The following chapters are, in a sense, the execution of a bequest. No less a man than Karl Marx had made it one of his future tasks to present the results of Morgan's researches in light of the conclusions of his own—within certain limits, I may say our—materialistic examination of history, thus to make clear their full significance." Marx had died in 1883.

CHAPTER 5. THE GIFT

1. A selection of Perls' tapes available from Big Sur Recordings, 117 Mitchell Blvd., San Rafael, California 94903.

2. Leo Litwak, "Joy Is the Prize," *The New York Times Magazine*, December 31, 1967, p. 31.

3. Sigmund Freud, *Civilization and Its Discontents*, trans. by James Strachey (New York, 1962), p. 69.

4. *Ibid.*, p. 60.

5. *Ibid.*, p. 70.

6. *Ibid.*, p. 73.

7. *Ibid.*, p. 59.

8. *Ibid.*, p. 78.

9. Sigmund Freud, *Moses and Monotheism* (London, 1951), p. 131.

10. Norman O. Brown, *Love's Body* (New York, 1966), p. 3.
11. Herbert Marcuse, *Eros and Civilization* (Boston, 1955), p. 60.
12. Freud, *Civilization and Its Discontents*, p. 58.
13. A. T. W. Simeons, *Man's Presumptuous Brain* (London, 1960).
14. S. L. A. Marshall, *Men Against Fire* (New York, 1947), pp. 50, 78, 79.
15. Leonard, *Education and Ecstasy*, p. 71.
16. Marcuse, *op. cit.*, p. 30.
17. Leo Srole and others, *Mental Health in the Metropolis: The Midtown Manhattan Study* (New York, 1962).
18. Alexander H. Leighton, "The Stirling County Study: Some Notes on Concepts and Methods," in *Comparative Epidemiology of the Mental Disorders*, Paul H. Hoch and Joseph Zubin, eds. (New York, 1961).
19. Robert W. White, *The Abnormal Personality* (New York, 1964), pp. 240–241.
20. O. Fenichel, *Psychoanalytic Theory of Neurosis* (New York, 1945) pp. 454–57.
21. Karl A. Menninger, Martin Mayman, and Paul Pruyser, *The Vital Balance: The Life Process in Mental Health and Illness* (New York, 1963), summarized in Hoflind, Leninger, and Gregge, *Basic Psychiatric Concepts in Nursing* (Philadelphia, 1967), p. 210.
22. René Dubos, *Man Adapting* (New Haven, 1965), p. 239.
23. *Ibid.*, p. 275.

CHAPTER 6. GRAHAM CRACKERS FOR OUR CHILDREN

1. Sylvester Graham, *Lectures on the Science of Human Life*, Vol. 1 (2 vols., Boston, 1839), p. 190.
2. Sylvester Graham, *Lecture on Chastity*, quoted by Stephen Nissenbaum in "The New Chastity in America, 1830–1840," u.p., p. 14.
3. *Ibid.*, p. 33.
4. *Ibid.*, p. 35.
5. *Ibid.*, pp. 34, 35.
6. *Ibid.*, p. 33.
7. *Ibid.*, p. 31.
8. Stephen Nissenbaum, *op. cit.*, p. 52.
9. D. Yellowlees in *Journal of Mental Science*, 22 (1876), p. 336, cited by Alex Comfort in *The Anxiety Makers* (London, 1967), p. 97.
10. Page Smith, *Daughters of the Promised Land* (Boston, 1970), pp. 134–135, quoting Catherine Beecher in *Letters to the*

People on Health and Happiness (New York, 1855) pp. 24, 124, 133.

11. Arthur C. Clarke, *Profiles of the Future* (New York, 1962), p. 14.
12. Jay Forrester, "The Counterintuitive Behavior of Social Systems," in *M.I.T. Technology Review*, January, 1971, pp. 53–68.
13. Tom Wicker, "The Greening of the Press," *Columbia Journalism Review*, May–June, 1971, p. 7.
14. *Ibid.*, p. 10.
15. George B. Leonard, "Youth of the Sixties: The Explosive Generation," *Look*, January 3, 1961, p. 17.
16. Dr. George Gallup and Evan Hill, "Youth: The Cool Generation," *Saturday Evening Post*, December 30, 1961, p. 64.

CHAPTER 7. CHANGE AND FLOOD CHANGE

1. Thomas S. Kuhn, *The Structure of Scientific Revolutions* (Chicago, 1962), p. 69.
2. *Ibid.*, p. 155.
3. *Ibid.*, pp. 149–150.
4. *Ibid.*, p. 116.
5. *Ibid.*, p. 24.

CHAPTER 8. CIVILIZATION AND MAGIC

1. B. Malinowski, *Myth in Primitive Psychology* (1926; reprinted in *Magic, Science and Religion* New York, 1955, pp. 101, 108).
2. George M. Foster, *Tzintzuntzan* (Boston, 1967), pp. 122–152.
3. Cambridge, King's College Library, Keynes MS. 38, fol. 9v-10r; an abstract of "The Epitome of the Treatise of Health, written by Edward Generosus Anglicus innominato who lived Anno Domini 1562."
4. Peter Farb, *Man's Rise to Civilization* (New York, 1968), p. 47.

CHAPTER 10. GLEAMINGS ON THE WATER

1. Carlos Castaneda, *A Separate Reality* (New York, 1971), pp. 131, 194.
2. Alan Vaughan, "Interview: Captain Edgar D. Mitchell," *Psychic Magazine*, September–October, 1971, p. 32.

CHAPTER 11. BEYOND INCEST

1. *Pro Football Weekly*, October 16, 1971, p. 1.

2. George B. Leonard, *The Man & Woman Thing and Other Provocations* (New York, 1970).
3. Leonard C. Lewin, *Report from Iron Mountain on the Possibility and Desirability of Peace* (New York, 1969).
4. Claude M. Summers, "The Conversion of Energy," *Scientific American*, September, 1971, p. 160.
5. A. W. Clausen, Address to The Conference Board's Sixth Annual Financial Conference, New York, February 18, 1971.

CHAPTER 12. THE PAIN AND JOY OF THE CHANGE

1. Dennis L. Meadows and others. *The Limits of Growth: A Report for the Club of Rome's Project on the Predicament of Mankind* (New York, 1972).

Index